Studies in Economic Ethics and Philosophy

Christopher Cowton · Michaela Haase

Trends in Business and Economic Ethics

Springer

Prof. Christopher Cowton
The Business School
University of Huddersfield
Queensgate
Huddersfield
HD1 3DH
United Kingdom
c.j.cowton@hud.ac.uk

PD Dr. Michaela Haase
Freie Universität Berlin
Marketing Department
Otto-von-Simson-Str. 19
Berlin 14195
Germany
Michaela.Haase@fu-berlin.de

ISBN 978-3-642-09838-3 e-ISBN 978-3-540-79472-1

DOI 10.1007/978-3-540-79472-1

Studies in Economic Ethics and Philosophy ISSN 1431-8822

Library of Congress Control Number: 2008930088

Softcover reprint of the hardcover 1st edition 2008

Cover design: WMX Design GmbH, Heidelberg

Printed on acid-free paper

9 8 7 6 5 4 3 2 1

springer.com

Contents

CONTENTS

Introduction

Christopher J. Cowton and Michaela Haase

A Developing Field

A growing number of academics and other specialists are paying attention to ethics in business. The fall of the Berlin Wall and the associated attempts to establish market economies in Central and Eastern Europe; business 'scandals' such as Enron and WorldCom in the USA and Parmalat in Europe; the increasing pace of internationalization of trade and supply chains; and the urgency on many fronts of calls to respond to global climate change: all these factors and more have added to the momentum behind attempts to analyze, critique and reform business and economic activity in ethical or ethical-economic terms. Many voices are now heard – not only business practitioners and academics, but also consultants, politicians, NGOs and other critics and commentators.

For academics there are issues about both what is researched and what is taught, and how those tasks are to be approached. Like business and management studies in general, business ethics is not an academic discipline as such but a field of study. In the field of business ethics there is no unique *business-ethical* theoretical framework from which research questions follow simply by means of direct application of the main theory. Indeed, many different disciplinary perspectives can fruitfully be brought to bear on business ethics. The chapters in this volume reflect this as they draw on economics and other social-scientific disciplines, on philosophy, or on knowledge harking back to management theory, which itself is multi-disciplinary. In addition, and as explored by some of the authors in this volume, some of the issues at stake are not, or not only, determined by the specific research programmes of theories but also influenced by the intersections between them. Furthermore (and at least as important), the practices of businesses and managers themselves are – or should be – an important influence.

What might be expected of business in terms of ethical or socially responsible behaviour, and what might be the appropriate contribution of research and teaching, are still subject to considerable debate – issues relating to scope and impact abound. However, what is clear is that ethical issues relating to business are seen as increasingly important by many, and the myriad questions associated with them need to be addressed with both urgency and rigour.

Thus, as both a management activity, broadly conceived, and as a scholarly endeavour, business ethics is increasingly seen as important for both current and future generations of managers, entrepreneurs, and other economic actors. But it is not without its problems and challenges. New insights, clarifications and developments are needed, but the complexity of the issues and the interested nature of what is at stake mean that progress will not be a simple task. Academically, there have been notable advances with respect to the integration of the field's topics in business schools' curricula, especially in the USA. Yet even there, there is a need for consolidation of what has been achieved, and much remains to be done. Furthermore, the different economic, social, political and academic contexts in other parts of the world – including Europe – mean that insights developed in the USA are likely to require a degree of adaptation when transferred elsewhere. The particularities of the US context also mean that some issues relating to business and economic ethics, that might be considered important in (parts of) Europe, have received scant or, so far at least, lesser attention in the USA. For example, the treatment of the workforce, organizational issues and the environmental responsibility of business are three areas in which European scholars have developed notable expertise. Moreover, a particular feature of many non-US perspectives is the systematic treatment of business as part of the economic and social system.[1]

Against this backdrop, a major conference took place in May 2006 in Berlin, Germany. This book's origins lie in that conference. Hosted by the School of Business and Economics at the Freie Universität Berlin, "Ethical Aspects of Management in Theory and Practice" (EAMTP) drew together a wide range of international speakers and delegates to discuss the relationship between economics, business economics and management studies, on the one hand, and ethics (economic ethics and business ethics) on the other. Within that broad agenda, more than 40 speakers (38 papers) contributed to the Conference, addressing the Conference's main themes of:

1 Hence our reference in places to 'economic and business ethics', which we usually elide to 'business ethics'.

- the scope of ethical and moral action within the economy and theories about it;
- approaches to teaching ethics within the business and management curriculum; and
- the dialogue between (management) scholars and practitioners.

All the chapters in this book are written by authors who participated in the EAMTP Conference. Most of them were initially presented in one form or another at the Conference itself, and all have been gone through a process of double blind review which (we hope our contributors will agree) has led to significant development and improvement. We trust that what we have as a result is a set of thought-provoking papers that address important issues in business and economic ethics. Of course, the individual chapters speak for themselves, but in this introductory chapter we wish to explain briefly the structure of the book and provide an overview of its contents.

Overview of the Book

As befits a multi-disciplinary, developing field, the chapters are written from a variety of perspectives. The subsequent papers are characterizable by their focus on issues related to economic ethics (Koslowski, Shionoya), economics and philosophy (Hodgson, Lenz), and the interaction of business ethics with other disciplines, fields of study (economics, philosophy, corporate finance, etc.), or even business practice (Cowton, Brink, Soppe, Gilbert and Rasche, Haase).

The first chapter, Christopher Cowton's *On Setting the Agenda for Business Ethics Research*, reflects on the many influences that can come to bear on research or scholarship in business ethics and thus, in some senses, prepares the way for the other chapters in the book. His chapter begins with an understanding that business ethics is not an established academic discipline as such, but rather a field of study (like business or management studies). If, as Cowton argues, research is necessary not only for pragmatic reasons but also in order to become an accepted academic field, then it is an urgent as well as justified question to ask about the set of research questions addressed, their coherence and sources. Generally speaking, besides problems identified by the theories which form the theoretical basis of business ethics approaches, problems identified by businesses and firms, and by management studies, are part of business ethics' research agenda, as well as problems related to the curriculum and teaching of business ethics. This analysis seems to be close to one that could also be given for the field of management studies in general. Cowton also, in effect, identifies two dangers for business ethics: sacrificing relevance for rigour, familiar from discussions in management studies; and using methods and applying analytical skills for their own sake, an issue familiar from economics. However, business ethics can develop a strategy with respect to its theoretical development, its applications, and its teaching, and thus form its own coherent identity as a field.

The next four chapters provide a basic and systematic treatment of issues in economic ethics or of the relationship between economics and ethics, respectively. Peter Koslowski and Yuichi Shionoya each generate a framework for economic ethics with respect to concepts, principles and approaches. After this, Bernard Hodgson and Hansrudi Lenz detect conundrums and diagnose conceptual incoherences or even contradictions which accrue from the conceptualization of individual action and decision in economics or its comparison to ends in ethics, as for example norm justification.

Peter Koslowski's *Some Principles of Ethical Economy* concentrates on the development of an ethical economy (or theory thereof) located at the intersection of economics and ethics. Koslowski outlines two strands of economic-ethical investigation that arise if one addresses issues of interest in economics from the point of view of ethics and vice versa. He delineates the interface between economics and ethics based on the multiple meanings of the concept of good and on the problem of the incompleteness and speculative character of choice. From his point of view, the meaning of the term "good" in the economic and technological sense (as the efficient and effective), can neither be equated with the meaning of the term "good" in the moral sense nor completely separated from it. The three meanings of "good" are complementary. Koslowski develops the synthesis of ethical economy as the economic theory of ethics and as the theory of the ethical presuppositions of the economic. He introduces several principles that are relevant for ethical and economic theory at the same time. The paper provides some fundamental thoughts on the formal relation between economic and ethical theory.

Yuichi Shionoya's *Economic Ethics: A Systematic Integration* deals with the intersection of economics and ethics. Shionoya directs his effort at the preparation of the field for both a positive and a normative virtue ethics. It is his goal to construct a system of economic ethics which is able to "develop the idea of virtue economics in positive and normative senses to shed light on a neglected issue, i.e., virtuous utilization of resources for the development and self-realization of human beings". The author characterizes economics: first, with respect to the allocation, distribution and utilization of resources; second, by distinguishing between statics, dynamics and sociology; and third, by a broad concept of good. Economics addresses resources mainly in the light of the end-means relationship between good (in the sense of goodness) and goods (in the sense of commodities) necessary for human life. Compared to that, ethics explores what a good life is and postulates a set of norms to evaluate it from multiple angles. Shionoya constructs a system of ethics by coordination of fundamental ethical values (good, virtue and right) and the main objects of evaluation which (at least in part) already play a role in the institutional strands of economics – namely act, being and rule. From Shionoya's point of view, economic ethics derived by the juxtaposition of the systems of economics and ethics as characterized above will be able to provide valuable norms which bring us closer to the achievement of ends like just distribution, virtuous utilization and efficient allocation of resources.

Both Koslowski and Shionoya elaborate on the distinction between the economic and the ethical good. As regards their meaning, the concepts remain distinct from Shionoya's point of view; that notwithstanding, they are related by the acts performed by the economic actors. For this reason, Koslowski would add, humans should take up a stance on their action (and, as Hodgson would add, this requires intentional morality). What can be drawn from both papers is that, if there is an intersection between the economic and the ethical good, with it is opened up a range for self-interested ethical action.

Bernard Hodgson's *The Conundrum of Moral Evaluation in Economics* addresses some of the moral or value dimensions of classical and neoclassical economic theories. Hodgson diagnoses a "severe conundrum in the standard interpretation of the 'mainstream' tradition of classical and neo-classical theory". Since a moral interpretation of individual decision and action should be able to take precedence over claims of self-interest, it should be able to come into conflict with a point of view completely based on self-interest. This is neither fulfilled by a conception of economic-ethical integration located at the individual level of analysis that equates the moral and the rational (in the sense of the Rational Sceptic discussed by Hansrudi Lenz in the subsequent paper) nor by one that ascribes morality to unintended action results *and* legitimizes it ex post in terms of understanding such purely rational, self-interested action as expressing an ethical point of view. If this viewpoint is right, then the purely methodical interpretation and treatment of the assumptions related to individual action in the tradition of Gary S. Becker possesses – from an ethical point of view – a problem: the implementation of moral values at the micro-level of analysis requires intentional morality. If the market mechanism could do all the work, no ethics requiring the exercise of a rational will would be needed (at least not for the realization of the ethical good). In some sense, this strand of argumentation in Hodgson's paper, addressing the micro-macro level interaction from an ethical point of view, is complementary to Lenz's interpretation of the ethical status of the economic "reference individual".

Hansrudi Lenz's *Why Act Morally? Economical and Philosophical Reasons* can be located within a field of study that Koslowski in his earlier chapter named "the economics of ethics". Lenz addresses the constitution and origin of the reference individual to which ethical or economic-ethical analysis could or should refer. As is well-known, the rationality assumption, often criticized because of its regard to self interest, is a fundamental principle in economics. Philosophers have addressed how this assumption relates to ethics and which consequences result from this for the generation and justification of ethical norms. Is there a material steering function of moral norms for rational individuals? The hypothetical figure of the Rational Sceptic that harks back to Peter Stemmer has achieved particular attention in this context. According to this figure, "a moral norm is rationally justified if and only if a Rational Sceptic could be convinced" to act in accord with it.

Lenz argues that this kind of justification of moral norms based on both strict rational and purely selfish individuals leads to a conceptual contradiction of the concept of moral norm based on ethics. Moral norms are senseless for the Rational Sceptic because he would only follow them if they were in accordance with rationality. Thus, the moral dimension of a norm that is acted on by reasons of rationality is superflous. Koslowski's position, that the moral cannot be subordinated to the economic, relates to this. Instead of the Rational Sceptic, Lenz recommends that philosophers interested in work at the intersection of economics and ethics should base their work on the conception of an individual equipped with a minimal concern for the interests of other beings. The Rational Sceptic should thus be replaced by that minimal moralistic, non-purely selfish individual. In order to find a sketch of the constitution and behaviour of this new reference individual, philosophers should consult recent empirical findings in, for example, experimental economics and game theory. Lenz argues that both philosophers and economists stand to benefit from this change in the presuppositions of research or conception of the reference individual for economic-ethical analyses.

It is well-known that economic ethics and business ethics' approaches give different answers to the question of the reconcilability of, roughly speaking, markets and morals. In addition, many economists are sceptical concerning a closer connection of business ethics and economics. They regard (at least some streams of) business ethics as being hostile to economics or normative, respectively. The first reason for their reluctance relates to assumptions in economic theory (like those belonging to *homo oeconomicus*); the second is the alleged or actual conflict with Max Weber's postulate concerning value judgements in the social sciences (one aspect dealt with by Hodgson's chapter).

Alexander Brink's *Business Ethics and the Rhetoric of Reaction* may provide a guideline for an anticipative reaction to resistance and reactions like these and others. His paper includes the idea that what are called the 'functionalist' and the 'corrective' approaches in business ethics are not necessarily in opposition to each other: if ethics has become an integrative part of economics (this refers to the functionalist idea), then ideas based on corrective approaches can be implemented without provoking "reactionary" opposition from mainstream economics.

Brink's chapter addresses the strategic interplay between business ethics and other disciplines. The paper asks if business ethics can make use of Albert O. Hirschman's idea of the historic interplay between "reactionary" and "progressive" tendencies. (The terms "reactionary" and "progressive" bear no negative or positive connotations; they simply express a mechanical backwards and forwards direction of forces within historical developments, which themselves do not lead automatically to progress.) Based on Hirschman's "Rhetoric of Reaction", Brink discusses three main theses that the reactionary forces bring to bear in order to push back the forces related to change and renewal in history. Business ethics should not wait for the "reactionary" reactions in particular of mainstream economics but instead proactively formulate its progressive strategy of defence. With respect to the strategic development of its interactions with other disciplines or fields of study, Brink suggests a means for putting business ethics in the driving seat in terms of its historical development.

Dirk Ulrich Gilbert and Andreas Rasche's *A Critical Perspective on Social Accounting – The Contribution of Discourse Philosophy* addresses accountability standards (in particular SA 8000), which they assume are not yet adequately represented in today's business ethics literature. Based on Habermasian discourse ethics, the authors introduce a "discursively informed version of SA 8000" that is an appropriate tool to better support the institutionalization of social accounting standards in firms (they particularly refer to multinational corporations). The authors draw on discourse ethics in a double sense: first, with respect to the justification of norms advocated by SA 8000; and second, with respect to the implementation of these norms in organizations. As the authors point out, "(w)hen meaningfully based on discourse ethics", SA 8000 supports multinational corporations, suppliers, and other stakeholders "to effectively communicate about conflicting issues to 'live' social responsibility". Gilbert and Rasche's discourse theoretical contribution can be viewed as supporting the recent discussion on the ethical nature of corporate ethics initiatives (e.g., internal codes of conduct and accountability standards).

Aloy Soppe's *The Stakeholder Equity Model* sketches a newly developing strand of research in economic ethics relating corporate finance, corporate governance and stakeholder theory. The paper deals with the economic foundations of corporate governance. Reflecting both the critical stance taken by many to the shareholder approach and also the emerging literature related to the stakeholder approach to strategic management, Soppe extends the basic ideas and concepts of corporate finance approaches from the shareholders to the stakeholders of the firm. Referring to a firm's efficiency and the structure of ownership of its stock, he argues that governance costs decrease if the majority of the firm's stock is assigned to its non-shareholder stakeholders. His argument is two-dimensional: first, the familiar relation between ownership, control and efficiency is extended from shareholders to non-shareholder stakeholders; and second, the answer to the question of who (from an efficiency point of view) should hold shares in a firm is given by consideration of the costs of market contracting faced by different groups of actors (like shareholders, the workforce, or managers).

The final chapter in the volume, Haase's *Theory, Practice, and Education: On the Role of Business Ethics for Management Education at Business Schools or Universities*, identifies an education gap with respect to the ethics education of future managers at business schools and universities and suggests the implementation of business ethics as a means of diminishing this gap. It discusses business ethics education from the more general perspective of management practice's knowledge sources. The implementation of business ethics can enhance business schools and universities' competences with respect to research and education. Business ethics both extends the classical competences of business schools and universities and contributes to the development of future managers' particular competences related to theoretical knowledge and its application, on the one hand, and ethical reflection and discernment, on the other.

Final Acknowledgements

Finally, as the Editors, we would like to acknowledge the encouragement and support provided by many people during the gestation of this book. First, we would like to thank Stefanie Geist and Christiane Weinreich for their help in making the EAMTP Conference in May 2006 such a success. Second, we would like to thank Peter Koslowski for his encouragement and guidance in producing this volume. Third, we would like to thank the Deutsche Forschungsgemeinschaft (DFG) for providing major financial support for the Conference, as well as Vodafone Group Research & Development, and Struwe & Partner. We would also like to thank Ernst & Young for their print subsidy. Fourth, as mentioned earlier, all the chapters here (and some other papers that have not been included) went through a double blind review process. We thank for their invaluable help those who generously gave of their time and expertise:

Paul Anand
Kurt Annen
Johannes Brinkmann
Nick Collett
Paul Gibbs
Markus Gmür
Diana Grosse
Ursula Hansen
Shaun Hargreaves Heap
Peter Koller
Gael McDonald
Bruce Macfarlane
Domènec Melé
Eleanor O'Higgins
Joakim Sandberg
Peter Ulrich
Johan Verstraeten
Radu Vranceaunu
Ben Wempe
László Zsolnai

Chapter 1

On Setting the Agenda for Business Ethics Research

CHRISTOPHER J. COWTON

I. Introduction

Business ethics as a field of academic endeavour has made significant progress over the past two or three decades. It now boasts a substantial body of scholarly literature, which is a major resource in which much time and effort have been invested and from which much can be gained. However, there is still much work to be done, and the dynamic nature of both academic life and the world beyond it ensures that new issues and opportunities will continue to emerge. Business ethicists, individually and collectively, through the allocation of their limited research resources (especially time), will govern how well the field progresses and meets future challenges over the years to come. In particular, through our decisions about what we do or do not study and write about, we will determine the future shape of the scholarly literature – what it addresses successfully and on what it remains silent or inadequate.

Implicitly or explicitly, individually and collectively, choices are made, and some are presumably better than others.

This paper is a reflection on the progress of business ethics as an academic enterprise. Of course, the development of business ethics as a focus of academic interest has been marked by several review papers already (e.g. Hosmer 1996; Werhane/Freeman 1999), some reflecting underlying concerns consistent with Enderle's (1996, p. 43) comment that "in its present stage of development, business ethics appears to be far from being an established academic discipline". Some might question whether something like business ethics can ever be an academic discipline as such, and for the purposes of this paper it will be helpful to distinguish between *disciplines* – such as philosophy, economics and psychology – and *fields* (such as business and management) to which the concepts and methods of academic disciplines can be applied. Nevertheless, whatever kind of academic activity business ethics is taken to be, there are significant issues relating to its academic status.

An important element in the project to promote the academic standing of business ethics is research, which "is needed to establish business ethics on an equal footing not only with other management subjects, but also with other topics in applied ethics" (Collier 1995, p. 6). Research needs to be done, and it needs to be up to the standards of cognate fields and disciplines. Worries about whether this is the case have led to some of the previous reviews of business ethics, particularly (in the early 1990s) of empirical research carried out in its name (e.g. Brady/Hatch 1992; Fleming 1990; Randall/Gibson 1990; Robertson 1993; Weber 1992). Such concerns are legitimate, not only for reasons of academic respectability (see Cowton 1998b) but also because poorly conducted research, in whatever tradition, is a waste of resources and possibly seriously misleading. However, it is not sufficient for research to be conducted according to established academic standards; the choice of question or issue to be addressed is also important. Thus, in addition to attention being paid to *how* business ethics is researched, it is important that sight is not lost of *what* is researched. It is with the latter that this paper is principally concerned.

One approach to advancing the consideration of what is researched in business ethics would be to develop a comprehensive catalogue and critique of the contents of the literature as it currently stands and to make recommendations regarding the focus of future work. However, such an endeavour would be a massive undertaking given the extent of developments since 1990 (Enderle 2003), and it might turn out to be of dubious benefit. The approach taken here is rather different. Instead of attempting to list the agenda items for future scholarly activity, I will take a step back to consider the process by which that agenda comes to be set, wittingly or not. In other words, how do we, as business ethics scholars, come to choose what we do – and do not – write about, particularly in academic journals? I address this question in the hope that progress in answering it will enable business ethicists, individually and collectively, to recognize more clearly the actual and potential influences to which we are subject and hence to make better choices about our work than we might otherwise do. In the next two sections of the paper I identify various possible influences upon the agenda of business ethics research, divided into those influences which are primarily academic and those which emanate from beyond the academy. I discuss the pertinent features of each one in turn, identifying both their strengths and – of particular importance when they become too strong an influence – their shortcomings.

II. What to Research: Some Academic Influences

The references above to research quality and academic respectability demonstrate the powerful influences emanating from the academic context in which business ethics researchers are principally located. But this context might influence not only how we research, but also what is researched. In this section I identify and discuss five possible academic influences; previous business ethics literature, debates in academic disciplines, business and management research, research resources, and the curriculum.

1. Previous Business Ethics Literature

Clearly it is important, in order to publish, to cite relevant previous work, thus anchoring the work in a stream (Bain 1995). But in addition to helping us to explore independently chosen topics, the reading of literature helps to shape our agenda. It is the means by which we often get our research students started on choosing a research topic, advising them to read the journals, perhaps within a broad remit. As we keep up to date on the literature or delve in to back issues of journals, we can generate ideas for our own responses and hence contributions to the literature. Thus building on previous literature can either be part of a deliberate approach to deciding what we are going to research, or its influence can be more serendipitous, an element in a more emergent strategy (cf. Mintzberg/Waters 1985).

Good business ethics scholars try to be well-read in their claimed area of expertise, and previous literature in the field is a naturally strong trigger for the reflective reader, prompting the identification of topics, problems and potential contributions. This in itself is not a bad thing, but a literature can develop a life of its own, characterized by contributions of diminishing value which pile up 'footnotes to footnotes' of interest only to the protagonists involved. As Sorell (1998, p. 83) comments, 'One piece of armchair applied ethics can provoke another,' particularly given the pressures on academics to publish. Thus, although it is desirable to possess a cumulative body of knowledge or insights on a particular topic, over-reliance on existing business ethics literature in setting the agenda could result in an inbred corpus of work which, while perfectly competent according to conventional scholarly criteria, could have a significant opportunity cost in terms of alternative uses of the time and effort expended on it. Vast areas of business and management studies could lie unanalyzed in ethical terms. For example, it is possible that the interests pursued in a specialist academic literature will diverge more and more from those generated by the world of business and management practice, which displays considerable dynamism (see below).

It is also possible that the business ethics literature could become intellectually introspective, failing to connect with wider academic developments, not just practical ones. However, as a relatively new, interdisciplinary field, this is less likely, because – for reasons briefly explained in the introduction – its scholars tend to belong or relate to at least one other academic discipline. The potential influence of other academic disciplines is discussed next.

2. Debates in Academic Disciplines

Business ethics scholars tend to read more widely than just business ethics, in many cases seeking to keep abreast of at least some of the developments in whatever they consider to be their academic disciplinary home. Awareness of what is happening in traditional academic disciplines is thus likely to influence research in the applied field of business ethics. This might occur as part of a deliberate strategy, whereby business ethics scholars intentionally seek to apply concepts, frameworks, tools or whatever in the context of the ethics of business. On the other hand, the influence might be more subtle, as business ethics scholars respond subliminally to advances and debates in relevant academic disciplines, absorbing changes in the intellectual climate. Thus intellectual activity in the academic environment, while not directed specifically at the ethics of business may, through the way in which business scholars identify and frame the issues they address, come to have an impact on the agenda for business ethics research. As these disciplines develop and make progress, the potential for building business ethics on sound theoretical foundations is enhanced.

Theology has a long tradition of contributing to the ethical analysis of aspects of business (De George 1987), but many of the leaders of the modern growth of business ethics have a background in philosophy. Thus developments in philosophy – particularly moral philosophy – are likely to be significant. A pertinent example is virtue ethics, which enjoyed a major revival in moral philosophy and has subsequently been taken up with some enthusiasm in business ethics (e.g. Whetstone 2001).

Although such an influence might be taken to imply or confirm the derivative nature of business ethics, the forging of strong links with disciplines might be mutually beneficial, for the exercise of exploring recent academic developments in a business or management context might not only generate new insights for business ethics but also provide an opportunity to make a contribution to the original discipline, particularly if there is substantive work to be done rather than 'mere application'. For example, Freeman (2000) contends that the best work in business ethics (and biomedical ethics) is helping to change (has 'rewoven') the very fabric of ethical theory. One of the areas in which this can happen is in the development of 'bridge concepts', such as conflict of interest or autonomy, that are needed for the application of ethical theory (Bowie 2000). Thus the development of philosophical business ethics can stand as a challenge to moral philosophy, contributing to its own agenda.

In addition to the substantive benefits that progress in such work might bring, there is the further advantage that it can enhance the academic respectability of business ethics and business ethicists (see earlier discussion). Another possible benefit is that it might help to stimulate further business-related conversation in philosophy and perhaps increase the degree of interest shown in business and management by the wider philosophical community, taking advantage of philosophy's having 'tilted again towards the "real world"' (Solomon 1991, p. 354) and thus increasing the resources applied to our area of interest.

There seem to be good reasons both to expect and to welcome the influence of academic disciplines such as philosophy. However, any of the influences identified in this paper can, if unchecked, entail problems too. Stark (1993), for one, thinks that the influence of academic philosophy on business ethics is harmful; though if there is merit in Stark's charges, it may be more to do with the way philosophy is sometimes done than anything inherent in its nature (see Crisp 1998). Sorell (1998, p. 83), for example, charges that, '[i]n order to prove its academic credentials, some writers of business ethics have felt obliged to pursue the subject with as much theoretical apparatus as they can bring to bear, with the result that few business people can follow what is being said.' In other words, to employ a distinction used earlier, there exists the possibility that, through perceived pressures to attain academic respectability, a particular "how" comes to trump "what". Style can come to dominate substance. Stark's well-known broadside against business ethics contains a similar point: "Unfortunately, academic insecurity is causing business ethicists to direct their work away from addressing the real needs of managers and toward satisfying the perceived rigors of academic science in their field" (Stark 1993). Thus there is a risk – depending on what developments have been taking place in philosophy (and theology perhaps) and how they are applied – that business ethics becomes disconnected from its object of study.

However, the 'sustained and cumulative' normative contribution (Robertson 1993) of the philosophers has been augmented by the introduction of various social scientific perspectives, most often from social psychology and organization theory (Victor/Stephens 1994); also from economics (Hosmer/Chen 2001) and politics perhaps. Again, these offer the potential for rigorous analysis and theoretical development. Furthermore, a feature of social science disciplines is that they bring with them an orientation towards empirical research, which might suggest a stronger connection with the 'real world' and thus reduce the risk of irrelevance, which could happen with more abstract theorizing. Many business schools, particularly those with strong research profiles, have a commitment to social scientific research (see below).

In spite of the importance of root disciplines, though, Hosmer (1996) is disappointed by, and critical of, the relative lack of reference to basic normative and descriptive theories. However, it should be acknowledged that this does not mean that those theories do not have an impact on business ethics research. For example, they might influence the background thinking of scholars, in particular through their manifestation in more fully developed frameworks and ideas. Thus more detailed conceptual understandings, whether normative or descriptive, might act as 'intervening variables', not least because – like Bowie's 'bridge concepts' (Bowie 2000) – they are more likely to be capable of relation to the particular concerns of business ethicists and hence of greater analytical value.

From the perspective of this paper, the real contribution of academic disciplines is that they provide a sound foundation for *how* we undertake business ethics research – whether that be philosophical argumentation, abstract theorizing or empirical testing, or whatever. They might also suggest avenues for *what* we research, but the risk is that a research agenda over-determined by academic disciplines will fail to address many important issues. One possible way to control this is to pay attention to research in business and management studies, some of which may well reflect factors related to the practice of business and management, in addition to drawing on developments in academic disciplines.

3. Business and Management Research

Collier (1995, p. 6) notes that in academic terms business ethics 'represents both a field in applied ethics and a legitimate area of management studies'. If we take our cue from business and management research, it might be reasonable to expect business ethics research to be at less risk of becoming divorced from its domain of application than if it is more in subjection to academic disciplines such as philosophy.

Business and management is a diverse area, and it is likely that some aspects will be more interesting for, and amenable to, ethics research than others. For example, ethical issues frequently surface in human resource management, in one guise or another, and it is relatively easy to identify ethical questions in relation to advertising. There are plenty of topics that can easily attract the attention of someone with an interest in ethics.

However, although some other areas might also be ripe for ethical consideration, it might be harder to identify the significant issues or to tackle them convincingly, perhaps because the area is thought to involve matters that are technically challenging and therefore relatively difficult to deal with without the requisite expertise. For example, Boatright/Peterson (2003, p. 265) note that 'business ethics scholars have devoted comparatively little attention to financial topics'. Some financial topics are undoubtedly complex in practice, but since its capture by neo-classical economics, academic finance has also become increasingly abstruse (Whitley 1986) and the dominant paradigm tends to subordinate or bury ethical issues, making them less obvious both to many experts in the field (who possess and pursue a constrained 'how' in research terms) and to observers with limited understanding of the technicalities (who will find it difficult to discern the 'what' to study).

Nevertheless, many business ethics researchers, particularly if they work in a business school, already possess the requisite technical background, since many are well versed in a business discipline (even finance in some cases) rather than, or in addition to, an academic discipline, to use the distinction made earlier.[1] Such expertise will not only enable them to pursue known ethical issues but, particularly if they are keeping up to date with their field of academic business expertise, to identify new, emerging issues. Alternatively, for those business ethics researchers who do not possess the requisite technical expertise, it might be possible for them to collaborate with suitable experts – who might be able to identify important ethical issues and who might have a concern for them, but who lack the specialist competence or confidence to pursue that interest on their own.

When thinking about undertaking research, it is normal to think in terms of conducting new projects, but another possibility is for a business ethics expert to help a subject expert to re-analyze their existing research in ethical terms. It might even be possible for a business ethics researcher to re-analyze existing research in business and management studies without the help of the original researcher, using published accounts of the work and/or data archives – a kind of 'silent collaboration'. Ethical commentary on the substance of a body of existing research should certainly be possible and is probably highly desirable in many cases. Producing ethics perspectives on authoritative review papers on particular topics in particular fields might be a fruitful way of doing this. Thus previous research in business and management studies might have some influence on the agenda for business ethics research by its very availability, particularly if it is awareness of that availability, on the part of either a business ethics researcher or a subject expert, that prompts the new 'ethical commentary' work.

---

1 COWTON/CUMMINS (2003) found that the growth of business ethics teaching in the UK over the previous decade was accounted for by the enthusiasm of staff in business schools or equivalent departments who had originally been appointed to teach another subject and continued to do so.

One of the interesting issues that arise is where such research should be published. Given the focus of this paper on the success of business ethics as an academic endeavour and the development of a valuable body of knowledge, the most obvious destination for submitting papers is one of the main business ethics journals. However, the strong relationship with business and management research, which is the focus of this section, implies that publishing in journals in fields like marketing or accounting might also be possible – or even preferable. This might be of particular importance if the business ethicist is collaborating with a subject expert, depending on the view that expert takes of managing their curriculum vitae. This might be in addition to publication in a business ethics publication, given appropriate writing-up to pursue a different 'angle' in the respective literatures. One of the benefits of publishing in journals dedicated to particular business disciplines is that it enhances the potential for ethics to be incorporated into mainstream subjects. It might also enhance the academic respectability of business ethics and the standing of the individual business ethics scholar. However, the 'leading' journals in some areas of business and management enact a construction of appropriate research that does not admit ethical analyses, except in the most constrained social scientific terms. Such definitions of rigour and respectability are strongly enforced in certain areas of business and management research. Nevertheless, it is an avenue worth exploring.

It is also apparent that researchers in other areas of business and management publish their current work in business ethics journals without the help of an expert in business ethics. This is one of the ways in which research in business and management comes to influence the content of business ethics journals, and it is likely to increase as the status of business ethics grows, thus making publication in its outlets more attractive to scholars. This is not the place to assess whether the full potential of those papers, in business ethics terms, is exploited, but if it is not, then such contributions can be picked up and developed further by business ethics scholars, responding to work that is now part of the business ethics literature (see first influence). And having been published in that literature, it is likely to be easier to develop in ethical terms than work published in other parts of the business and management literature, as at least *some* of the ethical work should have been done already for publication in a business ethics journal.

Taking our cue from business and management research might not be as valuable as expected though. According to Ciulla (1991, pp. 213-214), "[o]ne of the first things you hear upon entering a business school is references to something called the 'real world' ... which dictates what you can and can't do." Yet business schools, notwithstanding their apparently vocational mission, have received criticism from some quarters for the poverty of their relationship with business and management practice, in particular the alleged 'irrelevance' of much of their research. Their research has been criticized for prizing rigour over relevance, perhaps in pursuit of social scientific respectability in the same way that business ethicists can feel themselves subject to academic disciplinary pressure. 'Leading' business schools have been pursuing academic respectability for the past forty years or so by conducting 'rigorous' social science research (Cowton 1998b; Whitley 1986), which has resulted in a 'technical, scientifically-inspired regimen' (Donaldson 1994, p. 4). It seems that academic rewards and resource allocation systems are not configured in such a way as to guarantee research that is respected outside the academy. Therefore, although existing business and management research has a great deal to offer as an influence upon business ethics research, including as a possible corrective to an over-reliance on academic disciplines for setting the agenda, it is not necessarily an infallible guide to ensuring that the agenda will not miss certain important issues.

4. Research Resources

It was noted at the beginning of this paper that, whether we are actively conscious of it or not, research resources for business ethics are limited. What influences the allocation of those resources, particularly time, is the theme of this paper, but it should be acknowledged that research resources can themselves be directed towards particular ends or become available in such a way as to facilitate particular aspects of business ethics research. In the previous section mention was made of the analysis of existing research in business and management. The two other resources to be considered here are money and data.

First, there are funding agencies, of various sorts (e.g. government, foundations, commercial organizations, universities) which either seek to have particular types of research done or, in responsive mode, fund or reject particular project proposals. As such, they mediate, amplify or suppress concerns that emanate from beyond the walls of the academy, some of which will be discussed below. Although business ethics does not receive a large amount of research funding compared to other areas, it receives some. To the extent that it does so, the decisions of funders will influence the agenda for business ethics research. If a particular funder became over-dominant, or if an unduly homogeneous agenda came to exist across funders, problems could be entailed for business ethics researchers – though that is probably a more welcome problem than having little or no research funding.

Second, existing data can be a resource for business ethics research. Mention was made in the previous section of the possibility of re-analyzing from an ethical perspective research data from studies already conducted, but the availability of secondary data more generally is a potential influence on research in business ethics. For much of the time, the unavailability of data acts as a constraint, because appropriate data of adequate quality are difficult to obtain for the investigation of many ethical issues. However, where they do exist, data can act as a prompt to research; secondary data can play a serendipitous role in the initiation of research (Cowton 1998a). Many types of such data exist, including company accounts and other material, government statistics, reports from regulatory agencies and newspapers.

One of the interesting features of secondary data is that they contain the seeds of the solution to the question that they stimulate in the minds of the researcher. (Even if they are insufficient for scholarly purposes, some of them help make scholars aware of significant issues.) Another is – as I have argued elsewhere via a notion termed 'eavesdropping' (Cowton 1998a) – secondary data provide opportunities for avoiding some of the problems associated with collecting primary data on sensitive issues. However, taken too far, the risk with using secondary data is that we research what is convenient rather than what is important, or we fail to address satisfactorily the real issue because the secondary data are inadequate proxies for the primary data that we would wish to collect. Nevertheless, the significant point for this paper is that secondary data *can* act as an influence on what we research.

5. The Curriculum

Directly or indirectly accessing the research interests of academic colleagues in business and management was mentioned earlier as a way of guiding business ethics research, but the vast majority of academics do not spend all or even most of their time conducting research. Teaching is important. The precise nature of the relationship between teaching and research is often debated (e.g. the importance of research activity for the vitality of teaching), but there seem to be two important dimensions relating to the concerns of this paper.

First, the teaching of business ethics itself provides opportunities for research. Such pedagogic research (I am not referring to students as proxies for "proper" research subjects) is common in many fields and disciplines. The challenges of teaching business ethics (often to sceptical students), its unusual nature when compared to many other business school courses, and its relatively recent appearance in many curricula mean that questions worthy of research are likely to occur to academics relatively frequently in the course of their teaching. Indeed, the business ethics journals contain many scholarly contributions to the debate on how to teach business ethics and its effectiveness. In addition to learning more about the process of business ethics teaching and learning, shortcomings in teaching material might stimulate research work that might generate mainstream research findings as well as resources for students. As Collier (1995) comments, research is needed to provide a knowledge base for the expansion of business ethics teaching. For example, many writers have pointed out the need to generate non-US material, not only to provide appropriate material for students outside the USA but also to help internationalize the curriculum in US business schools (Cowton/Dunfee 1995). Thus, one might argue, business ethics might be expected to generate a relatively large amount of pedagogic and related research. The only problem is that such research is often viewed as lower status than research into the subject itself, thus compounding the possible status problems of researching business ethics at all (see earlier discussion). There seems to something of a tension here: for a relatively new academic field such as business ethics, pedagogic research is likely to be of more value than in more conventional business school subjects; but given the relatively low status of pedagogic research there may be an opportunity cost in terms of building the academic respectability of – and hence curriculum opportunities for – business ethics.

Second, and returning to the more tactical tone of some of the earlier comments, one of the desires of many business ethicists is to have ethics integrated into mainstream courses within the business school (Dunfee/Robertson 1988). Taking our research cue from what our colleagues teach might be one way of achieving this. As Murphy comments:

> Most of us "doing ethics" would be less than honest if we didn't recognize that there is still substantial resistance to business ethics within most schools of business. These critics are often not only vocal, but also productive and respected faculty members. They will probably never embrace the notion of eth-

> ics in the curriculum or as a field of study, but we cannot ignore them. Involving them in team teaching of a case or as part of a *joint research topic* are ways to begin the dialogue. (Murphy 1994, pp. 387-388, emphasis added)

Of course, it is often asserted that the curriculum is already too full – across and within courses – to find room for business ethics. The excuse might not be a good one, but it is often deemed sufficient. A possible response is for business ethicists to work on emerging issues in particular subject areas: "New business practices are constantly evolving, the ethical nature of which is not always or immediately clear" (De George 1991, p. 44). Analysis of techniques and methods being promoted in more practice-oriented journals, such as *Harvard Business Review* or *McKinsey Quarterly*, might be a good starting point. If room is left for current issues or space is made for important new topics in the curriculum, and hence new teaching material is being generated, material on ethics is more likely to find a foothold. Indeed, it might even be welcomed by subject specialists as they seek to get to grips with a novel topic and develop a new lecture or seminar. If the new issue or topic is one that the business world is also grappling with, such an approach is also going to do no harm to the perceived relevance of business ethics research. That world beyond the academy is itself a source of potential influences upon the agenda for business ethics research, and is the subject of the next section.

III. What to Research: Some Influences from Beyond the Academy

Janus-like, the scholarly community of business ethics faces two ways; towards the academy of which we are members, as discussed above, and towards the world beyond the academy. Perhaps it is the case that 'non-academic' factors have less influence on the business ethics research agenda than might be expected or desired by some commentators. However, as Sorell (1998) notes, there are several ways in which the distance between business ethics and the business world can be diminished. Without any claim to exhaustiveness, this section will attempt to highlight some of the main ways in which 'real world' influences might bear upon the research agenda of business ethics, beginning with businesses and their managers and radiating outwards through stakeholder concerns and the wider society.

1. Businesses and Their Managers

It would be strange indeed if business ethics had no contact with businesses and other types of organization that are usually considered to come with its purview, and the identification by business (in the broad sense) of issues that it considers to be of ethical significance is a potential influence upon business ethics research. There are many ways in which business ethics researchers might come to learn of these issues, but a basic division would be between direct and indirect methods.

The ethical concerns of organizations and their managers can be picked up on an opportunistic basis just from interacting with people from the business world, in the classroom or beyond. This can lead to interesting and perhaps important research. Individual case studies, perhaps developed for teaching purposes, can also be a useful source of ideas. On the other hand, the ethical issues that confront business and managers could be established on a more systematic basis. At one level it could be viewed as a kind of market research to 'poll' managers on what they consider the most significant ethical issues facing them. An example is to be found in the work of Waters *et al.* (1986), who asked managers "What ethical questions come up or have come up in the course of your work life?" Similarly, Fisher/Lovell (2000) conducted fieldwork to discover from practising management accountants what kinds of ethical problems they had faced. The concerns and work of managers, such as ethics officers, who have formal responsibility for helping to manage the corporate ethics agenda, might be particularly relevant. Such research would not only identify ethical issues but might also aim to prioritize them according to some criteria, which is difficult to do if a more casual approach is taken. Professional associations might be another useful source of such insights. This is not to say that practitioners will be the only source, but as I have suggested elsewhere (Cowton 1998b), although it might be thought that practising managers are not necessarily adept at such exercises (which also raise some research challenges), that is no reason for ignoring them. Instead, their replies should be treated with circumspection as well as respect.

A less direct approach is not to ask businesses but to listen to what businesses say 'anyway', or to observe what they do. This is not just to save the trouble of doing more systematic research; direct 'polling' research can entail 'leading' or socially desirable response bias (Fernandes/Randall 1992; Randall/Fernandes 1991). To cite an obvious example, codes of ethics are one of the most visible manifestations of the addressing of ethical issues in the world of business. There are debates about their efficacy, and to the extent that they ignore important issues, they will have limitations as an influence upon the business ethics research agenda. Nevertheless, what they do cover is a useful indicator of significant topics. Thus codes of ethics might not only be a subject of research in their own right (e.g. how widespread or effective they are) but they can also help identify topics and issues for further research and analysis. It might be hoped that business people would, other things being equal, take more notice of such research since they have already 'gone public' on the relevant focus of attention.

2. Stakeholder Concerns

The approaches briefly described above might be characterized as seeking to discover problems *for* managers. However, there are also problems *of* managers and the institutions of which they are part. Put another way, business ethics research can take both a 'decision-making' and a 'critical' perspective (Macfarlane 1996); or, as Collier (1995, p. 6) comments, research of the right kind will ideally 'serve the needs of companies *and stakeholders* alike' (emphasis added). Thus if business ethics is to be more than managerial ethics, its agenda also needs to be influenced directly – rather than derivatively via managers' discomfort – by the concerns of other organizational stakeholders, such as non-managerial employees and consumers. Some of these might already have some coverage in the less managerialist elements of the business and management literature. In the case of 'silent stakeholders', such as the environment or third world workers in the supply chain, NGOs acting on their behalf can play an important role in highlighting issues for business ethicists to address.

Such an orientation brings with it a wider conception of 'relevance' than is often apparent when business schools and business ethicists are criticized for a lack of relevance in their research and writings. There is nothing in the foundation documents or funding sources of the institutions in which most academic research takes place to suggest that business ethics research should not be critical of businesses and their managers. Quite the contrary; universities etc. are generally intended to pursue some notion of the public interest, and that might well involve identifying and attempting to solve the problems *of* managers, attending to the ethical issues that modern management tends to cause. Thus the relevant question regarding relevance is: relevant to whom?

As Sorell (1998, p. 81) remarks, "might not even a business ethics without credibility among business people be picked up by institutions whom business people do take seriously – legislatures, say, or regulatory agencies, or the media?" Business ethics research needs to avoid being unduly 'descriptive' (De George 1991) and should maintain, where appropriate, a critical edge. Taking a non-managerial stakeholder perspective can be a way of ensuring that the research agenda possesses that quality in addition to its interest in addressing the problems *for* managers.

3. Societal Issues

The stakeholder approach represents an attempt to identify and give weight to the social impact of a business, beyond its financial returns to the owners of its share capital. In some cases there will be particularly widespread and important issues that affect all or many stakeholder groups, and some of these will provide a possible prompt to business ethics research to the extent that business is in some way responsible for causing, promoting or alleviating the relevant trends. Carroll (2000) noted that one way in which we can think about ethical challenges for business in the new millennium is to think of what new issues will arise. Important though they are, it is easy to lose sight of such issues and their relevance to business ethics.

Various issues or trends have been suggested in the literature. For example, Carroll mentions technology, as does Frederick, who notes that it is infrequently discussed by business ethicists – even though it is

> a transformative force in human culture, bringing people together and splitting them apart in bewildering ways, thrusting fierce and poignant moral questions forward, generating strikingly new and dazzling dimensions of communication and sensing and experiencing and intellectual exploration (Frederick 2000, p. 162).

Fuelled in part by technology, globalization is another major force, posing ever greater and more complex practical and theoretical challenges (Enderle 2003). Although there has been a growth in the general area of international business ethics, "the achievements of business ethics have fallen considerably short of what is required," according to Enderle (2003, p. 531). Other possible major themes or issues in modern society include risk, the environment and climate change, population change (e.g. growth and aging) and poverty/inequality (Ciulla 2000). In this context, it is interesting to note that

Collins (2000), in his analysis of the first 1500 articles published in the *Journal of Business Ethics*, entitles his article 'The quest to improve the human condition'. This title provides an arresting corrective to overly narrow debates, mentioned earlier, regarding the 'relevance' of business ethics to the 'real world' of managers.

Of course, many of these issues can come to be reflected in the political domain. The relationship between ethics and the law or other forms of regulation is not a simple one, but proposed and enacted regulations provide scope for business ethicists to provide research-based analysis and, as such, can be an influence upon the research agenda. Legal cases and scandals can also provide pointers for business ethics research, though the latter are probably a two-edged sword for the progress of business ethics. Scandals are as much about social perception as they are about what happened, and they can lead to moral panic and hence over-reaction, diverting attention from other, perhaps less spectacular but equally important, issues.

IV. Conclusion

In this paper I have attempted to highlight the possible influences active in the setting of the business ethics research agenda, and I have indicated some of the advantages and possible disadvantages of those influences. From within the academy I have suggested influence coming from previous business ethics literature, debates in academic disciplines, business and management research, research resources, and the curriculum; while from outside the academy I posited influences running from businesses themselves through stakeholder groups to social issues. Perhaps there are other influences too, and advantages and disadvantages other than those I have identified. Further analysis, including systematic research into the impact of those influences and their interrelationship, might refine the points made in this paper. However, there is a limit to what can be accomplished within the constraints of a single paper. This paper will have achieved its purpose if it stimulates and helps to promote reflection and conversation on how the business ethics research agenda has come to be the way it is and on what it might be in the future. I cannot imagine any business ethics researcher maintaining that we have enough time and other resources for all the research we could do. The literature we create as scholars is a major investment and the resources available for creating and improving it are finite. It is important, therefore, that we think seriously about the research agenda that we develop – even if, perhaps, one conclusion is that no more papers like this one are required!

Acknowledgements

I am grateful to John Boatright, Tom Dunfee, Michaela Haase and Henk van Luijk for comments on earlier versions of this paper.

References

BAIN, W. A.: "Ethical Problems in Ethics Research", *Business Ethics: A European Review*, 4 (1995), pp. 13-16.

BOATRIGHT, J. R., PETERSON, J.: "Introduction: Special Issue on Finance", *Business Ethics Quarterly*, 13 (2003), pp. 265-270.

BOWIE, N. E.: "Business Ethics, Philosophy, and the Next 25 Years", *Business Ethics Quarterly*, 10 (2000), pp. 7-20.

BRADY, F. N., HATCH, M. J.: "General Causal Models in Business Ethics: An Essay on Colliding Research Traditions", *Journal of Business Ethics*, 11 (1992), pp. 307-315.

CARROLL, A. B.: "Ethical Challenges for Business in the New Millennium: Corporate Social Responsibility and Models of Management Morality", *Business Ethics Quarterly*, 10 (2000), pp. 33-42.

CIULLA, J. B.: "Business Ethics as Moral Imagination", in: R. E. FREEMAN (Ed.): *Business Ethics: The State of the Art*, New York (Oxford University Press) 1991, pp. 212-220.

CIULLA, J. B.: "On Getting to the Future First", *Business Ethics Quarterly*, 10 (2000), pp. 53-61.

COLLIER, J.: "Business Ethics Research: Shaping the Agenda", *Business Ethics: A European Review*, 4 (1995), pp. 6-12.

COLLINS, D.: "The Quest to Improve the Human Condition: The First 1500 Articles Published in Journal of Business Ethics", *Journal of Business Ethics*, 26 (2000), pp. 1-73.

COWTON, C. J. (1998a): "The Use of Secondary Data in Business Ethics Research", *Journal of Business Ethics*, 17 (1998), pp. 423-434.

COWTON, C. J. (1998b): "Research in Real Worlds: The Empirical Contribution to Business Ethics", in: C. COWTON, R. CRISP (Eds.): *Business Ethics: Perspectives on the Practice of Theory*, Oxford (Oxford University Press) 1998, pp. 97-115.

COWTON, C. J., CUMMINS, J.: "Teaching Business Ethics in UK Higher Education: Progress and Prospects", *Teaching Business Ethics*, 7 (2003), pp. 37-54.

COWTON, C. J., DUNFEE, T. W.: "Internationalizing the Business Ethics Curriculum: A Survey", *Journal of Business Ethics*, 14 (1995), pp. 331-338.

CRISP, R.: "A Defence of Philosophical Business Ethics", in: C. COWTON, R. CRISP (Eds.): *Business Ethics: Perspectives on the Practice of Theory*, Oxford (Oxford University Press) 1998, pp. 9-25.

DE GEORGE, R. T.: "The Status of Business Ethics: Past and Future", *Journal of Business Ethics*, 6 (1987), pp. 201-211.

DE GEORGE, R. T.: "Will Success Spoil Business Ethics?", in: R. E. FREEMAN (Ed.): *Business Ethics: The State of the Art*, New York (Oxford University Press) 1991, pp. 42-56.

DONALDSON, T. J.: "Introduction", in: T. J. DONALDSON, R. E. FREEMAN (Eds.): *Business as a Humanity*, New York (Oxford University Press) 1994, pp. 3-8.

DUNFEE, T. W., ROBERTSON, D. C.: "Integrating Ethics into the Business School Curriculum", *Journal of Business Ethics*, 7 (1988), pp. 847-859.

ENDERLE, G.: "A Comparison of Business Ethics in North America and Continental Europe", *Business Ethics: A European Review*, 5 (1996), pp. 33-46.

ENDERLE, G.: "Business Ethics", in: N. BUNNIN, E. P. TSUI-JAMES (Eds.): *The Blackwell Companion to Philosophy*, Oxford (Blackwell) 2003, pp. 531-551.

FERNANDES, M. F., RANDALL, D. M.: "The Nature of the Social Desirability Response Effects in Ethics Research", *Business Ethics Quarterly*, 2 (1992), pp. 183-205.

FISHER, C., LOVELL, A.: *Accountants' Responses to Ethical Issues at Work*, London (Chartered Institute of Management Accountants) 2000.

FLEMING, J.: "A Survey and Critique of Business Ethics Research, 1986", in: W. C. FREDERICK, L. E. PRESTON (Eds.): *Business Ethics: Research Issues and Empirical Studies*, Greenwich, CT (JAI Press) 1990, pp. 1-23.

FREDERICK, W. C.: "Notes for a Third Millennial Manifesto: Renewal and Redefinition in Business Ethics", *Business Ethics Quarterly*, 10 (2000), pp. 159-168.

FREEMAN, R. E.: "Business Ethics at the Millennium", *Business Ethics Quarterly*, 10 (2000), pp. 169-180.

HOSMER, L. T.: "5 Years, 20 Issues, 141 Articles, and What?" *Business Ethics Quarterly*, 6 (1996), pp. 325-358.

HOSMER, L. T., CHEN, F.: "Ethics and Economics: Growing Opportunities for Joint Research", *Business Ethics Quarterly*, 11 (2001), pp. 599-622.

MACFARLANE, B.: "Reflections on Business Ethics", *Economics and Business Education*, 4 (1996), pp. 171-174.

MINTZBERG, H., WATERS, J. A.: "Of Strategies, Deliberate and Emergent", *Strategic Management Journal*, 6 (1985), pp. 257-272.

MURPHY, P. E.: "Business Ethics: A Mature Product", *Business Ethics Quarterly*, 4 (1994), pp. 383-389.

RANDALL, D. M., FERNANDES, M. F.: "The Social Desirability Response Bias in Ethics Research", *Journal of Business Ethics*, 10 (1991), pp. 805-817.

RANDALL, D. M., GIBSON, A. M.: "Methodology in Business Ethics Research: A Review and Critical Assessment", *Journal of Business Ethics*, 9 (1990), pp. 457-471.

ROBERTSON, D. C.: "Empiricism in Business Ethics: Suggested Research Directions", *Journal of Business Ethics*, 12 (1993), pp. 585-599.

SOLOMON, R. S.: "Business Ethics", in: P. SINGER (Ed.): *A Companion to Ethics*, Oxford (Blackwell) 1991, pp. 354-365.

SORELL, T.: "Armchair Applied Philosophy and Business Ethics", in: C. COWTON, R. CRISP (Eds.): *Business Ethics: Perspectives on the Practice of Theory*, Oxford (Oxford University Press) 1998, pp. 79-95.

STARK, A.: "What's the Matter with Business Ethics?" *Harvard Business Review*, 71 (1993), pp. 38-48.

VICTOR, B., STEPHENS, C. U.: "Business Ethics: A Synthesis of Normative Philosophy and Empirical Social Science", *Business Ethics Quarterly*, 4 (1994), pp. 145-155.

WATERS, J. A., BIRD, F., CHANT, P. F.: "Everyday Moral Issues Experienced by Managers", *Journal of Business Ethics*, 5 (1986), pp. 373-384.

WEBER, J.: "Scenarios in Business Ethics Research: Review, Critical Assessment, and Recommendations", *Business Ethics Quarterly*, 2 (1992), pp. 137-159.

WERHANE, P. H., FREEMAN, R. E.: "Business Ethics: The State of the Art", *International Journal of Management Reviews*, 1 (1999), pp. 1-16.

WHETSTONE, J. T.: "How Virtue Fits Within Business Ethics", *Journal of Business Ethics*, 33 (2001), pp. 101-114.

WHITLEY, R.: "The Transformation of Business Finance into Financial Economics: The Roles of Academic Expansion and Changes in U.S. Capital Markets", *Accounting, Organizations and Society*, 11 (1986), pp. 171-192.

Chapter 2

Some Principles of Ethical Economy

PETER KOSLOWSKI

Aristotle states that everything worth doing is worth doing well. The economist James Buchanan claims that this is not the principle of economics, which states rather that it is not worth it to do everything well. Aristotle founded his ethics on the principle of *arete* or excellence, literally bestness.

The human being should aim at excellence in all actions. Economics, however, is founded on the principle of efficiency. Everything worth doing should be done efficiently. It is not efficient to do too well, and there are actions and things that should not be done or made too well. Therefore, not everything worth doing is worth doing well. It is worth making mass products, but it is not worth making them in such a way that they are as good as possible. It would be rather beside the point to make mass products so well. They would be too expensive and not mass products anymore. The economist has to adopt his actions to economic demand, not to conceptions of intrinsic excellence. It is also, economically speaking, not good to produce goods that are excellent but do not succeed in the market.

Ethics and economics seem to be inimical brothers.[1] They are brothers since they are both theories of human action and decision-making. They both ask the questions: "How can I make sure that I will act appropriately" and "Have I acted appropriately?" And both, ethics and economics, have a prospective and retrospective dimension.

Ethics and economics are inimical brothers since their normative content seems to be contradictory. In ethics, the task of the human, *to ergon tu anthropu* as Aristotle says, is to realize the best. In economics, the task is to realize the efficient; in technology, to realize the effective. If we look closer, however, ethical and economic theory are not as contradictory as first appears. Doing the best for mass demand means not producing the best but producing the best suited to the needs of the market, i.e. consumer demand. On the other hand, it is also a postulate of ethics to consider the circumstances that might distinguish the best in a given situation from the best as a whole. It might under given circumstances, for instance, be the best to realize a solution that is considered to be only second best if circumstances are improved. It is worth realizing mass production well, although the result of the action will not be the best possible product but a mass product.

---

1 The author uses arguments in this paper from his earlier publications (see Appendix). The present paper is the revised version of the inaugural lecture that the author gave as Professor of Philosophy at the Vrije Universiteit Amsterdam in Amsterdam on 9 December 2005.

I. The Good and the Speculative as Bridges Between the Ethical and the Economic

The concept of the good as the moral good and as the economic good leads to the link between ethics and economics. The good as the common ground of ethical and economic reasoning is the first phenomenon that makes the intrinsic link between ethics and economics visible. The other phenomenon is the not-well-structured decision and the inevitability of the speculative in economics and ethics. The lack of well-structuredness of many decisions causes the paradox of choice that we only know the consequences of our actions precisely when they do not have many consequences, if they are well-structured. We do not know them well, however, if they have grave consequences and are, therefore, badly structured. Decisions can be badly structured and uncertain in its consequences for two reasons: first since they are badly structured in economic respect as the arguments of the utility or profit calculus are not well-defined, or secondly since they are morally relevant and touch upon something unconditional. The two bridges towards the synthesis of ethics and economics, the good and the speculative will be discussed in the first part of this paper.

In the second part, the synthesizing theory of ethical economy will be analyzed as comprising two fields, the economic theory of ethics and the ethical theory of economics. The first part of ethical economy discusses the impact of the economic method for ethical theory, the second part the impact of ethical principles for the theory of individual decision-making and for the coordination of human action in the market.

1. The Principle of the Threefold Nature of the Good: the Unconditionally Good, the Effective, and the Efficient

Plato discusses the question in *Hippias Minor* whether a bad person can do bad well. He comes to the conclusion that this is possible and that it aggravates the problem of evil. The good person can do good badly and can do good well. The bad or evil person can do bad or evil excellently and badly. If the bad person does bad very well the outcome will be worse than if the bad person does bad poorly. The worst case is that the very bad person does very bad things very well. The proverb *corruptio optimi pessimum*, the corruption of the best is the worst, captures this perversion of good and bad in doing bad excellently. Apparently, it is not sufficient to do something well. It must also be the right thing that is done well. The intention to do something well matters. Intentionality does usually also imply the taking of position, the *Stellungnahme*. In acting consciously, human beings take a position to their action and to its consequences. They are not neutral towards their actions. Human beings take an affirming or disapproving position to their actions. *Stellungnahme*, taking position, is, as Eduard Spranger showed, a key concept of the humanities.

Economics and ethics are also concerned with the conflict between intention and success, effort and outcomes. Intention and outcome might diverge. The good person intends the best but achieves a bad outcome. The bad person intends the not-so-good and realizes the good outcome. This divergence between intention and outcome or between moral intention and economic success has prompted questions of theodicy since the story of Job. Why does sometimes the not-so-moral person meet with economic success in life whereas the moral person often suffers economic disadvantage? The problem of theodicy concerns, strictly speaking, the suffering of the innocent that is not caused by individual moral shortcoming or guilt but by circumstances beyond the moral intention of the individual. In the case of Job, the person struck by mischief is described as being particularly moral. The contingency of happiness and economic success upon moral worth is one of the central topics of religion as the activity of mastering contingency, or *Kontingenzbewältigung* as Hermann Lübbe coined it. The contingency of the harmony between merit and success is a central problem in ethics and is therefore also an aspect of ethical economy: Why is the ruthless (business) person sometimes economically more successful than the moral one?

There are theories of economic ethics, such as the one introduced by Karl Homann, which claim that the contingency of the disharmony between intention and success can only obtain as long as the right economic order is not yet installed (Homann 2002). In the right economic order, the proper institutions would make sure that intentions and rewards would not diverge. Although it is the necessary and legitimate aim of the economic order to create incentive-compatible business norms and business ethics, it seems likely that conflicts between intentions and results and between moral motivation and economic incentives will persist.

There are two kinds of divergences between morality and advantage possible: firstly, systematic divergences: An immoral action can appear to be and be more advantageous than the moral one. This is the more serious case for ethical economy. Secondly, accidental or contingent divergences: A moral action that appeared to be advantageous can turn out to be disadvantageous due to a change of the circumstances of the action in question. The change of circumstances might be brought about by changes in the behavior of others as will be discussed below.

A totally incentive-compatible economic order and business ethics is yet another economic utopia. For now, it seems to be a realistic economic and ethical premise to assume that economic incentives and moral motivation or economic and moral motivation do not always converge and are likely to be in conflict from time to time. It is as wrong to assume that moral and economic imperatives always diverge as to assume that an economic order is possible in which they never diverge. Even if moral intention and incentive on the one hand and economic motivation and incentive on the other are harmonized and point to the same choice of action, the problem of evil remains. Evil can be intended against moral and economic imperatives and incentives. Free will can intend the immoral and the non-economic, and evil will usually intend the morally and economically bad.

The economic dimension adds a third dimension to human action beyond the technically and morally good: the dimension that something is done efficiently in relation to the demand of others. The good person can do good effectively and still fail to satisfy consumer demand of those for whom the action is done. Someone might produce a good car with good technology, but the car fails to satisfy consumer demand. The action of producing it is therefore inefficient and not good.

There are three dimensions of good: the moral good, the effective, and the efficient. A good action should be done well in the sense of morally good, effectively good and efficiently good. Three imperatives correspond to these three meanings of good: the categorical imperative, the technical imperative, and the economic or pragmatic imperative. The moral good is categorically, not hypothetically good in the sense that its being good is not conditional or hypothetical on a given good or goal like the economic. It is not sufficient when realizing good to follow only one of the imperatives. To follow the goal of the categorically moral good without consideration of the technical and pragmatic or economic imperatives is as bad as following the technical or economic/pragmatic imperatives without consideration to the categorically good.

The simple word "good" is the unifying concept of the moral good, the technically effective, and the economically efficient. G. E. Moore contended that the word "good" cannot be defined and has only an intuitive meaning. This impossibility theorem about the definability of the word "good" is exaggerated but it does point to the fact that good has three dimensions that are to be distinguished and sometimes hard to recognize in the concrete case. The central one of these dimensions is the morally or ethically good, which defines an ultimate and unconditional or categorical norm that is the measure of higher commitment as compared to the other meanings of good.[2] The other two meanings of good, the technically good and the economically good or efficient, are good only under the condition that the morally good is not violated.

It is not always clear – and there is certainly no consensus about – what the categorical imperative implies in the real choice of actions. The definition of the moral is subject to disagreement and historical development. It belongs, however, to the grammar of the word "good" that we cannot subordinate the moral to the economical. The economic good is conditional on the non-violation of the moral good, rather than the other way around. The moral good is not conditional on the economically efficient. If someone said that it is immoral to kill an innocent person and at the same time claimed that it is economic to apply euthanasia and kill someone for the good economic reason of saving resources, he would be considered not to have understood the meaning of the word "good". The economic good cannot overrule the moral good since the economic good is conditional on an end, whereby the consumption of means for attaining this end should be minimized or the goal attainment for using the given means should be maximized. The moral good is not to subordinate the moral good to the economic good, although it is furthered by the efficient action adopted to realize it. It is a category mistake to overrule the moral good by the economic good.

Good cannot be exhausted by describing a functional relationship, i.e. of being functionally good for fulfilling a function. In the case of a knife, the good can be described by a functional relationship: a good knife is a knife that cuts well and thus fulfills the function of cutting well. With human beings, it is more difficult. They cannot be described by one function alone. A good person is not a person that fulfills a function well. The function might

2 In this sense, the moral good can also be described as a „hypergood" (CHARLES TAYLOR 1989) or „hypernorm" (DONALDSON/DUNFEE 1994, p. 264).

be a perverse function but be performed excellently, or it might only be one function among many.

If the quality of the ethical and the economic coincide in the word "good", they must be related, even if they are not identical. The theory of ethical economy aims at understanding this interface of the economic and the ethical in the word "good". It insists that there can be neither a lasting opposition between the economically and the ethically good nor a simple identity between them. The moral is the unconditionally good in the sense that is not conditional on a given goal as the economic good is. Its concretization will, therefore, always be debated and contested since it is not conditional on something else. The morally good and ethical is, as Niklas Luhmann has rightly stated, "polemogenous", "generating war", or, if not war, so at least generating moral strife. The polemical character of the moral is due to its character of being the unconditionally good.

The unconditional character of the morally good promotes questionable features of morality such as moral aggression or the aggressive moralization of morally neutral realms of action. The economy, on the other hand, is not usually a field of moral contention for the unconditionally good, but of economic contest over goods or commodities, which are conditional on the demand of individuals and not conditional on violating or not violating moral norms. It is a category mistake to moralize economic efficiency conditions of human action if the unconditional is not touched.

To argue morally against firms that move their production to countries where labor is less expensive, for instance, is a category mistake since it is not immoral to lower one's costs. Since it is not expected of workers that they make economic sacrifices to maintain the firms for which they work, it cannot be expected of the firms' owners that they sacrifice their wealth to maintain the production sites. None of the two parties, neither the employer nor the employee, can be expected to make economic sacrifices for the long-term survival of their firms. Both can undergo reductions of their future remunerations in wages or in profits, but they both cannot accept a severe loss of wealth by subsidizing their firm.

The semantics of the word "good" imply that ethics cannot be introduced merely functionally, in order to attain something completely outside of the moral. The ethics must be generally valid at core, not simply specific to a firm or a single group, be it employers or employees. There can, of course, be firm-specific forms of corporate culture,[3] habits, customs, etc. But the general rules of business ethics cannot be firm-specific in the sense that they are valid only for the firm in which they are created because they are good only for this firm. Attempts to introduce firm-specific codes of business ethics that are only useful functionally for the financial goals of the firm in question face the same objections as functionalist foundations of ethics in general.

Ethical theories that are introduced in order to serve functionally a purpose that is outside ethics per se are always in danger of not achieving their purpose, because people see through their purposefulness, with the consequence that the ethics are not accepted as binding. Functional foundations have the weakness that they argue – and must argue – with functional equivalents. Something is good for the fulfillment of a function. But something else can likewise fulfill the function, so that something *else* can always take the place of that which the function fulfills. If ethics are introduced only in order to attain something external to ethics, i.e. the purpose at hand, like in the case of the firm higher profits, the ethics will have no power of persuasion with the workers. If ethics is not also acknowledged as valid in itself and desirable by all members of a firm, including its managers and owners, it will not be convincing and effective. If ethos and ethics are used as means for something completely different and are not recognized as intrinsic and unconditional, as a challenge for the person's free moral decision, they have no power of persuasion.

Functionalistic foundations are insufficient for the development and expansion of a theory of economic ethics, since – in business ethics as in general ethics – human freedom must be at the same time acknowledged as an end in itself. Ethics must portray the fact that, in Kant's words, one must never regard oneself or others simply as a means, but always, at the same time, as an end in itself. That does not mean that one may *never* consider other persons and ethics as a means to something else. Such hypermoralism would make the idea of economic cooperation and the division of labor impossible.

Kant stated that the categorical imperative is only one and one among all of its formulations "Do not use another as a means only, but always consider him or her as an end in itself". The categorical imperative demands that one

3 Cf. for the ethical aspects of institutionalizing a corporate culture in a firm VAN GERWEN (2000) and on personal, moral and professional integrity MUSSCHENGA (2002).

may never use a person and ethics *only* as a means. When applied to economic ethics, this means that business ethics can and should be beneficial to economic purposes, but that they may never be founded only on economic purposes and may never be made completely instrumental to business purposes.

To use a person as a means only implies in the business context severe violation of business morals, such as breach of contract, fraud, systematic discrimination on the grounds of race, sex, religion and age, and systematic exploitation.[4] It does not imply minor and nonsystematic variations in the price ratio (such as underpaying or overcharging at a minor rate), laying staff off due to a lack of demand, or relocating production. Changes in business relationships, such as laying workers off, might be economically disadvantageous or unpleasant, but they are variations in contractual relationships that are due to economic, not moral, reasons. They should not be moralized over since they do not conflict with the moral dignity of people. Business ethics cannot be used to argue against changes in the market conditions and in favor of compensation for damages caused by these changes. Business ethics are a means to argue against non-compliance with the rules of the economy, not against economic changes in market conditions.

2. The Speculative as a Bridge Between Ethics and Economics: Choice as Transcending the Infinity of Opportunity Cost and Negation

Ethical economy is not a hybrid of subsystems of a different kind or genus, but a conceptual synthesis. It is a combination of the ethical and the economic mode of thinking. Both methods have to overcome their mistrust of each other. Economics is notoriously suspicious of ethics since it assumes that it will interfere with its assumed clarity and univocal character. Economics is based on the economist D. H. Robertson's warning that the economist must economize on love and ethics, i.e. economize on unselfish motives since they are not robust, but weak, and are a most scarce resource. We just do not have such a wealth of unselfish motives that we can waste them. Ethics in turn must overcome its suspicion of economics, of the "dismal science"

4 Whether the Kantian principle to treat human persons never as means only requires "a vast democratization of the work place" (BOWIE 2002, pp. 12ff.) and the adoption of the stakeholder approach to corporate governance (EVAN/FREEMAN 1993) as Bowie as well as Evan/Freeman postulate is very doubtful. It is rather a negative principle of excluding actions than demanding positive action.

which reduces everything to scarcity and money. Since any course of action excludes another opportunity for action, every action has a cost which can, in one way or another, be expressed by its opportunity costs in terms of money.

It must be acknowledged not only by economics but also by ethics that in a finite world every course of action excludes other actions and opportunities and that this opportunity cost is of ethical and economic relevance. The cost for an opportunity forsaken is not the same as a cost actually occurred since we never know exactly how much another opportunity would have cost in real terms since it has not occurred yet and will never occur. Nevertheless, opportunities forsaken imply a forsaken utility and therefore an opportunity cost for economic and an opportunity forsaken for ethical theory. This is particularly true for irreversible decisions in which the opportunity cost of the decision cannot be revised at any cost. Irreversible decisions are particularly ethical decisions since they encounter prohibitive costs of revision.

The concept of opportunity cost resembles but is not identical with the principle of negation. Spinoza introduced the principle of negation of which Hegel made ample use: *omnis determinatio est negatio*. Every determination is negation. Hegel extended this Spinozan principle to the principle of determined negation, of *bestimmte Negation*, in his metaphysical logic. The world is nothing than the process of an original partition, *Ur-teil*, and the consecutive infinite process of negation. Translated into the logic of choice, Spinoza's principle implies that every decision is the negation of other decisions, every outcome chosen the negation of all other possible outcomes, every chosen profit opportunity the negation of all other possible profit opportunities.

The idea, however, that determination and decision are negation cannot stand philosophical and economic criticism as the critique of Spinoza's and Hegel's ontology demonstrates. If determination or decision-making is the negation of all other attributes, possibilities, or decision outcomes it will never reach the point of determinedness or decision since there are just infinite possibilities to be negated. Hegel's principle of determined negation implies that we know how often we have to negate to reach the positive. This is, however, just what we should like to know but do not know from the principle of negation alone.

The logic of determination and the logic of decision are similar in logics, ethics, and economics. In the logics of logics and in the logics of choice, negation is a central principle, but it is not the only and ontological or metaphysical principle of reality or decision-making. To make negation the origin of the totality of being implies to move the spirit of evil at the origin of being, as Immanuel Hermann Fichte, the son of the older Fichte, said. It identifies *den Geist, der stets verneint*, the spirit who always negates, as the origin of being. The Spinoza's pantheism of negation as the principle of reality is a questionable import and re-import by and from German Idealism from and to Amsterdam.[5]

By making an ethical or economic decision we do not negate infinite other possibilities but negate only a finite number of alternatives or opportunities. We negate the opportunities that we are able to imagine and that are actually open to us. It requires all our imagination and analysis as well as all our ethical honesty to recognize what our opportunities really are and which of these opportunities we shall forsake.

In the ontology of determined negation, on the other hand, we would face infinite opportunity costs as infinite alternatives forsaken. Infinite alternatives forsaken imply that we ought not and can not act at all since we only lose by any action taken. By not acting, however, we also face infinite opportunity costs. As a result, decision-making would be made impossible if non-acting implied infinite opportunities forsaken and a decision for a concrete course of action implied also infinite opportunities forsaken. Decision-making in ethics and economics demands to identify the relevant and real opportunities we actually have, it does not demand to negate all possible opportunities in all possible worlds.

As acting persons we are not omniscient negators of all the other possibilities we might have. Only for God is this determined negation possible. God is able to choose the best of all possible worlds by negating all other possible but suboptimal worlds, as Leibniz demonstrated in his *Theodicy* (cf. Koslowski 1985). God can negate all the other non-optimal worlds by choosing the best of all possible worlds which is the existent one since God can only choose the best. Therefore, the existent world must always be the best possible one. Only possible non-existent worlds can be suboptimal worlds.

Humans, in contrast, are decision-makers acting under relative uncertainty and facing the "paradox of choice" (Shackle 1979, p. 19). In his book *Imagination and the Nature of Choice,* G. L. S. Shackle formulated this deep paradox most elegantly. If our actions after a decision have no influence on the course of the world, we have no genuine choice. Everything is already

5 Abraham Kuyper, the founder of the Vrije Universiteit Amsterdam, already pointed to the Pantheistic common ground between Spinoza, Kant, Hegel and Schelling.

predetermined. If we have, however, genuine choice and our decision changes the course of the world, we cannot know in detail which effects our actions will have, since the determined course of the world is interrupted by our action. The decision is based on freedom, not on negation of opportunities. It breaks through the infinity of negated opportunities in favor of the one chosen opportunity. In this sense, Johann Gottlieb Fichte was right when he called freedom the rock at which the surge of the universe is broken: *Freiheit: der Fels, an dem sich die Brandung des Universums bricht.*[6]

Applied to the problem of economic choice according to a maximization rule, the paradox of choice implies that when genuine opportunities for choice exist, the maximization calculus, understood as a precise calculation procedure, is not applicable, since the arguments of the equation for the utilities of the future outcomes are unknown. When the maximization calculus is, on the contrary, applicable, it is of little use, because the equations of the constraints of the maximization by the environment are completely known and the environment is parametric. The decision problem is then not a real decision problem at all, but instead a transformation of known relations between parameters and variables that are not really unknown. We can choose the option with the highest expected utility or the minimum opportunity cost only in well-defined contexts of decision-making. When our decision is of real impact on the environment of our action this environment ceases to be parametric and the isolation of the one opportunity cost minimizing decision becomes impossible or at least very difficult.

To act in the real economy or in business as a producer and consumer implies more than being an economizing individual, a cost minimizer or goal attainment maximizer. The economy, the world of business, as a realm of human interaction and of innovation in production and in consumption is not a calculating machine but a realm with a speculative side, a realm in which calculation and speculation interact. The speculative element cannot be reduced to calculation since the arguments of the calculation are not completely given ex ante. By the creation of new production techniques, new markets and new goods, the entrepreneur engages in an activity that is characterized best as speculative. The entrepreneur calculates on the basis of given knowl-

---

6 KRINGS (1980) expressed this problem by the dialectics or paradox of freedom and system thereby referring to SCHELLING (1809). Freedom requires a system of freedom and rationality and must at the same time be free of it.

edge about reality and speculates on that a new economic reality may materialize which will yield a future profit.

If we look at a long-run investment from the short-run point of view of returns on investment and of economizing means for given ends, new goods and new techniques imply creative destruction of given structures and the expenditure of more means than the continuation of the habitual production scheme requires. Investment is speculative since it assesses that a new detour in production will yield a higher return on investment in the future. In the reality of updating the mode of economic production, a highly uneconomic, ever renewed effort of recreation and innovation is necessary and is, indeed, encountered. Economic progress is the result of a permanent effort of recreation that is uneconomic in the short-run but might prove to be superior in the long run.[7] The mere application of the economy principle to realize the optimum or the greatest success with the least outlay is a technique oriented on formal rationality and economizing. It is not the speculative work of re-creating the conditions of production. Business is the effort of re-creation, the process of creative destruction and recreation – to use a Schumpeterian term –, it is not just rational calculation.

Speculation is the anticipation of a reality that cannot be recognized by mere empiricist experience or by conclusions from given axioms and observations. If one compares speculative philosophy and theology (cf. Koslowski 2003) with speculation in the economic context the common speculative element in theological-philosophical and in business and financial speculation becomes visible. Both modes of knowledge and speculation try to gain knowledge from limited empirical observation, to imagine new possibilities from this incomplete empirical knowledge, and to draw "speculative" conclusions without having complete knowledge or data. The observation of the incompleteness of the data for far-reaching strategic business decisions does, however, not refute the business rule: "In God we trust, everyone else brings data to the table."

---

7 MAX WEBER (1922, p. 199) identified art as the frequently "most uneconomic product of a permanent labor of recreation and simplifying reduction to the essential" (*Kunst ... ein höchst unökonomisches Produkt immer erneuter vereinfachender Umschaffensarbeit*) and distinguished the economy of art from the economy of business. In contrast to the economy in Weber's time, the contemporary economy has become more and more artistic, imaginative and "creative".

II. Ethical Economy as a Synthesis

Ethical economy is a theoretical synthesis of ethics and economics. Most deep choices have an ethical and an economic dimension. The optimization of a decision requires doing justice to both of these dimensions, to the ethical and economic one. Ethical economy is the theory of this synthesis. It is more than applied ethics. Rather, it is a foundational theory of its own kind, not an application of ethical principles to concrete cases. A number of general and rather abstract principles are derived from this theoretical synthesis and serve in turn to make the combination of ethical and economic criteria operational. They will be developed in the following second part of the paper.

1. The Double Nature of Ethical Economy as the Economy of Ethics and the Theory of the Ethical Presuppositions of the Market Economy

The principles of ethical economy can be applied to various fields of decision-making, particularly to business and medical decisions. If the theory of ethical economy is applied to business and economic organizations it is the ethical economy of business and comes close to what is usually called business ethics. If it is applied to medical decision-making it becomes the ethical economy of medical practice and allocation ethics in medicine.[8]

Since any synthesis of theories can be approached from both sides and focus on each of the two terms of this synthesis, the theory of ethical economy is relevant for both of the synthesized theories, for economics and for ethics. Ethical economy can focus on either of the two parts of its synthesis.

If ethical economy focuses on the relevance of ethics for economics it is an ethical theory of economics. It analyses the ethical presuppositions of economic coordination, of the market, and of efficiency. I shall examine some aspects of the ethical theory of economics, the need for the third person in economic coordination and the problem of incomplete contracts.

If ethical economy focuses on ethical theory it forms an economic theory of ethics, of the efficiency and economy of ethics. It analyses the economic or efficiency conditions under which the ethical can be realized. The economy of ethics has two sides, a motivational and a systemic one.

8 Cf. Koslowski (1981 and 1983).

2. Ethical Economy as the Economy of Ethics

a) The Principle of the Aspired Compatibility of Morality and Advantage

The first question of the economics of ethics concerns the conditions under which efficient rule adherence can be expected. Under which conditions do individuals have incentives to follow the ethical norm? Ethical economy as the economy of ethics gives an answer to the question for which economic reasons individuals are motivated to follow ethical norms.

Approaches to business ethics, like Karl Homann's economic ethics or incentive ethics, cover this aspect of ethical economy that is an economy of ethics, and of it one part, namely how to formulate ethics in such a way that it is incentive-compatible or congruent with self-interest. The motivational part of the economy of ethics is concerned with the question how ethics can be made effective by harmonizing it with economic incentives. Economic ethics demands avoiding situations in which ethical demands are incentive-adverse and contradict the incentives individuals have. In contrast to situations in which ethical motivation and rule are contrary to self-interest and economic incentive, ethical economy as the economy of ethics proposes that the social and ethical order are instituted in such a way that, by following the ethical rule, the persons acting in the economy face no net loss of wealth, do not violate their self-interest.

The economy of ethics can also be interpreted as a traditional theme of philosophical ethics since Plato. As Plato stated in his works on political philosophy, in his *Republic* and in his *Laws*, society should be instituted in such a way that there is no conflict between what is moral and what is good for the individual. Plato was, however, aware of the fact that in its totality this goal can only be reached by a transcendent retribution, which induced him to have recourse to a myth. He relates the myth of Er, about the judgment of souls after their death. In the myth of Er, the complete harmony of moral motivation and happiness is assumed to be realized by the operation of the transcendent compensation of merits and moral failure. Only by this transcendent retribution of acting morally during the whole life span is an incentive-compatible ethics thought by Plato to be viable.

b) The Principle of Universal Weighing of Goods as Consequentialist Utilitarian Ethics

The second part of the economy of ethics concerns the question of which ethical rules are efficient in the sense of returning the highest yield or economic return or benefit. Extended cost-benefits analysis or the universal weighing of goods that include ethical arguments as well as utilitarian consequentialist theory belong both to the economy of ethics and form the part of ethical economy that could be called the consequentialist economy of ethics.

An example of the impact of ethical economy as the economy of ethics and a central issue at the interface of ethics and economics is the question of the degree to which the universalization of rules is economically efficient or what level of universalization should be aimed for.

An illustration for the case for an economic theory of ethics as a theory of the efficiency of different regimes of universalization is as follows. Parking a car in Amsterdam is difficult; there are just too many canals or *grachten* where you cannot park a car. Since it is not a good idea to fill up these *grachten* with sand to create more parking lots for other reasons, very strict rules for parking have been made and are enforced with great vigor. These rules for parking are now so strict and the price for parking meters so high that many parking lots are usually empty and unused. This is certainly not an efficient solution. The City of Amsterdam could do two things. It could lower the price for parking in the streets where the high price has the effect of creating an over-incentive not to park there and parking lots remain, therefore, unused. The municipal authority might not want to introduce different prices for parking since it does not wish to spoil the price in Amsterdam; however, on other occasions, the municipal authority may practice price differentials in parking fees by, for instance, making the parking fees very low in certain shopping quarters to attract consumers to these places.

Alternatively, the municipal authority could reduce the degree of universalization enforced and permit exceptions so that certain risk-loving drivers could park there and run a reduced risk of catching a ticket. This, in turn, might not be approved by the City Council since it creates exceptions and contradicts the principle of equality. The result is that, under strict universalization, the dilemma of unused parking lots and a certain inefficiency of the outcome persist and offer a good example of how complete universalization and the enforcement of universalization lead to a suboptimal outcome from the point of view of ethical economy as an economic theory of ethics.

Another example is the problem of universalization of new and very expensive therapies in medicine: Which degree of universal application of such a therapy is desirable, i.e. ethically required and economically efficient? Is it ethically admissible to postpone the universal use of a therapeutic means for economic reasons of efficiency until the costs of a therapy have come down?

3. Ethical Economy as the Theory of the Ethical Presuppositions of the Market Economy

The other part of ethical economy is the complement to the economic theory of ethics and forms the ethical theory of economics, the ethical economy of the ethical preconditions and presuppositions of the market economy.[9]

In the market economy, the price is not the only parameter for competition. The goods supplied in the market are not homogeneous for all suppliers when new goods or modifications of goods enter the market. New goods and services create unique offers for which there are no adequate substitutes yet and for which the price is not the only criterion in competition.

Perfect competition is the case of an ideal market following the criteria of microeconomic theory. It is an instantiation of actual markets or a market type that is more an ideal than a reflection of the actual shape of markets. Under perfect competition with a large number of suppliers and consumers, the goods offered by different suppliers become homogeneous. There is a uniform market price which is the same for all suppliers and consumers. Suppliers and consumers are price takers.

Perfect competition has no need for ethics since the market price and the quality of the goods are perfectly transparent, the theory of perfect competition assumes. Furthermore, perfect competition tends to squeeze out non-remunerative incentives in the labor market since all suppliers have to provide the same working conditions to attract labor. It drives out non-remunerative incentives in the market for goods since consumers have no other incentive but the market price if the goods offered by suppliers are the same. Consumers can only differentiate in the quality of goods being sold on the market by moving to substitutes of the goods in question.

David Gauthier describes the ideal market of perfect competition as a "morals-free zone" (Gauthier 1985). There is no need for morals in a perfectly transparent market situation in which all goods are perfectly recognizable in their qualities, have no hidden qualities and are available in any part of the market at the same market price. In such a market, the price is the only decision parameter in the market interaction, and this price is determined by factors outside the control of the market participants. Monetary price incentives are the only incentives in a market of perfect competition. There are no

---

9 J. M. Buchanan subsumes parts of what is called here "ethical economy" under the concept of "the constitutional economics of ethics" (cf. BUCHANAN 1992).

buying incentives introduced by unique features of goods and services. Under perfect competition, there is no incentive for the buyer to buy above equilibrium price and no incentive for the seller to sell at a lower price.

It must be understood that the market of microeconomic theory describes an interaction of the market participants that is free of imposition and free of any distortion of the scarcity ratios. It reflects adequately the scarcity conditions and the suppliers' and consumers' preferences. In this respect, the perfect market is an ideal form of social coordination. The theory of the competitive market assumes that market participants are driven by self-interest and do not use force, power or collusion in their interactions. The price of the competitors is parametric in this model. The price is set beyond the control of a single supplier and therefore is not dependent on supplier discretion. The suppliers control only their own production and cost functions, the consumers only their budget. There is no coercion to enter into or maintain a contract. The market of perfect competition is a model of free interaction and satisfies conditions of freedom and optimality. These features render it far superior to any model of centrally planned and therefore coercive interaction.

a) The Principle of Self-Interest and its Ambiguity: *Homo Homini Deus* or *Homo Homini Lupus*?

The self-interest theorem as the driving motive of market interaction has been emphasized by Adam Smith in his famous dictum that it does not depend on the benevolence of the butcher but on his self-interest whether we shall have meat or not. Smith had, however, a Dutch predecessor who introduced the idea of the invisible hand of the market. More than one hundred years before the publication of Smith's *Wealth of Nations* in 1776, Pieter de la Court contended that self-interest is central and presented the concept of an invisible hand for a republic and market in his book of 1662 *The True Interest, and Political Maxims of the Republick of Holland and West-Friesland.*

Pieter de la Court writes that "the good government is not that where the well or ill-being of the subjects depends on the virtues or vices of the rulers; but (which is worthy of observation) where the well or ill-being of the rulers necessarily follows or depends on the well or ill-being of the subjects". (De la Court 2003, p. 10f.) According to de la Court, we have no other choice than to realize self-interest since the rulers or governments will always prefer and follow their own self-interest. "We must believe that in all societies or assemblies of men, self is always preferred." (De la Court 2003, p. 11) He concludes, quite in anticipation of the critical public choice perspective on government, about the self-interest of governments: "So all sovereigns or supreme powers will in the first place seek their own advantage in all things, tho' to the prejudice of the subject." (*ibid.*)

Fortunately enough, there is an invisible hand in politics and economics that turns the pursuit of the self-interest of the government into freeing the pursuit of the private good by the citizens. It also transforms the citizens' pursuit of their private good into the public good of the government.

> But seeing on the other hand true interest cannot be compassed by a government, unless the generality of the people partake thereof; therefore the publick welfare will ever be aimed at by good rulers. All which very aptly agrees with our Latin and Dutch proverb, that, *Tantum de publicis malis sentimus, quantum ad privatas res pertinet*; i.e. We are only sensible of publick afflictions, in so far as they touch our private affairs. (*ibid.*)

Pieter de la Court's gives a very early defense of a market in a republic that frees the self-interest of the citizens and thereby realizes the public interest since the pursuit of the citizens' self-interest will lead to the realization of the public interest and the pursuit of the government's self-interest will lead to furthering the private good of the citizens. This theory also links the republican form of government with the market form of the economy. Both are founded on the freeing of self-interest and on turning the pursuit of self-interest in the realization of the public interest, "so that *homo homini deus in statu politico*, one man being a god to another under a good government". (De la Court 2003, p. 23)

In the Dutch republic, it does not hold true what holds true for the kingdom of England, for the Leviathan of English absolutism: that *homo homini lupus*, that man is a wolf to man, as Hobbes stated it. In Holland, man is a God to man. In an impressive critique of Hobbes's absolutism eleven years after the publication of Hobbes's *Leviathan* of 1651, de la Court formulates the republican counter-principle to Hobbes in a country where the population is even more crowded and the citizens are closer to each other than in England.

> It is an unspeakable blessing for this land, that there are so many people in it, who according to the nature of the country are honestly maintain'd by such suitable or proportionable means, and especially that the welfare of all the inhabitants … from the least to the greatest, does so necessarily depend on one another. (De la Court 2003, p. 23)

De la Court (2003, p. 24) concludes: "*A furore monarcharum libera nos Domine* God preserve Holland from the fury of a monarch, prince, or one supreme head." As a radical republican, de la Court did not foresee that future generations of Hollanders would find a constitutional compromise that reconciled the status of the citizen and of the subject in the Dutch *onderdaan* (subject, in German *Untertan*).[10]

The comparison of Hobbes's, de la Court's and Adam Smith's understanding of the self-interest theorem shows that the self-interest theorem assumes quite different meanings and causes quite different conclusions about human nature. The interpretation of self-interest reaches from Hobbes's *homo homini lupus* to de la Court's *homo homini deus*. The self-interest theorem is not univocal. It embraces several possible interpretations of human nature that reach from an extreme pessimism to an extreme optimism about human nature and the effects of human self-interest.

b) The Principle of the Need for an Internalized or External Third in Contracts

There is a difficulty in the model of the market of perfect competition which concerns the workings of the invisible hand in the coordination of self-interested action. The business contracts might not be self-enforcing even under perfect competition. They seem to require a third party to enforce them.

In his *Leviathan*, Hobbes writes about the nature of humankind's desires:

> So that in the nature of man, we find three principall causes of quarrell. First, Competition; Secondly, Diffidence; Thirdly, Glory. The first, maketh men invade for Gain; the second, for Safety; and the third, for Reputation .... Hereby it is manifest, that during the time men live without a common Power to keep them all in awe, they are in that condition which is called Warre; and such a warre, as is of every man, against every man. (Hobbes 1909, p. 43).

Human beings need a third party to control their desire to invade each other for gain, greater safety, or more glory. Human beings understand that they can improve their lot by entering into agreements not to invade for greater gain, safety, or reputation, but their rational self-interest to come to mutual

10 This constitutional compromise turns even the EU citizen living in the Netherlands into an "*EU Onderdaan*". Since the author's Dutch permit of residence (Dutch *Verblijfsdocument*) describes his status as *EU Onderdaan* or EU subject the term raises the question whom the *EU Onderdaan* is *onderdaan* or subject to.

agreements might be not as strong as their reluctance to keep these agreements. Their readiness to observe contracts is unstable as long as there is not a third party to control their permanent temptation to break agreements or contracts. This is why a social contract of association, a contract between two parties, Ego and Alter, is not sufficient for a civil state of contract compliance. Anyone living in a civil state cannot be prevented from leaving it any time he or she considers it expedient. Without a third party who enforces compliance, human beings are always tempted to breach their contracts. The war Hobbes talks about does not consist in actual hostility but in an assured insecurity, in the knowledge of the fact that all contracts can be breached at any time.

> So the nature of War, consisteth not in actuall fighting; but in the known disposition thereto, during all the time there is no assurance to the contrary. … And the life of man, solitary, poore, nasty, brutish, and short. (*ibid.*)

The assured insecurity surrounding contracts is the reason why a social contract of association is not only unstable for the civil state or commonwealth but is also unstable for the contract of civil law between two parties, Ego and Alter, in the realm of business. Everyone living under civil or public law in a civil state cannot be prevented from leaving the social contract or the private contract at any time that he or she considers this useful.

Any contract of association must be supplemented by a contract of subjection to a third party whom the power is granted to enforce the contract of association. This third party can either be the law and its courts or an internalized ethics. Without a contract of subjection under the authority of legal or ethical enforcement, any contract of association is weak if not useless. The contract of two always implies a third, the third party of contract enforcement or of self-commitment to the general rule of keeping contracts. When you are two, you are actually three.

With Hobbes, ethical economy shares the skepticism about the idea that the will to associate and to enter an agreement already guarantees the will to fulfill the agreement. In contrast, both Hobbes and ethical economy assume that agreements need the enforcing third party. Franz von Baader remarked that not only the social contract but also any contract, even the business contract, presupposes the enforcing third party, either of law and religion or of ethics and religion. Therefore, ethics and the law are present in all contracts and stabilize every contract.

Hobbes believed that human beings find their way out of the state of nature because they are rational beings. Each human being should be willing to honor contracts and to pursue peace when others are willing to do the same, while retaining the right to continue to breach a contract or pursue war when others fail to observe contracts or pursue peace. By being reasonable and by recognizing the rationality of this basic precept of reason, human beings can be expected to construct a social contract consisting of a contract of association between the first and the second person, and of a contract of submission between the two or the many and the third that consists in the submission of the first and second person to the authority of the third person. Thus, according to Hobbes, when different interests are at stake, and that means in every agreement, it is rational to sign away your right to the self-enforcement of contracts to a third party or power, be it a juridical court or a sovereign power or an ethical rule of observing contracts regardless of one's desire to breach them. Since we are never able to judge our own interests objectively and will always be tempted to interpret the contract in our favor, we are always in need of a third party, as the third impartial judge of our agreements. In most cases, this third party will be the ethical principle of the duty to observe contracts.

In the instability of our interest to keep a contract, there is no self-enforcing contract and no difference between civil and public law. This is one of the consequences of Hobbes's theory. If we need the third party in public law, we also need the third party in civil or common law. All agreements, be they civil or public, need the third party to guarantee their fulfilment and to ensure certainty of expectation, which is the core of legal safety. Without the third party, Ego and Alter have no certainty that their agreements will be observed and that their expectations about the future will be fulfilled. They cannot plan for the future without an external or internalized third party guaranteeing observance of the contracts.

The civil state or the state of law is the state in which agreements between the first and the second party always imply a third. The ethical rule of the duty to observe contractual agreements is the preparation of the law.

Adam Smith has assumed that, by the invisible hand of the market, self-interested actions are transformed into the common good: into an efficient general economic outcome that does not involve the interference of a third party. Adam Smith's business contracts need no contract of submission to a third party, although Smith assumes that the judiciary will enforce contracts. His theory uses the invisible hand of self-interested market transactions and the visible hand of the legal enforcement of contracts. There remains a residue of skepticism about the working of the invisible hand of the market in Adam Smith in that he assumes that, even under conditions of an invisible hand at work, the visible hand of the law and of contract enforcement remains necessary. Smith's theory of the market relies on courts and on the invisible hand, not on the invisible hand only. It relies on double control measures. As American lawyers say: any contract must use double measures – must use, metaphorically speaking, a belt and suspenders to make sure that the trousers hold.

c) The Principle of the Ethical Assurance of Loyalty to Contracts

The competitive market works perfectly well if there is transparency in interactions and the interactions are carried out simultaneously, under the condition that compliance with the contract can be monitored easily by the contracting partners. As soon as there is a time lag between contracting and serving the contract, uncertainty enters as to whether the contract will be observed as agreed upon. This uncertainty is reduced by a third party, be it the legal guarantor of contracts, long-term business relationships and repeat business, or an effective business ethics code. The legal monitoring and enforcement of contracts is costly. Legal costs occur, and the contract enforcement is only realized later when the damage caused by the delay in honoring the contract and by the non-realization of the contract-based expectations about the future have already occurred. Even if the law enforces a contract, the plans of the contracting partner for the future made on the basis of the contract have already been disrupted.

Long-term business relationships and repeat business do not rely on ethical considerations, but on the formation of habits and the expectation of lower transaction costs by replicating the same business. The same process that creates economic advantages and the formation of trust, however, is also subject to the possibility of being exploited by both sides. The more often a business transaction is repeated and a habit of doing business is established, the more both sides are locked into the business relationship. They cannot circumvent it except at high cost. They become quasi-monopolists for each other, with the consequence that both sides can extract a monopoly profit from each other due to the fact that their partner is locked into the business relationship. Repeat business is economically and ethically ambivalent. Not only does it create cost-saving opportunities but also the possibility of losses from being locked into a relationship and being exploited in it.[11]

Contractual relationships in the market can be monitored by more than fear of legal punishment or the establishing of long-term business relationships. Ethical codes and ethical convictions serve as a substitute for legal enforcement and monitoring, and as a way to reduce the exploitation potential in long-term business relationships. An ethos of observing contracts leads to a market environment that is superior to an environment where only lawyers or mere habits ensure that contracts are served.

Pacta sunt servanda is a central norm of the economy that is not secured by self-interest alone. Every time business partners can get away with opportunistic behavior, they will engage in it unless they are restrained by respect for the principle of observing contracts. Even in a market with well-functioning legal enforcement of contracts, there are many contracts that are incomplete, ill defined, or indeterminate with regard to the contractual obligations. Ethics and religion are a means to give substance to the expectation that the contracting partner will observe the contract and keep the promises made in the contract.

Reliability and mutual trust on the part of business partners result in reducing the costs of economic exchange. Trust reduces transaction costs, since the contracting partners can come to an agreement more rapidly. They face fewer monitoring costs.

Individuals may react in three ways to this relationship between trust and freedom of contract:

First, individuals can behave unconditionally morally. They understand the common economic need in ethical behavior as the *motive* for their *own* behavior. The persons turn common interest into their own interest, i.e. the persons behave morally irrespectively of the behavior of the others (*Case 1*). For example, firm employees try to do their best irrespective of what the others achieve, or businesspersons try to remain fair even if widespread forms of unfair behavior are to be found in the industry.

11 In a famous business case, the so-called "Schneider bankruptcy" in Germany, the owner of a building firm, Jürgen Schneider, had been able to attract large sums of credit through his position of trustworthiness acquired through long-term business relationships with large banks, which at some point in time had simply stopped controlling whether the real estate existed that he had given as security for loans.

Second, a person can behave conditionally morally. Individuals are ready to follow ethical rules if the others or the majority also follow them, but violate the rules if they feel that they alone "will be the fool" (*Case 2*). The contracting partner fulfils the contractual obligations only if everybody else does so as well.

Third, persons may appreciate that the better situation for everybody is achieved if everybody follows the rules, but consider the best situation a situation in which everybody but them follows the rules (*Case 3*). This is the pattern of behavior assumed by the famous prisoners' dilemma in game theory. A firm knows that it is best for the industry if every firm sticks to the rules and no bribing of business partners or other form of corruption takes place, but it prefers to make an exception for itself and to support contracting by doing favors for business associates.

Case 3 of the behavioral options presents a typical dilemma situation in which one cannot remain. The dilemma describes a situation in which everybody benefits if *everybody* follows the rules and in which each person is interested in being the only one who can violate the rules in the hide. As a consequence, the rule will be violated if it is not enforced by external control and sanctions, or if it is not affirmed by the individuals on ethical grounds. Case 3 will be transformed either into the ethical options of case 1 or 2, or into a system of external monitoring and enforcement.

Case 2 that one acts morally if everyone else does so, too, is a typical intermediate situation that seems to be acceptable to most people. One behaves morally if others do the same; one stops behaving morally if one feels oneself to be the only person behaving morally. Ethics is a means to transform the situation of a prisoners' dilemma into a situation of trust or assurance. The general acceptance of and compliance with ethical rules would transform the isolation paradox, named so by Amartya Sen (1967, p. 112), of case 2 into a situation of relative certainty. The isolation paradox implies that individuals will not follow the rules under conditions of isolation and uncertainty about the others' behavior since they are afraid of being deceived, although they are actually ready to follow the general rule in other circumstances.

However, case 2 is not stable, as the certainty that all the others or at least most of them follow the rules is always vague and limited. Sen, though, assumes that generally acknowledged moral values transform case 3, the situation of the prisoners' dilemma, into case 2, the situation of certainty or assurance, into an "assurance game". When moral values are generally acknowledged, the individual is no longer uncertain about the moral preferences of the others. But Sen's position is begging the question – a *petitio principii* remains. If one says that individuals have further motivation to behave morally if ethical behavior is general, i.e. that "values" are recognized, this begs the question of whether the values are indeed generally acknowledged. How is it possible to make sure that moral "values" are generally acknowledged, that the others also behave morally and that the individuals make the rule their motive? The element of uncertainty remains here; assurance is only relative. Case 2 is more stable than case 3, as in case 2 the individuals are at least partially moral and cooperating, but case 2 cannot ensure absolute certainty about the moral behavior of the others and provide secure grounds for trust.

In case 2, in the situation of the isolation paradox, two questions arise: "How long will the individuals be ready to follow the moral rules if most of the others violate them or if they are not certain about the others' actual behavior?" and "How may the uncertainty about the behavior of the others be reduced?" Both questions cannot be solved by ethics alone. Answering the questions by pointing to the need for a general ethics leads again and again to the *petitio principii* that the ethics will be accepted by the individuals and find general recognition if this already enjoys general recognition and that the isolation paradox of the acceptance of ethics may be overcome if the ethics is already generally effective.

Case 2 shows that the prisoner's dilemma and isolation paradox may be solved by ethics only if individuals recognize the moral rule naturally and irrespectively of the behavior of the others – if they make the moral rule their individual motive also. As uncertainty about the others' behavior cannot be eliminated, the moral rule can win recognition only if it is recognized despite the others' behavior.

The failure of ethics requires a corrective. Kant, in his *Critique of Practical Reason*, sheds light on this problem of ethics failure. If a moral individual follows the categorical imperative while all the others follow the rule of personal happiness, the harmony between one's own morality and pursuit of happiness is destroyed. Kant thought that this problem could be solved by the "postulates of practical reason". The postulates of practical reason – God, liberty and the immortality of the soul – restore trust in the meaningfulness of moral behavior, and in the harmony between morality and advantage. Religion here is a postulate guaranteeing the exigency of being moral. It helps build up a social capital on which trust can be founded.

The religious belief can transform ethics failure into trust in the effectiveness of ethics. It transforms the empirical uncertainty of the isolation paradox into the belief that morality is a common phenomenon and that it is useful to be moral. Religion accomplishes what Sen ascribes to ethics: the transformation of situations of prisoners' dilemma and of the isolation paradox into situations of assurance (in game-theoretic terms: into an *assurance game*). Assurance and trust in the advantage of being moral are not fully attained on the basis of ethics, but on the basis of religion. There is a sequence of compensations for failure. When self-interest fails, there is ethics; when ethics fails, religion. This structure of failure compensation has been analyzed in greater detail in the author's *Principles of Ethical Economy* (Koslowski 2002).

The ethical economy of the relationship between the individual's utility calculus and the individual's readiness to act morally has been discussed in different epochs of the history of philosophy. In Kant, religion gives reason to the belief in the final harmony between moral behavior and happiness in the form of the postulates of practical reason. In Plato, it is "the idea of the good" and of the myth of the trial of the soul after death that assures the human being that morality and happiness converge. It guarantees trust even in situations in which the individual is unsure of the behavior of the others, such as in the situations of isolation and the prisoner's dilemma.

The theory of the link between economics, ethics, and religion seems to violate the rule that the scholar has to renounce the use of God in scientific discourse. The theory developed here is, however, first a positive, non-normative theory of the link between ethics and religion. The response against the objection that religion should not be used in scientific discourse is quite simple: Social science has to include religion if religion is a motivational factor in the actual human behavior and is shared by many individuals in a society. Religion is than a socially effective force even if its truth value in the scientific sense remains open. Religion is real in its consequences if it has consequences for the individuals' behavior.

The result of the analysis of the relationship between economics, ethics, and religion can be interpreted in a threefold way. First, it can be interpreted as an empirical nexus between religious and ethical motivation that exists in many humans but not in all. Secondly, it can be interpreted as an argument for the economic and ethical usefulness of religion.[12] Thirdly, it can be inter-

12 RATZINGER (1985) also emphasizes the conditionedness of economics by ethics and of ethics by religion. – Pope BENEDICT XVI refers in his paper to KOSLOWSKI

preted as an argument for the existence of God. In the last sense, it demonstrates that if God is the condition for the congruence of ethical and rational self-interested behavior and if this congruence cannot be proven by rational calculus alone there is an ethical-economic argument for the existence of God or an argument from ethical economy for religion as the compensation for the failure of ethical motivation.[13]

The aim of the argument developed in the present paper is not metaphysical but ethical and economic. It is satisfied by proving that economics is conditioned and "improved" in its efficiency by the validity of ethics and that ethics is conditioned and "improved" in its effectiveness by the validity of religion.

d) The Principle of Double Effect: Handling Externalities of Economic Action

The assumption of market theory is that the market price includes or internalizes all benefits and costs caused by the exchange to both sides. Both sides confirm that all benefits and costs are internalized by their consent to the exchange. Third parties that are not part of the exchange are not concerned. There are, however, exchanges that have side-effects or externalities on others that are not internalized in the exchange like environmental pollution. When pollution on third parties originates from a contract of two parties the principle of internalization is violated.[14]

Side-effects are a classical problem of moral philosophy and of economics. Moral philosophy and moral theology, particularly in the Catholic tradition, developed the theory of the principle of double effect which can be con-

---

(1985b), an earlier version of the argument developed here. The argument about the usefulness of religion as a guarantee for that being ethical is also useful for the individual is expanded further in KOSLOWSKI (2007).

13 Cf. for this ethical-economic argument for the existence of God KOSLOWSKI (2008).

14 A tragic example for an action with double effect is the "three-strikes laws" in the United States, under which a third felony conviction yields life imprisonment. These laws are intended to deter repeat offenders. However, they may encourage repeat criminals to kill witnesses – since the sentence for murder is no worse than the sentence for a lesser third offense. Cf. JOHN SLOAN III, TOMISLAV V. KOVANDZIC, LYNEE M. VIERAITIS: "Unintended Consequences of Politically Popular Sentencing Policy: The Homicide-Promoting Effects of 'Three Strikes' in U.S. Cities (1980-1999)", in: *Criminology & Public Policy*, 1 (2002).

sidered to be a transcendental principle of handling side-effects. As a transcendental principle of handling side-effects it is also a central principle of ethical economy and of business ethics.

The principle makes it possible to analyze and assess decision situations under uncertainty and expected (negative) side effects. It is a decision principle for ill-structured and ambiguous decisions. Most ethically relevant decisions in business do in fact have side effects and, therefore, are ill-structured decision problems under uncertainty. They cannot be converted into well-structured decision situations by calculi unless with unrealistic, scientistic premises, such as premises that the results of actions can be known with certainty or that the probability distribution of the possible effects of actions and outcomes is known. The probabilistic principle of action with side effects or double effect[15] is therefore especially applicable in economic ethics and decision theory, and is able to penetrate the ill-structured economic-ethical decision situation and to reduce it to a better defined structure. The principle of double effect is, in contrast to the principle of the categorical imperative, concrete and makes it possible to perform comparisons of goods. It is, therefore, an important complement to the universalization principle, which is weak in judging the concrete case.

The principle reads: An action with negative side effects is sensible and permitted, if the following four conditions are met:

15 On the problem of actions with double effects, see PETER KNAUER: "The Hermeneutic Function of the Principle of Double Effect", in: *Natural Law Forum*, 12 (1967), pp. 132-162; RICHARD MCCORMICK: "Das Prinzip der Doppelwirkung einer Handlung", in: *Concilium*, 12 (1976), pp. 662-670; R. A. DUFF: "Absolute Principles and Double Effect", in: *Analysis*, 6 (1976), pp. 68-80; JOSEPH M. BOYLE, JR., GERMAIN GRISEZ, OLAF TOLLEFSON: *Free Choice*, Notre Dame (Notre Dame University Press) 1976; ROBERT SPAEMANN (1977, pp. 167-182); JOSEPH M. BOYLE JR.: "Toward Understanding the Principle of Double Effect", in: *Ethics*, 90 (1980), pp. 527-538; L. J. MCNAMARA: *Direct and Indirect*, Ph.D. Thesis, University of Oxford 1980; J. L. MACKIE: *Ethics*, London (Penguin) 1977, pp. 160-168; S. S. LEVY: *The Doctrine of the Double Effect*, Ph.D. Thesis, University of Michigan 1982; G. E. M. ANSCOMBE: "Action, Intention, and 'Double Effect'", in: *Proceedings of the American Catholic Philosophical Association*, 57 (1983), pp. 12-25. On judgment of consequences, cf. RAINER SPECHT: *Innovation und Folgelast*, Stuttgart (Frommann Holzboog) 1972.

1) The goal of the action must be good and sincere (i.e. the acting person may not intend a bad and impermissible effect). The side effects must be unintended, must be *praeter intentionem*.[16]

2) The type or form of the action must be intrinsically good.

3) The negative side effects must be true *side* effects. They must objectively have the character of accidental effects arising in the pursuit of other goals, and may not serve as means to the good effect.

4) There must be a proportionately grave reason to perform the action. The acting person may not be obligated by other duties to refrain from it completely.

This list of conditions summarizes the formulations of the principle by John of Saint Thomas,[17] from whom the first complete version of the principle is derived, and by Jean Pierre Gury.[18] Conditions 1), 3) and 4) are the same for both authors. Condition 2) has been expanded by Gury, in order to ensure that the principle is not applied in the sense of a universal comparison of goods that does not differentiate effects and side-effects. The principle of double effect is not identical to an uncritical, universal comparison of goods, with which the good and bad effects of *all* actions, including actions of an unambiguously unethical character, are taken into account, and the least evil of several evil actions is chosen. With condition 2), Gury attempts to guarantee that intrinsically-evil actions are excluded from the comparison of goods.

The question is discussed within general ethical theory whether the principle of double effect can be united with various normative, basic convictions, or whether it is a prerequisite of a normative ethical theory that judges certain actions as intrinsically evil and excludes them from comparing main effect and side effects according to the principle of double effect. Joseph Boyle holds the view that the principle of double effect can be united with any normative theory that assumes that there are types of actions that are good and types that are evil. Every ethical theory that makes such a distinction can make use of the principle of double effect.[19]

---

16 On *praeter intentionem*, see JOSEPH M. BOYLE JR.: „Aquinas on Praeter Intentionem", in: *Thomist*, 42 (1978), pp. 649-665; and M. MÜLLER: *Ethik und Recht in der Lehre von der Verantwortlichkeit*, Regensburg (J. Habbe) 1932.

17 JOHN OF SAINT THOMAS: *Cursus Theologicus*, Madrid 1645-56, tom. VI, disp. XI, a. 6, cap. 39 &. 42.

18 JEAN PIERRE GURY: *Compendium theologiae moralis*, Regensburg 1857, 2nd edition, tr. I, cap. II, n. 9.

19 BOYLE: "Toward Understanding the Principle of Double Effect", p. 537.

This position, of course, shifts the debate, from the question whether there are actions that are intrinsically good and evil and whether the answer to this question is a prerequisite for being able to apply the principle of double effect, to the question, *which* actions are intrinsically good or evil.

Elizabeth Anscombe is of the opinion that the principle does not say what one can or should do, but instead what one may not do, and thus that its applicability is restricted. The principle does not read that the predominance of good over bad/evil makes an action permissible and recommends it, but instead requires that the side effects stand in a reasonable relation to the good. It permits only *good* actions with negative side effects, and only actions with which the negative side effects stand in an appropriate relationship to the (good) primary effect.[20]

The principle has been further explicated as follows: The necessity of tolerating negative side effects must be proportional larger, if:

1) the primary goal is by nature closer to the negative effect,

2) it is certain that the evil effect will follow, and

3) there are fewer ways to avoid the evil than there would be if the goal or primary effect were first to occur.[21]

Additional support for decision-making that can be derived from the principle of double effect, is:

1) How closely is the bad result or side effect dependent upon the action?

2) Is the damage that would result from the omission of the intrinsically-good action greater than the evil side effect that would result from performing the action?[22]

The principle and its explications do not remove the burden of judgment and of evaluating the internally assumed probability, the *probabilitas interna,* from the decision-maker, but they help to penetrate the decision to be made.[23] The analysis of side effects and the principle of double effect form a

---

20 ANSCOMBE: "Action, Intention, and 'Double Effect'".

21 COLLEGIUM SALMANTICENSIS: *Cursus Theologicus* (*Comm. in S. Thomae s. th.* II-II, q. 64, a. 7), (= *Tractatus de bonitate et malitia actuum humanorum*), edited by Domingo de Santa Teresa, Paris 1878, tom. 7, tract. XIII, disp. 10, dub. 6, n. 214-47. See also J. T. MANGAN: "A Historical Analysis of the Principle of Double Effect", in: *Theological Studies*, 10 (1949), pp. 41-61.

22 NIKOLAUS SEELHAMMER: "Doppelwirkung einer Handlung", in: *Lexikon für Theologie und Kirche*, Freiburg im Breisgau (Herder) 1959, Vol. III, pp. 516-517.

23 See for an application of the principle of double effect to a business ethics case P. KOSLOWSKI: "Hoe om te gaan met de neveneffecten van bierleveranties?", in:

bridge between ethics and economics. The principle is a crucial instrument of the analysis and judgment of ethical economy.

e) The Principle of Hyper-Motivation: Incentives of Self-Justification as Economic Incentives

The idea of the right structure of incentives and contributions is a central concept of economic and management theory.[24] There exist, however, not only incentives but there exist right and wrong incentives in business, science and technology. A remuneration of managers according to the rise or fall of the share price of the firms they manage creates incentives to arrange their performance primarily on this goal and to neglect other duties of their work. A remuneration of scientists only according to their ability to attract funds from third sources has the effect that they pay attention particularly to the third party's interests and neglect independent, long-term, original, creative research.

Motivation structures and contributions can be intensified in their effect through motivation boosters as the history of entrepreneurship, of technological invention and of scholarship demonstrate. German Idealism turned the scholar into the agent or fiduciary of the absolute spirit. J. G. Fichte believed that the scholar is the vessel of the absolute. The scholars of historism and of the historical school of the humanities as the successor of idealism followed a similar path of enforcing motivation. They were confirmed in their urge to creative research by the conviction that the absolute realizes itself in history, in the historical spirit of cultures and nations, and that they illuminate this self-realization of the absolute. The illumination of the historical phenomena became by this conviction a work on the realization of the absolute, *Arbeit am Absoluten*. For the phase of the blossom of the German humanities in the 19th century, these aggrandizement of the scholar's own work by a pantheistic metaphysics had a motivation- and creativity-amplifying effect. This effect was at the same time boosting research and its results and problematic since it caused a self-aggrandizement of the scholar with the dangers of forming the ideal-type of the mandarin-scholar.

Business competition increases motivation and creativity as does the competition between nations. Japan was stimulated to high performance since

---

WIM DUBBINK, HENK VAN LUIJK (Eds.): *Bedrijfsgevallen. Morele beslissingen van ondernemingen*, Assen (Koninklijke Van Gorcum) 2006, pp. 126-132.

24 Cf. COLEMAN (1993).

the end of the 19th century by the incentive of catching up, by the motto „make up, catch up, overtake." (*Einholen, Aufholen, Überholen*).

Max Weber's Calvinist entrepreneur becomes creative and is motivated for high performance through religious incentives. Because he understands his economical success as a proof of being in the state of grace he experiences additional religious incentives to be successful in business. Max Weber's *The Protestant Ethic and the Spirit of Capitalism* (1905) shows that cultural and economic incentives and motives overlap and that culturally defined incentives enhance economic creativity and business performance. The Calvinist teaching on justification undergoes a revision. Justification is finally in part redefined as economic success.

The insecurity in Protestantism whether the Protestant believer can be certain to be in the grace of God is eased by economic success interpreted as a sign of grace. Justification becomes only visible through economic success since in Calvinism even faith is no guarantee of being chosen. According to the Westminster Confession of 1646, God chooses those predestined to eternal life "out of His mere free grace and love, *without any foresight of faith or good works* (italics by PK), or perseverance in either of them, or any other thing in the creature as conditions or causes moving Him thereunto".[25] Neither faith nor good works make a human being deserving the state of grace. The only proof of being predestined to the state of grace can be given, as Weber (1905) showed in his analysis of Calvinism, through being economically successful. This re-interpretation of economic into religious success is presumably one of the most powerful and subtle incentives and amplifiers of motivation and creativity that humankind ever experienced.

The difference in the effect of the Calvinist and the Lutheran teaching on justification cannot be overestimated. Whereas the Lutheran is justified *sola*

25 *Westminster Confession,* Chapter III. Of God's Eternal Decree, § 5: "Those of mankind that are predestinated unto life, God, before the foundation of the world was laid, according to his eternal and immutable purpose, and the secret counsel and good pleasure of his will, hath chosen in Christ, unto everlasting glory, out of his free grace and love alone, without any foresight of faith or good works, or perseverance in either of them, or any other thing in the creature, as conditions, or causes moving him thereunto; and all to the praise of his glorious grace." Online edition: http://www.reformed.org/documents/index.html?mainframe= http://www.reformed.org/documents/westminster_conf_of_faith.htm
Weber (1905, p. 57) quotes the Westminster Confession extensively as one of the central historical and theological documents for his thesis.

fide, only by faith,[26] the Calvinist is even unsure about his or her justification by faith.

The German Lutheran contempt for "good works", for religious good works, affects also the economic good works and economic success. The weakness of economic thinking in the German intellectual tradition is influenced, if not caused, by the Lutheran teaching on justification and good works. This teaching renders the success of actions irrelevant for the justification of the human being as compared to mere faith. It also justifies a right of every one to every kind of social benefit since no good or success is "deserved" – a position which opens somehow a right to everything. The attitude toward economic success and good works is different in Calvinism where the radicalization of predestination made the recourse to justification *sola fide*, only by faith, impossible. Success in the world becomes the only assurance of being chosen in Calvinism which, theologically speaking, remains a doubtful assurance.

Re-interpretation and aggrandizement of meaning are central phenomena of cultural and economic enforcement of motivation. One can call this meaning enforcement a „hyper-motivation" by cultural incentives. Since the external world as such does not have enough meaning for the human being, humans are in need of cultural-religious boosters of motivation in their economy of creativity.

f) The Size of the Market and the Need for an Ethics of Market Exchange

It is a frequently heard thesis that ethics is a phenomenon of small groups who, through their face-to-face control, can assure the effectiveness of ethics, which is by nature not legally enforced. Friedrich von Hayek, James Buchanan, and in the German discussion on business ethics Karl Homann defend the thesis that the ethics of small groups has been replaced in the modern market society by the formal coordination of the market process, which does not rely on goodwill but on market forces to make sure that individuals deliver for the good of all. Homann in particular goes so far as to say that only modernity has established and understood markets and that it has re-

26 Cf. *Augsburg Confession* (1530), Article IV. Of Justification: "…men cannot be justified before God by their own strength, merits, or works, but are freely justified for Christ's sake, through faith." Online: http://www.ctsfw.edu/etext/boc/ac/augustana04.asc

moved all ethics from actual market interactions to the frame order of the market, i.e. to the institutional rules of the market.

First, one must reply to this position that it is not necessary for the existence of a market and for acting in a market that market participants understand all aspects of what a market is. Rather, it is central that they do act in it. Particularly for the market, the Vico principle *Non intelligendo omnia facimus* (Not by understanding everything do we do everything) holds true. Even if we do not find an elaborate market theory in the history of ideas before Adam Smith, it is inconceivable hat the Roman Empire with its sea and land trade and with its civil law had no markets and that its citizens did not engage in far-reaching market exchange. One limitation on the development of a market society in the Roman Empire, though, was slavery and the non-market organization of labor. Slavery is a commodification of labor without the free marketability of it. Forced labor limited the development of a market economy in antiquity. In this sense, modernity brought a radical change.

Secondly, it must be emphasized that ethics as deliberation over the goodness of an action on a personal level developed precisely in a setting in which the small-group society grew to become the large-group society. As a theory of right action, ethics did not develop in traditional small-group societies but in societies in transition to a large-scale society. Plato's and Aristotle's ethics are not the ethics of small groups with face-to-face control but the ethics for human beings living in extended large groups. Plato emphasized in his *Gorgias* that ethics intervenes precisely at that point at which group control ceases. His example is the ring of Gyges, a ring that renders its wearer invisible. Plato asks the ultimate question of ethics: What could convince a human who can do everything invisibly to act ethically?

Finally, the development of the universalistic Christian ethics in the Roman Empire that transformed the particularistic ethics of nations and groups to an ethical universalism proves that ethics in not a small-group phenomenon. As Paul's letter to the Galatians 3.28 says: "There is neither Jew nor Greek … for ye are all one in Christ Jesus." Friedrich Schelling called this letter "the Magna Carta of Protestantism". Christian ethics belongs to a society in which the habitual morality of local habits and customs is superseded by a universalistic ethics.

Hayek introduced the argument that the market society replaces the society of small groups by an abstract order that renders ethics obsolete. This Hayekian argument is flawed and must be turned round. The market society requires personal ethics since it does *not* rely on the face-to-face control of small groups but on the formal rules of market coordination *and* on the ethics of observing contracts and of realizing mutual value creation. The ethos of *pacta sunt servanda* cannot be guaranteed by the legal system and mutual monitoring devices only.

It may be true that the market erodes certain features of ethics, but it is also true that the market accumulates features of a new ethos of contractual obligations. The constitutional state and the market economy do not only live on values that are prior to the state and the market. Nor do the constitutional state and the market only use up moral resources or moral capital. Rather, they also build up ethical resources since the individuals involved understand that ethics secures the working of the constitutional state and the market and that it must therefore be fostered in their individual motivation and action.

A good example of the anticipation of generalization in individual motivation is electoral participation. For years, public choice theory argued that, from the point of view of self-interest, a rational voter should not take the trouble of casting his or her vote since it is not worth the effort, as the voter's single vote has no influence on the outcome of the vote. Now, history reveals that voters do cast their vote. They act under anticipation of universalization. They seem to tell themselves: "The election works only if everyone votes; therefore, I shall vote."

The workings of the market also support the formation of an economic ethos by remunerating loyalty to contracts, reliability and the like, by furthering and putting a value on trust, reputation, and other non-monetary but valuable ethical assets.

Ethical economy interprets the ethical presuppositions of market interaction and exchange as second-order optimality conditions that must be added to the first-order economic optimality conditions of market interaction. Although market interaction needs to work – and actually does work – without strong ethical commitments and under the condition that individuals follow their narrow self-interest, it is improved by the ethics of contractual relationships. The need to economize on love in the market requires institutions that work without the resource of love. But this does not imply that institutions are required that work without the ethics of contractual relationships. Such institutions work even better if the resource of ethics is present.

***

I conclude with a short ironical biographical remark taken partly from Edmund Clerihew Bentley (1875-1956), *Biography for Beginners* (1905), and its entry on 'John Stuart Mill':

John Stuart Mill
By a mighty effort of will,
Overcame his natural bonhomie
And wrote 'Principles of Political
Economy'.

Peter Koslowski
By rehabilitating natural bonhomie
Wrote 'Principles of Ethical
Economy'.

References

BOWIE, NORMAN E.: "A Kantian Approach to Business Ethics", in: ROBERT E. FREDERICK (Ed.): *A Companion to Business Ethics*, Oxford (Blackwell) 2002, pp. 3-16.

BUCHANAN, JAMES M.: "Die konstitutionelle Ökonomik der Ethik", in: PETER KOSLOWSKI (Ed.): *Neuere Entwicklungen in der Wirtschaftsethik und Wirtschaftsphilosophie*, Berlin (Springer) 1992, pp. 21-46.

COLEMAN, JAMES S.: "Social Organization of the Corporation", in: THOMAS DONALDSON, PATRICIA H. WERHANE (Eds.): *Ethical Issues in Business. A Philosophical Approach*, Englewood Cliffs, N. J. (Prentice Hall), 4th edition 1993, pp. 172-190.

DE LA COURT, PIETER: *Interest van Holland* (*The True Interest, and Political Maxims of the Republick of Holland and West-Friesland*), 1662, 2nd edition 1669 under the title *Aanwysing der heilsame politike gronden en maximen van de republike van Holland*, Chapter IX. English translation of the 2nd edition by John Campbell, Nourse 1742, under the title *Political Maxims of the State of Holland*, reprinted in excerpts in: *Commerce, Culture, and Liberty. Readings on Capitalism Before Adam Smith*, edited by Henry C. Clark, Indianapolis (Liberty Fund) 2003.

DONALDSON, THOMAS; DUNFEE, THOMAS W.: "Toward a Unified Conception of Business Ethics: Integrative Social Contracts Theory", in: *Academy of Management Review*, 19 (1994), pp. 252-279.

EVAN, WILLIAM M.; FREEMAN, R. EDward: "A Stakeholder Theory of the Modern Corporation: Kantian Capitalism", in: THOMAS DONALDSON, PATRICIA H. WERHANE (Eds.): *Ethical Issues in Business. A Philosophical Approach*, Englewood Cliffs, N. J. (Prentice Hall) 4th edition 1993, pp. 166-171.

GAUTHIER, DAVID: *Morals by Agreement*, Oxford (Oxford University Press) 1985.

GERWEN, JEF VAN: "Corporate Culture and Ethics", in: JOHAN VERSTRAETEN (Ed.): *Business Ethics. Broadening the Perspectives*. Leuven (Peeters) 2000, pp. 43-78.

HOBBES, THOMAS: *Leviathan*, edited by W. G. Pogson Smith, Oxford (Clarendon Press) 1909. Reprint of the edition of 1651, Chap. XIII. Of the Natural Condition of Mankind, As Concerning Their Felicity, And Misery, reprinted as online edition in: The Online Library of Liberty, Liberty Fund 2005.

HOMANN, KARL: *Vorteile und Anreize*, Tübingen (Mohr Siebeck) 2002.

KOSLOWSKI, PETER (1985): "Maximum Coordination of Entelechial Individuals. The Metaphysics of Leibniz and Social Philosophy", in: *Ratio. An International Journal of Analytic Philosophy*, 27 (1985), pp. 160-177.

KOSLOWSKI, PETER (1985b): „Religion, Ökonomie, Ethik. Eine sozialtheoretische und ontologische Analyse ihres Zusammenhanges", in: PETER KOSLOWSKI (Ed.): *Die religiöse Dimension der Gesellschaft. Religion und ihre Theorien*, Tübingen (Mohr Siebeck) 1985, pp. 76-96.

KOSLOWSKI, PETER: *Principles of Ethical Economy*, Dordrecht (Kluwer) 2002, paperback edition. German original: *Prinzipien der Ethischen Ökonomie. Grundlegung der Wirtschaftsethik*, Tübingen (Mohr Siebeck) 1988.

KOSLOWSKI, PETER: *Philosophien der Offenbarung. Antiker Gnostizismus, Franz von Baader, Schelling*, Paderborn (Ferdinand Schöningh), 2nd edition 2003.

KOSLOWSKI, PETER: "What Is Christianity Good For?", in: *Philosophia Reformata. Orgaan van de Vereniging voor Calvinistische Wijsbegeerte*, 72 (2007), pp. 34-52.

KOSLOWSKI, PETER: "Argumentum ethico-oeconomicum. The Argument for the Existence of God from Ethical Economy", in: STEFANO SEMPLICI (Ed.): *Philosophy of Religion Today? In Memoriam Marco M. Olivetti*. Archivio di Filosofia – Archives of Philosophy, Pisa, Roma (Fabrizio Serra) 2008 (forthcoming).

KRINGS, HERMANN: *System und Freiheit*, Freiburg im Breisgau (Alber) 1980.

MUSSCHENGA, ALBERT W.: "Integrity – Personal, Moral, and Professional", in: ALBERT W. MUSSCHENGA, WOUTER VAN HAAFTEN, BEN SPIECKER, MARC SLORS (Eds.): *Personal and Moral Identity*, Dordrecht (Kluwer) 2002, pp. 169-201.

RATZINGER, JOSEPH (POPE BENEDICT XVI): *Marktwirtschaft und Kirche*, 1985, English translation: *Market Economy and the Church,* online in: http://www.acton.org/publicat/occasionalpapers/ratzinger.html.

SCHELLING, F. W. J.: *Philosophical Inquiries into the Nature of Human Freedom* (1809), translated by James Gutmann, La Salle, Illinois (Open Court) 1936.

SEN, AMARTYA: "Isolation, Assurance, and the Social Rate of Discount", in: *Quarterly Journal of Economics*, 81 (1967), pp. 112-124.

SHACKLE, G. L. S.: *Imagination and the Nature of Choice*, Edinburgh (Edinburgh University Press) 1979.

SPAEMANN, ROBERT: "Nebenwirkungen als moralisches Problem", in: R. SPAEMANN. *Kritik der politischen Utopie*, Stuttgart (Klett Cotta) 1977, pp. 167-182.

TAYLOR, CHARLES: *Sources of the Self*, Cambridge, Mass. (Harvard University Press) 1989.

WEBER, MAX: *Wirtschaft und Gesellschaft. Grundriss der verstehenden Soziologie*, Tübingen (Mohr Siebeck) 1922.

WEBER, MAX: *The Protestant Ethics and the Spirit of Capitalism* (1904/5), translated by Talcott Parsons with an introduction by Anthony Giddens, London (Routledge Classics) 2005.

Appendix

KOSLOWSKI, PETER: "Lebensverlängerung als Aufgabe und Begrenzung ärztlichen Handelns. Aus philosophischer und ökonomischer Sicht", in: *Medizinische Welt*, 32 (1981), pp. 1811-1814. Extended version: "Lebensverlängerung. Nebenwirkungen und Grenzen der ärztlichen Behandlungspflicht aus philosophischer und ökonomischer Sicht", in: P. KOSLOWSKI, PH. KREUZER, R. LÖW (Eds.): *Die Verführung durch das Machbare. Ethische Konflikte in der modernen Medizin und Biologie*, Stuttgart (S. Hirzel) 1983, pp. 83-100.

KOSLOWSKI, PETER: *Gesellschaft und Staat. Ein unvermeidlicher Dualismus*, Stuttgart (Klett Cotta) 1982.

KOSLOWSKI, PETER: "Ethics of Capitalism", in: PETER KOSLOWSKI: *Ethics of Capitalism and Critique of Sociobiology*. Two Essays with a Comment by James M. Buchanan, Berlin (Springer) 1996. German original: *Ethik des Kapitalismus*. Mit einem Kommentar von James M. Buchanan, Tübingen (Mohr Siebeck) 1982.

KOSLOWSKI, PETER: "Grundlinien der Wirtschaftsethik", in: *Zeitschrift für Wirtschafts- und Sozialwissenschaften*, 109 (1989), pp. 345-383.

KOSLOWSKI, PETER: *Gesellschaftliche Koordination: Eine ontologische und kulturwissenschaftliche Theorie der Marktwirtschaft*, Tübingen (Mohr Siebeck) 1991.

KOSLOWSKI, PETER: "Ethical Economy as Synthesis of Economic and Ethical Theory", in: PETER KOSLOWSKI (Ed.): *Ethics in Economics, Business, and Economic Policy*, Berlin (Springer) 1992, pp. 15-56. German original: "Ethische Ökonomie als Synthese von ökonomischer und ethischer Theorie", in: *Jahrbücher für Nationalökonomie und Statistik*, 208(2), (1991), pp. 113-139.

PETER KOSLOWSKI

KOSLOWSKI, PETER: "Economics as Ethical Economy in the Tradition of the Historical School. Introduction", in: PETER KOSLOWSKI (Ed.): *The Theory of Ethical Economy in the Historical School: Wilhelm Roscher, Lorenz von Stein, Gustav Schmol ler, Wilhelm Dilthey and Contemporary Theory*, Berlin (Springer) 1995, pp. 1-11.

KOSLOWSKI, PETER: "The Ethics of Banking. On the Ethical Economy of the Credit and Capital Market, of Speculation and Insider Trading in the German Experience", in: ANTONIO ARGANDOÑA (Ed.): *The Ethical Dimension of Financial Institutions and Market,* Berlin (Springer) 1995, pp. 180-232.

KOSLOWSKI, PETER: *Ethik der Banken und der Börse: Finanzinstitutionen, Finanzmärkte, Insider-Handel*, Tübingen (Mohr Siebeck) 1997.

KOSLOWSKI, PETER: "The Social Market Economy: Social Equilibration of Capitalism and Consideration of the Totality of the Economic Order. Notes on Alfred Müller-Armack", in: PETER KOSLOWSKI (Ed.): *The Social Market Economy: Theory and Ethics of the Economic Order*, Berlin (Springer) 1998, pp. 73-95.

KOSLOWSKI, PETER: "The Shareholder Value Principle and the Purpose of the Firm: Limits to Shareholder Value", in: STEPHEN A. CORTRIGHT, MICHAEL J. NAUGHTON (Eds.): *Rethinking the Purpose of Business: Interdisciplinary Essays from the Catholic Social Tradition*, Notre Dame, IN (University of Notre Dame Press) 2002, pp. 102-130. German original: "Shareholder Value und der Zweck des Unternehmens", in: PETER KOSLOWSKI (Ed.): *Shareholder Value und die Kriterien des Unternehmenserfolgs*, Heidelberg (Physica-Verlag) 1999, pp. 1-32.

KOSLOWSKI, PETER: "Contingencies, the Limits of Systems, and the Morality of the Market", in: GEOFFREY BRENNAN, HARTMUT KLIEMT, ROBERT D. TOLLISON (Eds.): *Method and Morals in Constitutional Economics. Essays in Honor of James M. Buchanan*, Berlin (Springer) 2001, pp. 504-528.

KOSLOWSKI, PETER: "Economics as Ethical Economy and Cultural Economics in the Historical School", in: HEINO H. NAU, BERTRAM SCHEFOLD (Eds.): *The Historicity of Economics: Continuities and Discontinuities of Historical Thought in 19th and 20th Century Economics*, Berlin (Springer) 2002, pp. 139-173.

KOSLOWSKI, PETER: "Wirtschafts- und Unternehmensethik", in: FRANZ X. BEA, BIRGIT FRIEDL, MARCELL SCHWEITZER (Eds.): *Allgemeine Betriebswirtschaftslehre,* Bd. 1: *Grundfragen*, 9th ed., Stuttgart (Lucius & Lucius) 2004, pp. 421-460.

KOSLOWSKI, PETER: "Business Ethics in Globalised Financial Markets," in: KARL HOMANN, PETER KOSLOWSKI, CHRISTOPH LUETGE (Eds.): *Globalisation and Business Ethics*, Aldershot, UK, Burlington VT, USA (Ashgate) 2007, pp. 217-236. German original: "Wirtschaftsethik in globalisierten Finanzmärkten", in: KARL HOMANN, PETER KOSLOWSKI, CHRISTOPH LÜTGE (Eds.): *Wirtschaftsethik der Globalisierung,* Tübingen (Mohr Siebeck) 2005, pp. 373-392.

Chapter 3

Economic Ethics: A Systematic Integration

YUICHI SHIONOYA

> "The question which leads us beyond the grave of our own generation is not 'how will human beings *feel* in the future' but 'how will they be.' In fact this question underlies all work in political economy. We do not want to train up feelings of well-being in people, but rather those characteristics we think constitute the greatness and nobility of our human nature.
> The doctrines of political economy have alternately placed in the forefront or naively identified as standards of value either the technical economic problem of the production of commodities or the problem of their distribution, in other words 'social justice.' Yet again and again a different perception, in part unconscious, but nevertheless all-dominating, has raised itself above both these standards of value: the perception that a *human* science, and that is what political economy is, investigates above all else the *quality of the human beings* who are brought up in those economic and social conditions of existence."[1]

This paper attempts to construct economic ethics or normative economics by a systematic reconsideration of economics and ethics. It starts with the identification of an interface between economics and ethics with the broad concept of good. While economics addresses allocation, distribution, and utilization of resources in light of the end-means relationship between good (in the sense of goodness) and goods (in the sense of commodities) necessary for human life, ethics explores what a good life is and postulates a set of norms to evalu-

1 MAX WEBER: "The National State and Economic Policy", Inaugural lecture at the University of Freiburg, 1895, in: WEBER (1999), pp. 128-129. (Italics in the original.)

ate it from multiple angles. The paper constructs a system of ethics by coordination of three grand ethical values (good, virtue, and right) directed to different entities of evaluation (act, being, and rule), on the one hand, and a system of economics consisting of economic statics, economic dynamics, and economic sociology, on the other. Economic ethics derived by the juxtaposition of the systems of economics and ethics provides the norms for just distribution, virtuous utilization, and efficient allocation of resources under a reasonable priority rule. It is emphasized that the future task of economic ethics will be to develop the idea of virtue economics in positive and normative senses to shed light on a neglected issue, i.e., virtuous utilization of resources for the development and self-realization of human beings.

I. Introduction

In order to discuss ethical implications of economic issues – to discuss economic ethics – it is necessary to start with a systematic, rather than ad hoc, reflection on the relationship between economics and ethics, and to formulate the tasks of economic ethics (or normative economics) with a well-defined vocabulary. The need for systematic approach to economic ethics is twofold: first, to provide a normative basis for evaluating economic activity and institutions, and second, to give a substantive content to abstract ethical theory. The standard view of contemporary economics is that, since ethical questions require value judgments, economics as a science cannot properly articulate ethical evaluation of economic activity and institutions. Since economics became independent from moral philosophy and recognized as a separate discipline, little effort has been made to unify the world of the economy and the world of morality. Economics and ethics are conceived as addressing two unrelated spheres.

As a result, when modern normative economics emerged in the neoclassical camp with the name of welfare economics, it had become concerned only with issues of productive efficiency, distributive justice, and the disharmony between them, as is exemplified in A. C. Pigou's welfare economics (Pigou 1932). Furthermore, speaking of the so-called New Welfare Economics after Pigou, economists have given up even discussing distributive justice, concentrating on productive efficiency. Amartya Sen, one of the contemporary proponents of economic ethics, argues that both modern economics and modern ethics have been substantially impoverished by the distance that has grown between economics and ethics (Sen 1987, pp. 7-9).

The economy and morality as parts of social reality are two basic schemes of social integration with remarkable universalizing capacities and wide coverage of human activities. As the starting point of inquiry, I contend, the concept of the "good" constitutes an interface of the two worlds. The first task of economic ethics is to analyze this interface so as to introduce broader ethical paradigms into economics through this channel. While economics addresses allocation, distribution, and utilization of resources for providing "goods and services" necessary for human life and is concerned with analysis and design of institutional conditions underlying the economic process, ethics explores what a "good" life is and postulates a set of norms to evaluate it from multiple angles. Thus, in dealing with human life, economics and ethics potentially have the same coverage of human activities. Since economics, however, has lost the abilities to discuss whole problems of value judgments as a result of its pretense of being a value-free science, we must now prepare a broader system of ethics for a systematic discourse of economic ethics. Moreover, lest a system of values should remain a mere abstract entity detached from social reality, ethics must be combined with knowledge about a material basis of society and implemented by a design of social and institutional frameworks. This paper attempts to provide such a theoretical system of values and institutions, drawing on Shionoya (2005a).

In both economics and ethics, the concept of the "good" is widely used explicitly or implicitly; it is an inclusive notion implying utility, welfare, well-being, happiness, and the like, based on interests, wants, desires, and preferences. In ethics, the concept of "good" has been defined in diverse ways; it is no exaggeration to say that how the good is defined signifies different viewpoints of ethical theories. All ideas of the desirable or valuable are likely to be expressed by a single concept of the good, which has created conflicts and confusions. In economics, by contrast, the concept of "goods" (in the sense of commodities) is defined as a means to bring about the "good" (in the sense of goodness) as an end, however differently the latter may be defined. While in the history of economics the normative standards of a good life swayed between physical goods (opulence) and psychological good (welfare), the concept of the "good" with its diverse ethical meanings was replaced by the single notion of utility.

As a result, despite the rich contents of the concept of the good in ethics, the scope of economic ethics supported by economic theory has been impoverished. The main issue is almost confined to the total quantity of the good (allocative efficiency) without regard to the differences of the good among individuals (distributive justice) and the differences in the quality of the good (human excellence). This is typically the case with utilitarian ethics, the most relevant ethical thought to economics, according to which the total welfare of a society should be maximized regardless of its distribution and its quality. It is the contention of this paper that a systematic inquiry of economic ethics should start with the concept of good which constitutes an interface between the world of the economy and the world of morality, and that the end-means relationship between the good and goods (*Gut* and *Güter*, or *bien* and *biens*) not only evokes the well-known conception of allocative efficiency, but also reveals further relationships between ethics and economics that remain to be explored, i.e., distributive justice and human excellence.

Thus having identified the concept of the good as the interface between economics and ethics, the all-inclusive notion of the good can now be decomposed into three basic components of values (i.e., *good* (in a narrow sense), *virtue*, and *right*) and a coordinated system of ethics will be developed (section II). The concept of good in this set will be defined in a narrow sense. On the other hand, the system of economics will be defined with respect to economic statics, economic dynamics, and economic sociology to coordinate with the system of ethics. I will present a systematic model for economic ethics by integrating economics and ethics thus defined, specifically proposing the coordination of Schumpeterian economic dynamics with the ethics of virtue (section III). Based on the tasks of economic ethics, I will focus on a market system as an institution with reference to business ethics (section IV). This paper proposes a new branch in economic ethics that might be called the *economics of virtue* (in addition to the economics of efficiency and justice), concluding with some observations for its development (section V).

II. Coordination of Ethical Thought

The history of ethical thought indicates that moral philosophers have dealt with three objects of moral evaluation: (1) the acts or behaviors of individuals, (2) the being or character of individuals, and (3) the rules or institutions of society. Corresponding to these three objects, there are three distinct approaches to moral philosophy, each with an exclusive emphasis on one of three basic value terms: (1) good, (2) virtue, and (3) right, respectively. These three approaches are typically represented, respectively, by utilitarian (or Benthamite), Aristotelian (or Greenian), and Kantian (or Rawlsian) moral theory respectively. In fact, these grand theories are not consistent but conflict each other because they claim that they are comprehensive doctrines that should be applied indiscriminately to all objects of moral evaluation. The applicability of the traditional three theories should be partitioned and localized with regard to the objects of evaluation.

It is useful to give further specifications to the three approaches for the sake of coordinating a moral vocabulary. The above value categories are very abstract, and an effective discussion in ethical theory needs more languages. In fact, a variety of value language is used in the practice of ethical discourse, and this pluralism also demands systematization and coordination of terminology. First, the basic values in the three approaches, (1) good, (2) virtue, and (3) right, are transformed into more operational values, (1) *efficiency*, (2) *excellence*, and (3) *justice*, so that they can be linked to a wider knowledge of moral and social theories. Second, it is also necessary to attribute axiomatic ultimate ends to basic values. By ultimate ends I mean that a type of meta-value is helpful as an ontological presumption underlying a specific paradigm of moral valuation. In the evaluation of (1) individual act, efficiency is defined in terms of utility maximization as the ultimate end, and this relationship is valued by the abstract concept of good. In the evaluation of (2) human existence, how a person should be is prescribed by the standard of excellence in order to cultivate human nature and capabilities and to realize a higher self as far as possible. This is the ethics of virtue. In the evaluation of (3) social rules, justice is defined with reference to the protection of the rights of individuals under the institutions in question, and this relationship is finally valued by the concept of right. Thus the underlying concepts of the ultimate ends are identified with (1) *utility*, (2) *capability*, and (3) *rights*, respectively.

This system of ethics is summarized in Table 1. It consists of (1) a utility-based moral theory of good for individual acts, (2) a capability-based moral theory of virtue for individual existence, and (3) a rights-based moral theory of right for rules. The idea underlying the coordinated system of ethics is that the traditional attempts at a comprehensive doctrine intended by a single overarching principle (e.g., utilitarianism) to cover all the different objects of moral valuation, often without distinguishing the different objects, are a perennial source of conflict and confusion in moral philosophy. To have a consistent system of ethics, it is necessary to achieve a consensus on the division of labor and the priority relations among the three branches of ethics. Such a system must have a structure and hierarchy of values.

Table 1. A System of Ethics

Value / Object	Basic value	Operational value	Ultimate end
(1) Act	Good	Efficiency	Utility
(2) Being	Virtue	Excellence	Capability
(3) Rule	Right	Justice	Rights

Human welfare is served by the plural values of (1) "act-good-efficiency," (2) "being-virtue-excellence," and (3) "rule-right-justice," not by a scalar value of, say, happiness or utility. The three branches of ethics should be complementary and coordinated in terms of objects and values. The inclusive, vague notion of the "good" is now decomposed into the quantity of good, the quality of good, and the distribution of good among individuals. This decomposition leads to the concepts of good in the narrow sense (efficiency), virtue (excellence), and right (justice); each is concerned with act, being, and rule, respectively, as the objects of moral valuation.

In this system of ethics, it is presumed that right takes priority over virtue and good, and that virtue takes priority over good. The moral reasoning for this hierarchy of values depends on two rationales: first, the primacy of right is a categorical imperative for accommodating plural conceptions of virtue and good; and second, the primacy of virtue over good is justified by the role of virtue to critically evaluate the quality of good. In other words, the values of the right and of virtue are imposed as constraints on the value of good at the interface between the economic world and the ethical world. The first rationale was developed by John Rawls in his theory of justice in opposition to utilitarianism and perfectionism (Rawls 1971); and the second was raised by Thomas Hill Green in his theory of perfectionism in opposition to utilitarianism (Green 1997).

It will be practical to relax the strict one-to-one correspondence between objects and values as described in Table 1. For instance, the value of good (efficiency) applies primarily to the valuation of individual acts and incidentally also to the valuation of individual being and of social institutions. Alternatively, while individual acts are primarily valued in terms of good (efficiency), they are also valued subordinately by the elements of virtue (excellence) and right (justice) embodied in individual acts. The overall relationship between values and objects is indicated in Table 2, implying the overall coordination and mutual reinforcement between all objects and all values. In this system there is no conflict between principal values in primarily evaluating a specific object.

Table 2. Relationship between Value and Object

Value / Object	Good	Virtue	Right
Act	⊙	○	○
Being	○	⊙	○
Rule	○	○	⊙

⊙: primary application ○: incidental application

III. Juxtaposition of Economics and Ethics

Having designed the three-layered system of ethics, we now consider how it may be linked with the system of economics. Generally speaking, economics is a science that relates to the processes of resource management (allocation, distribution, and utilization of resources) and the conditions promoting human well-being by material and institutional means. Despite competing directions and schools in economics, it is generally agreed that, broadly conceived, economics consists of three branches: (A) economic statics, (B) economic dynamics, and (C) economic sociology (or institutional economics). Formally speaking, each branch is defined by the identification of endogenous and exogenous variables, and exogenously given data became endogenous by moving from static theory to dynamic theory to economic sociology, consecutively. While economic statics focuses on static equilibrium with given preferences, technology, and quantity of resources, economic dynamics is characterized by changes in preferences, in technology and in the quantity of resources. Economic sociology relates to changes in social institutions, which are treated as fixed in the former two branches, and investigates the relationship between the economic activity and social and institutional constraints. In substantive terms, our definition of the three branches of economics is modeled after the framework of Schumpeter's universal social science (Shionoya 2004).

In terms of the history of economics, the basic paradigm of mainstream economics through classical and neoclassical economics is to explain an economic process and the mechanism by which the maximization of production and welfare is attained under given preferences, technology, and a fixed amount of resources: this is largely the task of economic statics. For Schumpeter, even where these data are changing, the static approach in terms of resource allocation is applicable as the extension of an economic logic as far as innovative behavior distinct from adaptive behavior does not exist.

In the design of economic dynamics, Schumpeter's approach deserves our special attention (Shionoya 1997, Chapter 3). He proposed to define the dynamic economy in terms of the dynamic man as the carrier of innovations in distinction from the traditional economic man who is typically concerned with adaptation to given conditions. This viewpoint enables us to establish a link between economics and ethics because the human typology relates to an evaluation of human existence. This is a unique romantic legacy to economics in emphasizing the individual creative spirit, but orthodox in keeping methodological individualism in comparison with other competing dynamic approaches in terms of saving-investment relations, monetary disturbances, period analysis, disequilibrium analysis, and expectations. For him, increases in capital and labor, changes in technologies and preferences, and growth of output are not dynamic phenomena per se, but merely indicate changes in exogenously given conditions to which agents are obliged to adapt. Adaptive behavior to the data is the core of static economic theory. For us, various approaches to economic dynamics have no ethical implication except for an ambiguous notion of "dynamic efficiency" measured by the growth rate of output.

Although economic sociology or institutional economics has not been regarded as mainstream, it deals with the institutional framework (economic, political, and social institutions) within which economic behavior takes place.

In other words, economic sociology is concerned with the significance of the institutional assumptions for static and dynamic economics and their changes in a historical context. The sociological direction in economics was pioneered by the German Historical School and developed by Max Weber's idea of *Sozialökonomik* and Schumpeter's idea of universal social science (Shionoya 2005b).

In light of the basic end-means (i.e., good-goods) relationship, economics addresses different aspects of the relationship between the well-being or happiness, on the one hand, and the goods, resources, and institutions as the means to the well-being, on the other. Economic ethics presented in the above provides normative knowledge about different aspects of the end-means relationship, i.e., (A) the efficient allocation, (B) virtuous utilization, and (C) just distribution of scarce resources. All of these relationships belong to the scope of economics because they are all concerned with different aspects of resource management. Importantly, they correspond with the three branches of the ethical system, respectively: (1) good (efficiency), (2) virtue (excellence), and (3) right (justice).

Table 3 summarizes how the branches of economics (A)-(C) are related to those of ethics (1)-(3) through the intermediary of economic ethics. By juxtaposing the two systems, we find, first, that economic statics represented by neoclassical economics with a focus on the allocation of resources motivated by utility and profit maximization through the market mechanism (modified by public policy) is the proper object of moral valuation in terms of the set of notions "act-good-efficiency-utility." This is what contemporary welfare economics has done by using the criteria of Pareto optimality as prescriptions for the efficient allocation of scarce resources.

Table 3. Juxtaposition of Economics and Ethics

Branch of economics	Task of economic ethics	Branch of ethics
(A) Economic statics	Efficient allocation	(1) Good (efficiency)
(B) Economic dynamics	Virtuous utilization	(2) Virtue (excellence)
(C) Economic sociology	Just distribution	(3) Right (justice)

Second, economic dynamics conceptualized by Schumpeterian innovations and entrepreneurship corresponds with moral valuation in terms of virtue ethics, consisting of the set of notions "existence-virtue-excellence-capability." From the ethical point of view, economic dynamics is concerned less with economic growth in terms of GDP based on changes in physical factors (such as capital, labor, and technology) than with innovations associated with the realization of human excellence, perfection, and quality of life through the virtuous utilization of resources. The dynamic nature of economic activities lies in the use of resources to signify and increase the virtues of human existence. Virtuous or perfectionist utilization of resources means that resources are directed to exert human capabilities and promote the self-realization of individuals. As T. H. Green's account of perfectionism explains, the vision of perfection is not a static ultimate state in which the moral ideal is realized, but a dynamic process of moral progress. "We have no knowledge of the perfection of man as the unconditional good," but "our life is directed to its attainment" (Green 1997, p. 206). Therefore, the maximization principle does not apply here.

Third, economic sociology, a science of social institutions, is primarily concerned with rules for the distribution of Rawls's "primary goods," including basic liberties, opportunities, social safety-net, social status, income, and wealth. It is the major counterpart of justice ethics, whose key notions are "rule-right-justice-rights." Although institutions embody several values, justice is the most basic value that should be inherent in the institutions of society as a fair system of social cooperation because the social institutions must assure the coexistence of plural values in a free society. Although the new institutional economics based on neoclassical economics attempts to explain the emergence of institutions by the criterion of efficiency, it may be an example of the incidental (not primary) application to social rules defined in Table 2. Otherwise, it is mainly concerned with institutions of technical nature such as money, exchange and markets.

The issue of efficiency versus justice, which has been well known to economists, is an economic version of the moral issue of good versus right, which was successfully dealt with in Rawls' critique of utilitarianism. In contrast, the issue of efficiency versus excellence is not discussed so much in contemporary economics, although it is of greater relevance to actual economic life. In a positive sense, excellence is realized by innovations in business; in a negative sense, corruption and greed are also deeply rooted vices in business. More basically, although human flourishing is conceived as the goal of economic activity, a preoccupation with economic efficiency, as evidenced by profits, is a perennial source of public critiques of the market and business. Developing virtue ethics in terms of economic practice is a new task of economic philosophy. It will lay a theoretical groundwork for the criticism of material- and wealth-oriented economic growth, for the promotion of the quality of life, and for the self-realization of the individual.

The critical field of business ethics is found in the economic ethics of virtue rather than in that of efficiency and justice. Robert Solomon developed a conception of business ethics on the basis of Aristotelian virtue ethics and emphasized the virtues of cooperation and integrity in business (Solomon 1992). The Aristotelian concept of excellence is defined by the superiority of individuals in the practice of the community to which they belong. Aristotle's central ethical concept is happiness or flourishing of life, which means sharing a good life with other members of the community. Thus the concept of virtue provides the conceptual linkage between the individuals and society, or between the concepts of individual good and social justice. In the virtue approach the corporation must be viewed as a morally responsible agent.

IV. Analysis of Market and Business Ethics

The economic, political, and social system of the contemporary world in developed countries can be studied to ascertain how ethical values could be implemented by actual institutions, and, specifically, to derive an insight on business ethics. The comprehensive view of the contemporary economic, political, and social system is represented by the notion of a "welfare state," which consists of a tripartite, grand system of capitalism, democracy, and social security. As far as the scope of the welfare state is concerned, this view agrees with the formulation by T. H. Marshall of the historical developments of citizenship: the welfare state has advanced through three stages of citizenship: "civil rights" for individual freedom developed in the eighteenth century; "political rights" for individual participation in public decision-making in the nineteenth century; and "social rights" for economic welfare and security in the twentieth century (Marshall 1964).

The outcome of these developments was what Marshall termed "Democratic Welfare-Capitalism" or the welfare state. This term means that the institutional constraints of democracy and of social security have been imposed on the workings of a capitalist market system. The fact that there is no longer a pure capitalist market economy is an underlying condition for discussing the structure and nature of business ethics.

Against the background of our formulation of ethical values, it can be argued that business ethics is a set of philosophical principles which should govern the conduct of business, the beings of economic agents, and the rules of economic activity, with its own topics of discussion. Although it may involve different ethical positions reflecting moral philosophy at the general level, business ethics or corporate social responsibility does not exist apart from the coordinated system of "good-virtue-right." Therefore, the consequences of the coordinated ethical system for business ethics will be developed.

Business ethics relates to the ethics of act, beings, and rules under capitalism as an institution, on which the institutional constraints of democracy and social security are imposed. The institutions of capitalism per se are defined as a competitive market system and its supporting arrangements. There has been a great deal of moral criticism of a competitive market economy, but the targets of that criticism are sometimes confused. The criticisms of many-faceted system of a market economy should be carefully identified. Three distinct aspects of a market system: (1) the motives (what moves people to emulation), (2) the rules (under what conditions people compete with others), and (3) the social ends (what is socially achieved as a result of competition) can be distinguished.

Whereas the first aspect characterizes market competition as such, the second and third aspects are not inherent in market competition but rather depend on how a market system is organized. As we conceive a contemporary system as consisting of capitalism, democracy, and social security, our ethical valuation of markets and business is related to how other components of the whole system supplement and amend a capitalist market system.

The motive of competition – the first aspect of a market system – is criticized for its egocentric or selfish viewpoint, which underlies all competitive efforts whatever their aims: wealth, power, fame, or innovation. Criticism that should be directed toward other aspects of markets is sometimes confused with criticism of the competitive motives. The maintenance of self-interest in social relations of a civil society requires a lot of effort. Hegel called it "the process of education" (Hegel 1967, p. 125.) The competitive motive of individuals is a reflection of their efforts to achieve freedom, spontaneity and self-development; it is the source of social vitality and efficiency, and the rational basis of social organizations. Self-love loosens the shackles of convention, laziness, and indulgence, stimulating progress and innovation. The virtues of self-love that underlie competition and rivalry, such as enterprise, diligence, and prudence, are intrinsic "goods," or the good of competition. Competition is a process consisting of various procedures and has intrinsic values as a motivational power to realize efficiency in achieving whatever may be accomplished.

A market economy is also criticized for its law of the jungle, where the weak are victims of the strong. The rules of competition – the second aspect of a market system – are concerned with this criticism. Indeed, free competition leads to unequal distribution of rewards among competitors because they are unequal in abilities, but it is unreasonable to reject the competitive motive because the results of competition are not desirable. The rules of market competition must solve the questions of how to construct the premise of competition, how to control the process of competition, and how to deal with the outcome of competition from the viewpoint of justice.

Finally, a market economy is criticized for its mammonism, hedonism, and materialism, but the direction of market competition is a matter of its social ends – the third aspect of a market system. Competition per se is instrumental and indifferent to what is achieved. If mammonism is to be despised, we must ask how the pursuit of more noble and virtuous objectives can be implemented and made workable in a market economy. This problem means a task of interpreting and molding the economy as a means to realize human and cultural values from the viewpoint of virtue. It is no use blaming the economy, which is a mere means.

The three aspects of a market economy constitute the viewpoints for evaluating the moral standing of markets and business and are subject to the three categories of ethical valuation. Formally speaking, while the private motive is an inner power of a competitive economy, the rules and aims which circumscribe a market economy are prescribed from outside of markets through the political and social institutions of democracy and social security. In fact, however, there are interactions between competitive motive and ethical considerations. The conduct of business should be examined from the overall viewpoint of designing a society with (1) goals of efficiency, (2) virtuous aims, and (3) just rules, under the priority constraints that good (efficiency) is subject to virtue (excellence) and right (justice) and that virtue is subject to right. Business ethics does not unilaterally impose moral duty on business; it must be considered as part of the morality of the economic, political, and social system based on the coordinated ethical system. Business should be moral in the sense of compliance with the three precepts of values. This means that there must be a market and a society in which moral business is rewarded: in other words, business that acts in conformity to justice and virtue can survive competitively and profitably.

Andrei Shleifer discusses how market competition encourages the spread of censured conduct, using several examples, and observes strategies for curtailing unethical behavior (long-run market pressure, moral suasion, and government regulation) (Shleifer 2004). His argument apparently does not assume the rule of justice and virtue in a society which effectively circumscribes business behavior in pursuit of efficiency and profit. If business circumstances are becoming moral, the ethics are likely to coincide with efficiency through competitive motive, as the author concludes. The articulation of structure and hierarchy of ethical values is most needed.

V. Conclusions – Toward the Economics of Virtue

Of the three ethical standards constituting an all-embracing concept of welfare, the notion of virtue (excellence) has completely disappeared from the literature of economics.

It is illuminating to examine the structure of moral philosophy in earlier ages when the specific disciplines of social science, though immature, were unified. An entry of "Moral Philosophy" in *Encyclopaedia Britannica* (1771) describes: "Moral philosophy is the science of manners or duty; which it traces from man's nature and condition, and shews [sic] to terminate in his happiness. In other words, it is the knowledge of our duty and felicity; or the art of being virtuous and happy" (*Encyclopaedia Britannica* 1771, vol. III, p. 270). If moral philosophy in the age of the Enlightenment was originally concerned with a system of rules based on man's rational power of becoming virtuous and happy, its focus was on the compatibility of virtue and good in designing the structure of the economy and society on the eve of industrialization. Although there are many earlier works of economics that could be mentioned on this matter, it suffices to refer to Adam Smith's *The Theory of Moral Sentiments*, which set the paradigm of economics on the basis of ethics (Smith 1976). As the industrialization proceeded rapidly in Western Europe, the interest of classical economists shifted to the problem of the distribution of income and wealth and the issue of the compatibility of justice and good, although the trace of virtue ethics was visible in J. S. Mill's discussion of the relationship between happiness and self-development (Mill 1977).

In the currently received scheme of economics, although individuals are regarded as pursuing their own good based on self-interest, the quality of the good attained is not questioned. What distinguishes human existence and its achievements is individual's character and capacities; a measure of quality is excellence. Furthermore, only virtue (excellence) of existence can mediate between right (justice) and good (efficiency), which are often in conflict, because the standards of virtue will change the quality of good entertained by people so that it accords with the precepts of justice designed by reason. This is the issue which John Rawls posited as the "stability" problem of a conception of justice in Part III of his *A Theory of Justice* (Rawls 1971, pp. 453-456). His interest was to base a coherent relationship between the good and the right on moral psychology in the context of Aristotelian virtue ethics. With regard to economic activity, the norms of virtue will change the nature of market competition from a "struggle-type" to a "record-type" in the sense of a typology of sports (Shionoya 2005a, pp. 133-171) and from a "business-oriented type" to an "industry-oriented type" in Veblen's sense (Veblen 1904).

Thoughtful thinkers such as Max Weber sometimes revealed an insight into the goal of economics as improving the quality of human beings by material means, as quoted at the outset of this paper. Writing a memorial to Alfred Marshall, A. C. Pigou remarked in the same vein: "So economics for him [Marshall] was a handmaid to ethics, not an end in itself, but a means to a further end: an instrument, by the perfecting of which it might be possible to better the conditions of human life. Things, organisation, technique were incidents: what mattered was the quality of man" (Pigou 1925, p. 82). However, because economics has long lacked the academic concepts of virtue, excellence, and perfection, the ideas of thoughtful scholars remained mere prose buried between the lines in economic works. In some cases, those ideas worked merely as a critique of mainstream economics; in other cases, they served merely as an excuse for absorption in scientific technicalities.

Where should we search for such tools for the economics of virtue? There is a need for positive and normative economics of virtue. Whereas mainstream economics has concentrated on the productive performance of the economy so that economic progress is conceived as the growth of wealth in terms of GDP, normative virtue economics will investigate the bilateral relationship or feedback effects between human nature and material wealth. Therefore, we must be attentive to how people act under both moral and economic constraints, what they consume and how they work in order to harmonize with life. For normative virtue economics, which tells people how to behave better, progress means improvements of human qualities by the virtuous utilization of wealth (e.g., education, research, and art). John Ruskin's work on the social and economic implications of art is a monumental contribution to the normative economics of virtue (Ruskin 2004). His basic philosophy was the conception of wealth as life: "There is no wealth but life" (Ruskin 1997, p. 222).

In national income analysis, three aspects of income (production, distribution, and expenditure) are regarded as equal by definition. In the paradigms of classical and neoclassical economics the analytical focus was always on production and distribution, although classical writers were much more concerned about the ethical implications of distribution than neoclassical writers. It was a distinction of Keynes to establish the role of expenditure (consumption and investment) in determining the volume of national income and employment as far as the full utilization of resources is concerned. Although Keynes's concern in economic theory was limited to the size of expenditure, his philosophical speculation about the coming age of economic abundance focused on the question "how to use his [man's] freedom from pressing economic cares, how to occupy the leisure, which science and compound interest will have won for him, to live wisely and agreeably and well" (Keynes 1972, p. 328). This question suggests the need of the normative economics of virtue which pays attention to kinds and qualities of expenditure from the viewpoint of improving human faculties and character, and of promoting human excellence.

Veblen's concept of conspicuous consumption contributed to disclosing the wasteful and non-virtuous utilization of resources in a market economy (Veblen 1899). He described the opposite of wasteful convention as "the instinct of workmanship" by the descriptive method of institutional economics. J. A. Hobson's concept of organic welfare, a desirable standard of welfare, depended on his view of society as an organic society, which led him to the concept of surplus value due to social cooperation (Hobson 1914). For him, organic surplus value was the economic source necessary for the self-realization of individuals. Specifically, his division of income into costs and surplus (each defined in terms of objective and subjective evaluation), instead of wages, interest, and rent, seems to be instrumental in combining Green's concept of self-realization with the virtuous utilization of economic resources. According to Amartya Sen, his capability approach to welfare depends on the philosophical standpoint affiliated to Aristotle, Adam Smith, and Karl Marx, but it can be interpreted legitimately as a version of Green's virtue ethics (Sen 1985). Along this line of approach, Martha Nussbaum suggests ten "central human capability": (1) life, (2) bodily health, (3) bodily energy, (4) senses, imagination, and thought, (5) emotions, (6) practical reason, (7) affiliation, (8) other species, (9) play, (10) control over one's environment (Nussbaum 2000, pp. 78-80).

Many more elements, though fragments, of virtue ethics will be found in the history of economic thought. Although little theoretical formulation has been given to the notion of virtue in economics, the idea that progress should mean improvements in the quality of individual lives has been latent in economic thought. Historians of economic thought might be interested in the rich reservoir of virtue ethics, for example, in Aristotle, Marx, Ruskin, Green, Nietzsche, Veblen, Hobson, and others to identify visions expressed in rhetoric and ideology for what might be called the economics of virtue. Among economists, Schumpeter is the rare bird who has ever attempted the development of the moral science of virtue into the economics of innovation, leadership, and entrepreneurship based on a typology of human nature (Schumpeter 1934). The ontological basis of his dynamic theory was the dichotomy of "static-hedonistic man" and "dynamic-energetic man." We might also cite Scitovsky's unfinished attempt of distinguishing between "stimulation" and "comfort" as leading to the positive economics of virtue (Scitovsky 1976). It is expected that the historians of economic thought will gather the filiations of thought on virtue, which has been overlooked by the historians of mainstream economic theory.

References

Encyclopaedia Britannica, vol. III, Edinburgh (Colin Macfarquhar) 1771.

GREEN, T. H.: *Prolegomena to Ethics* [1883], *Collected Works of T. H. Green*, vol. 4, ed. by Peter Nicholson, Bristol (Thoemmes Press) 1997.

HEGEL, G.W.F.: *Hegel's Philosophy of Right*, translated by T. M. Knox, Oxford (Oxford University Press) 1967. Original: *Grundlinien der Philosophie des Rechts*, 1821.

HOBSON, J. A.: *Work and Wealth: A Human Valuation*, London (Macmillan) 1914.

KEYNES, J. M.: "Economic Possibilities for Our Grandchildren" [1930], *The Collected Writings of John Maynard Keynes*, vol. IX, London (Macmillan) 1972.

MARSHALL, T. H.: "Citizenship and Social Class" [1950], in: *Class, Citizenship and Social Development. Essays by T. H. Marshall*, New York (Doubleday) 1964, pp. 65-122.

MILL, J. S.: *On Liberty* [1859], in: *Collected Works of John Stuart Mill*, vol. XVIII, ed. by J. M. Robson, Toronto (University of Toronto Press) 1977.

NUSSBAUM, M.: *Women and Economic Development: The Capabilities Approach*, Cambridge (Cambridge University Press) 2000.

PIGOU, A. C.: "In Memoriam: Alfred Marshall," in: A. C. PIGOU (Ed.): *Memorials of Alfred Marshall*, London (Macmillan) 1925.

PIGOU, A. C.: *The Economics of Welfare*, London (Macmillan) 1932.

RAWLS, J.: *A Theory of Justice*, Cambridge, MA (Harvard University Press) 1971.

RUSKIN, J.: *A Joy for Ever and its Price in the Market* [1857], Honolulu (University Press of the Pacific) 2004.

RUSKIN, J.: *Unto This Last* [1860], in: J. RUSKIN: *Unto This Last and Other Writings*, ed. by C. Wilmer, London (Penguinbooks) 1997.

SCHUMPETER, J. A.: *The Theory of Economic Development*, translated by Redvers Opie, Cambridge, Mass. (Harvard University Press) 1934. Original: *Theorie der wirtschaftlichen Entwicklung*, Leipzig (Duncker & Humblot) 1912.

SCITOVSKY, T.: *The Joyless Economy*, New York (Oxford University Press) 1976.

SEN, A.: *Commodities and Capabilities*, Amsterdam (North-Holland) 1985.

SEN, A.: *On Ethics and Economics*, Oxford (Basil Blackwell) 1987.

SHIONOYA, Y.: *Schumpeter and the Idea of Social Science: A Metatheoretical Study*, Cambridge (Cambridge University Press) 1997.

SHIONOYA, Y.: "Scope and Method of Schumpeter's Universal Social Science: Economic Sociology, Instrumentalism, and Rhetoric", *Journal of the History of Economic Thought*, 26 (2004), pp. 331-347.

SHIONOYA, Y. (2005a): *Economy and Morality: The Philosophy of the Welfare State*, Cheltenham (Edward Elgar) 2005.

SHIONOYA, Y. (2005b): *The Soul of the German Historical School: Methodological Essays on Schmoller, Weber, and Schumpeter*, New York (Springer) 2005.

SHLEIFER, A.: "Does Competition Destroy Ethical Behavior?", *American Economic Review*, 94 (2005), pp. 414-418.

SMITH, A.: *The Theory of Moral Sentiments* [1759], The Glasgow Edition, Oxford (Clarendon Press) 1976.

SOLOMON, R. C.: *Ethics and Excellence: Cooperation and Integrity in Business*, Oxford (Oxford University Press) 1992.

VEBLEN, T.: *The Theory of the Leisure Class: An Economic Study in the Evolution of Institutions*, New York (Macmillan) 1899.

VEBLEN, T.: *The Theory of Business Enterprise*, New York (Charles Scribner's Sons) 1904.

WEBER, M.: "The National State and Economic Policy (Freiburg Address)", in: R. SWEDBERG (Ed.): *Max Weber: Essays in Economic Sociology*, Princeton (Princeton University Press) 1999. Original: *Der Nationalstaat und die Volkswirtschaftspolitik*: Akademische Antrittsrede, Freiburg, Leipzig (Akademische Verlagsbuchhandlung von C. B. Mohr) 1895.

Chapter 4

The Conundrum of Moral Evaluation in Economics

BERNARD HODGSON

In addressing the question of the place for moral values in the construction of economics, one is challenged by a severe conundrum in the standard interpretation of the "mainstream" tradition of classical and neo-classical theory. On the one hand, under the influence of recent positivist doctrines insisting that normative and factual statements are different in kind, the prevailing "orthodoxy" among those concerned with methodological issues is that economic science is consistent with a canon of ethical neutrality, that its explanatory hypotheses are "value-free". On the other hand, even among those who agree that classical and neo-classical theory are "value-laden", the majority only acknowledge a certain anomalous character to the moral commitments of the theories. For it is distinctive of a moral point of view that it is unique, impersonal, and takes precedence over claims of self-interest which often conflict with those of morality. However, to the extent to which economics is internally concerned with ethical questions, it is contended that neo-classical theory continues the classical tradition of the "invisible hand" in affirming that "self-regarding utility maximizers" promote the common good of society, even though such a collective optimum is intended neither by the participating actors nor by state planning.

It is the aim of this study to critically review the above conundrum from two related perspectives. In the first place, I shall directly defend a thesis that neo-classical theory is not ethically neutral, that it does presuppose irreducibly moral ideals – most especially, in its core theory of rational choice. However, in the second dimension of my paper, I shall argue that any such moral valuations are systemically camouflaged and overridden by a reductive mechanistic form of theory-construction in conceiving human agency as, in Edgeworth's terms, that of a "pleasure machine". Or to respond to a position mentioned in the prospectus for this conference, that "if management acts to maximize profits, then it is automatically realizing ethical principles", it will be a primary implication of my analysis that such an understanding of the satisfaction of ethical principle is conceptually incoherent.

I. Rational Choice: The Standard Model

We may acknowledge the considerable achievement of economic science, especially that of "mainstream" or neo-classical economics, to have constructed a comprehensive, mathematically rigorous theory to conceptualize and explain the action-choices of instrumentally rational actors. In terms of the commonsense framework of ordinary language the exercise of instrumental rationality refers to the familiar choice of an action from amongst alternatives, which action offers the most efficient means for an agent to attain a given end. In terms of the canonical axioms of the neo-classical theory of rational choice, such rationality is analyzed as one wherein the agent's behaviour satisfies a set of principles for well-ordered preferences: first, he is never satiated with the current level of satisfaction of his desires for material goods; secondly, he can completely rank his options in terms of his preference or indifference between the consequences of any two choices of commodity-bundles; thirdly, he is consistent in his preferences in that he exhibits a transitive ordering across any three alternative choices: for instance, if he prefers bundle A to B and B to C, then he prefers A to C; and fourthly, he is parsimonious in his disposition to exchange relatively scarce goods for more abundant ones: the amount of one good he is willing to give up to get an additional unit of another good becomes progressively smaller as the quantity of the former diminishes. On the basis of such a "mental set", the rational economic man or *homo economicus* of orthodox economics is conceived as a "self-regarding maximizer" who regularly chooses an action that promises the greatest expected utility or the probability-weighted satisfaction he seeks to derive from the use of material goods.

The simplicity and formal elegance of neo-classical choice theory should not mislead one into believing that it has been deemed of rather narrow explanatory scope for human affairs; rather, one of the foremost features of contemporary intellectual culture has been the systematic effort to extend this economic model to a general theory of social life. Nevertheless, although intending comprehensive explanatory power, the theory claims moral innocence. For, according to the "official view", only hypothetical imperatives are countenanced by the theory: such imperatives take the valued ends of rational actors as given and simply recommend the most efficient means for attaining these ends. So interpreted, economic agency, in short, is fully conceived in terms of instrumental rationality. As so modestly limiting its conception of rationality, furthermore, it is believed that economic reasoning divests itself of moral content and thereby merits inclusion within the august domain of scientific reason. Allied to the alleged concentration on a merely instrumental conception of practical reasoning is the claim that a purely "formal" or "structural" interpretation of rational choice is being set forth. David Braybrooke summarizes such an interpretation in claiming that the neo-classical concept of utility refers to "nothing more than a quantitative metaphor for speaking of orders of preferences".[1] The interpretation claims ethical neutrality in that it intends no reference to the substantive evaluative bases or reasons for preference orderings, and where the economic subject can be conceived, as the economist Sean Hargreaves Heap puts it, as simply a "set of well behaved preferences"[2]. Thus, if an agent's strongest preference is for pornographic films as compared with classical opera or serious literature, but orders his preferences in a complete and consistent manner as specified by the neo-classical axioms, so be it, as far as such a "value-free" perspective is concerned. (We shall refer hereafter to the neo-classical theory of rational choice as outlined above as the "standard model".)

---

1 D. BRAYBROOKE: "Economics and Rational Choice", in: P. EDWARDS (Ed.): *The Encyclopedia of Philosophy*, New York (Macmillan and Free Press) 1967, Vol. 7, p. 455.

2 S. HARGREAVES HEAP: *Rationality in Economics*, Oxford (Basil Blackwell) 1989, p. 32.

II. The Ethical Content of "Formal" Structures

However, even if we were to concede the preceding formalist interpretation, it can be established that the so-called structural principles of the standard model are not, in any case, ethically neutral. Most critically, *the structure or form of the instrumental reasoning itself presupposes certain moral ideals.*

Consider, for example, the non-satiation principle that *homo economicus* always prefers more of available commodities; or as David Gauthier succinctly puts the structural logic of the situation… "Appropriation has no natural upper bound. Economic man seeks more".[3] It is evident that this principle tacitly aligns neo-classical economics with the *form* of maximization as it was defined within the framework of the type of Utilitarian ethics formulated by Bentham, wherein an agent's maximizing his utility is to be understood in an exclusively "expansionist" sense – that is, an agent is able to maximize his total utility only if he increases the quantity of his satisfied desires.[4] However, such a moral attitude is not logically or morally inevitable. There are open ethical alternatives to the expansionist form of utility maximization recommended and fostered by such Benthamite Utilitarianism. Such an option is encountered, for instance, in the Stoic imperative to achieve the greatest possible personal satisfaction by maximizing the *ratio* of one's satisfied to unsatisfied desires. Accordingly, such satisfaction might be represented by the formula:

$$\text{satisfaction} = \frac{\text{fulfilled desires}}{\text{unfulfilled desires}}$$

Under such a scheme, a morally rational agent could increase his satisfaction by either increasing the numerator or decreasing the denominator, or both. Hence, and most significantly, a truly rational consumer would sometimes be disposed to *contract* his desires for material goods in contravention of the Benthamite *cum* neo-classical formula.

3 D. GAUTHIER: *Morals by Agreement*, Oxford (Oxford University Press) 1966, p. 318.

4 J. BENTHAM: *An Introduction to the Principles of Morals and Legislation* (1789), London (University of London) 1970, p. 17 f.

Accordingly, as Epictetus advises:

> He who is entering on a state of improvement, having learnt from the philosophers that the object of desire is good, of aversion evil, and having learnt too that prosperity and ease are not otherwise attainable by man, than in not being disappointed of his desire, nor incurring his aversion, such a one removes totally from himself and postpones desire.[5]

Let us turn now to a scrutiny of the pattern or form of instrumental reasoning exercised in the other principles of the standard model of rational choice, especially the "consistency" of the transitivity postulate. Now, it is particularly crucial that this postulate should withstand criticism of its coherence and general truth. For intransitive preference orderings will express the fact that there will be no bundle of goods which is unambiguously highest in a subject's preference ordering. But, under these circumstances, no consistent utility function can be assigned to this individual, and, thus, his behaviour will be outside the range of the explanatory and predictive power of the standard model. Empirical observations have confirmed, furthermore, that such intransitive preference structures *are* sometimes exhibited in the behaviour of consumers.[6] Under which additional assumptions regarding consumer tastes, other than those explicitly stated in simplified codifications of the theory, is the transitivity axiom true of consumers and of whom the standard model would be competent to explain and predict their behaviour. In reply, we find that the common assumption appealed to by neo-classical theorists is that of the "constancy of tastes".[7] Thus, the "consistency" of consumers which neo-classicists claim to be implied by the transitivity postulate refers, roughly, to the fact that if S prefers A to B on one occasion, he will, given the same prices and income, exhibit the same ordering on other occasions. On the other hand, if a consumer's tastes and preference orderings were continually in a state of flux, then the standard model would be incapable of explaining or

5 EPICTETUS: *Moral Discourses and Fragments*, London (Dent) 1910, p. 10.

6 See, for example, B. CALDWELL: *Beyond Positivism: Economic Methodology in the Twentieth Century*, London (Allen and Unwin) 1982, pp. 150-88, for a discussion of experimental research on intransitive preference patterns.

7 See, for example, M. BLAUG: *Economic Theory in Retrospect*, 5th ed., Cambridge (Cambridge University Press) 1996, pp. 337-339, for a useful general scrutiny of the employment of the stability or constancy of tastes assumption. And see B. CALDWELL: *Beyond Positivism*, pp. 147-48.

predicting his choices. Of course, if the standard model were conjoined with auxiliary postulates explaining the evolution of material wants and their propensity to change, as "Institutionalists" and Marxist social scientists have strongly urged, then this model would no longer be so incapacitated when confronted by choices determined by volatile preference patterns. Neo-classical economists have, however, generally resisted such advice. But why? Surely sound recommendations as to the method for enlarging the explanatory scope of a theory are to be welcomed by serious scientists and taken into consideration in reconstructing the theory.

In my judgement, such revision has generally been avoided because of the covert *normative* content of the transitivity axiom, *even* as structurally interpreted, that is, irrespective of the evaluative grounds or reasons for preference rankings. Recourse has been taken to *criticizing* unstable wants from the evaluative perspective of the neo-classical concept of *homo economicus*. The transitivity axiom's presupposition of enduring tastes is to be understood as indicating that the standard model takes as its subject matter *only* the behaviour of *rational* economic agents. And at the centre of the proposed ideal development of human nature encompassed by the concept "rational economic man" is that of a severe "calculatedness". By definition, *homo economicus* formulates *deliberate* choices from amongst alternative actions. Such an attitude requires that a rational man exercise self-restraint in repressing the spontaneous satisfaction of his immediate impulses, thus introducing a degree of stability in his wants, which, in technical terms, permits a complete and transitive ordering of his preferences which, in turn, renders possible (the standard model's concept of) the maximization of his utility. Put another way, the transitivity axiom of the standard model formulates a principle of consistency for economic agents, and is to be understood as describing regularities in the behaviour of *homo economicus* who behaves thus consistently, not as describing the behaviour of impulsive, inconsistent consumers. As Lionel Robbins put the normative side of the general methodological posture of neo-classical theory-construction:

> And thus in the last analysis Economics does depend if not for its significance, at least for its existence, on an ultimate valuation – the affirmation that rationality and the ability to choose with knowledge are desirable. If irrationality, if the surrender to the blind force of external stimuli and uncoordinated

> impulse at every moment is a good to be preferred above all others, then it is *true* that the *raison d'être* of economics disappears.[8]

Robbins, of course, was writing in a methodological tradition whose articulation was given canonical expression in the *locus classicus* of neo-classical economics, the *Principles* of Alfred Marshall:

> The side of life with which economics is specially concerned is that in which man's conduct is most deliberate and in which he often reckons up the advantages and disadvantages of any action before he enters on it. And further it is that side of life in which, when he does follow habit and custom and proceeds for the moment without calculation, the habits and customs are themselves most surely to have arisen from a close and careful watching of the advantages and disadvantages of different courses of conduct.[9]

Most importantly, such calculatedness of the economic man implies that certain psychological dispositions or character traits are to be eschewed. The rational agent, as conceived by Marshall, never buys on impulse, constantly repressing any spontaneous urge to indulge himself in the purchase of "transient enjoyment' in preference to "lasting sources of pleasure".[10] He is, moreover, ever vigilant of the need to exercise self-control by patiently deferring present satisfaction in order to save his income for future use.[11] In fact, Marshall goes so far as to say... "it is deliberateness, and not selfishness, that is characteristic of the modern age."[12] Marshall's conception of economic

8 L. ROBBINS: *An Essay on the Nature and Significance of Economic Science*, 2nd ed., London (MacMillan) 1953, p. 157.

9 A. MARSHALL: *Principles of Economics*, 9th Variorum ed. (1st ed. 1890), Vol. 1, London (MacMillan) 1961, pp. 20-21.

10 MARSHALL: *Principles of Economics*, p. 120. See especially Book I, Chap. XII; Book II, Chaps. II and V; and Book VI, Chap. XIII, for Marshall's characterization of rational economic man in his consumer behaviour.

11 *Ibid*,, pp. 120 ff.

12 *Ibid*,, p. 6. The second axiom of the standard model presented on p. 2 above requires that the rational agent be able to compare any two combinations in terms of relative preference. And the fourth axiom requires that, as a rule, scarce goods are not to be relinquished for relatively plentiful ones. Hence, both of these postulates also demand the exercise of that family of virtues found in the "calculatedness" of *homo economicus*. However, as these character traits have already been required by the third "transitivity" axiom, I have dealt with them under the analysis of this postulate.

man, however, raises issues which present serious anomalies for the preservation of consistency in the use of fundamental tenets of neo-classical methodology – in particular, the conceptually related assumptions of ethical neutrality and instrumental rationality. Our discussion here may be understood as providing a case-study which confirms Imre Lakatos' caution, adapting Kant, that "philosophy of science without the history of science is empty, and history of science without the philosophy of science is blind".[13]

We might begin to address these issues by responding to an expected objection that the qualities of character displayed by *homo economicus* in formulating preferences according to the postulates of the standard model are not promulgated by neo-classical economists as genuine ethical ideals, that is, as qualities that ought to be desired for their own sake. Rather, the objection would continue, such (alleged) virtues of human temperament as deliberateness and self-control exhibited by *homo economicus* have *only* an instrumental value, and, therefore, "factual" status, which status fails to signify the use of (unavowed) moral judgments on the part of neo-classical theorists. The sole end posited by the standard model is that of the maximum satisfaction of given wants, whatever they may happen to be for any individual consumer. But this theory countenances no value-judgments as to the ethical desirability of alternative kinds of wants. Again, if an agent prefers pornographic films to classical opera, the standard theory must and does preserve its "neutrality" with respect to the moral value of such a preference-ordering. Of course, it is true that even a consumer whom moralists might denounce as being moved by a corrupt preference ranking must satisfy the axioms of the standard model if he is to maximize the satisfaction of the wants so ordered. And, if he is to behave consistently with the model, then he needs to manifest the "orderly personality" typical of rational economic man. But this last requirement merely records an instrumental truth concerning a means-end relationship. And empirical propositions concerning the comparative efficiency of means – in this case, dispositional traits of human character – for attaining given ends, do not transgress the scope of a value-free "positive science". In short, it would be argued, a claim of ethical presuppositions for the standard model is the reverse of the truth. The rational actor does not, by ordering his preferences in a complete and consistent manner, intend to avow an intrinsic value-

13 I. LAKATOS: "History of Science and its Rational Reconstruction", in: R. C. BUCK, R. S. COHEN (Eds.): *Boston Studies in the Philosophy of Science*, Vol. VIII, Dordrecht, Holland (D. Reidl) 1971, p. 91.

commitment in the form of exhibiting his allegiance to the moral virtues of calculatedness and self-restraint; rather, by developing such "firmness of character" he is able to satisfy the principles of the standard model with greater uniformity. Put differently, economic man, as defined by the model represents an ideal type in a normative, but *amoral* sense – the actions of *homo economicus* provide the standard for rational choice, but only in the sense of economic *efficiency*, that is, in specifying the optimal course of action for satisfying given wants. But whether these wants are *worthy* of satisfaction is beyond the economic universe of discourse.

The substance of the preceding argument is a familiar enough refrain and, no doubt, continues to record the "official view" of orthodox economists and economic methodologists. Nevertheless, it seems to me that the argument can only be sustained at too high a conceptual cost. In order to elucidate my rejoinder, it is instructive to observe that the contemporary viewpoint belies the status of neo-classical consumption theory as found in its historical roots in Marshall. For it is plain that, as Marshall saw it, it is not sufficient for the economic scientist to take consumer wants as *given* "data" upon which to construct theories of rational *qua* efficient processes for maximizing the satisfaction of such wants. On the contrary, according to Marshall, the problem of want satisfaction is of secondary and derivative importance within the scope of economics in comparison with an inquiry into what he calls "activities":

> It is not true that the theory of consumption is the scientific basis of economics. For much of the chief interest in the science of wants is borrowed from the science of efforts and activities.[14]

Now "activities" are understood by Marshall to refer to the distinct kinds of efforts and practices which are demanded of agents in their participation in the processes of different kinds of economic systems. And of primary concern for Marshall in the study of "activities" are the comparative qualities of human character which are expressed in different forms of these activities. With respect to the type of activities involved in the sphere of consumer behaviour, Marshall is intent on identifying the qualities of character manifest in the *systematic processes of instrumental reasoning* in which *homo economicus* engages prior to the optimal choice of a commodity-bundle. And consistently with the traits mentioned above, Marshall concludes that eco-

14 MARSHALL: *Principles of Economics*, p. 90.

nomic man would manifest a methodical, self-controlled character in his deliberative processes.

Most significantly, it is also clear that for Marshall such qualities are undeniably *moral virtues*, that is, categorically desirable dispositional traits of human character. The value or "welfare" of an economic process is not, from the highest point of view, to be judged according to the "efficiency" with which it satisfies given desires, but rather by the degree of moral excellence in the character traits of agents taking part in the process. Accordingly, the economic activities in which these virtues find their expression are also and primarily to be considered intrinsically desirable, that is, worth pursuing for their own sake, not merely as means to the realization of some future end. Thus, because they express the virtues of self-restraint and "firmness of character", the deliberative processes of the rational man outlined in Marshall's prototype of the standard model are, above all, to be desired as ends-in-themselves, and only secondarily as instrumental to maximizing the satisfaction of an agent's desires for material commodities.

In terms of current philosophical discussion, orthodox economists would be disposed to classify the structure of the deliberative processes issuing in the maximizing choices of the standard model as exhibiting instrumental, but not "expressive" rationality. For Marshall, however, such a classification would express a distinction without a real difference in the case of neo-classical agency – that is to say, the qualities of character manifest by economic man in his instrumental reasoning as to which action choices would most efficiently attain his material ends *give expression* to his self-identity as a moral agent. *A fortiori*, under his perspective, the ethical neutrality claimed for the concept of instrumental rationality within neo-classical theory would also be ill-founded. In Marshall's view, the instrumental reasoning of the standard model is itself informed by the expressive rationality of a moral self-identity.

Of course, it is open to contemporary followers of the general outline of Marshall's economics, who nevertheless disagree with his viewpoint concerning the "highest good" of economic processes, to appeal to the wisdom of historical perspective. Marshall, it might be claimed, was writing at a time when the exact logical grounds for separating "scientific" factual statements from pseudo-scientific value-judgements were, as yet, ill-understood; consequently, the (illegitimate) inclusion of moral attitudes in the construction of an economic science was only to be expected. We may grant that Marshall's economic theory embraces categorical moral imperatives of the form: "everyone ought to do A", recommending that certain kinds of deliberative activities are worth enacting for their own sake, as well as hypothetical imperatives of the form: "If anyone has (economic) want W, then he ought to do A to efficiently satisfy W". But, the criticism continues, we now more clearly realize that only the latter kind of imperative is acceptable to proponents of an "objective" or value-free science. However, certain aspects of economic processes which were evident to Marshall himself, but which appear to have escaped his disciples, discredit this appeal to contemporary enlightenment. There is a strict, though subtle, reason why the conceptual structure of the standard model cannot sustain value-freedom in the light of Marshall's conception of the model. And although Marshall himself failed to clearly recognize the philosophical implications concerning the value-freedom of economic science, the following quotation from the *Principles* reveals that the original codifier of neo-classical economics was at least cognizant of the substantive grounds of these implications:

> Speaking broadly, therefore, although it is man's wants in the earliest stages of his development that give rise to his activities, yet afterwards each new step upwards is to be regarded as the development of new activities giving rise to new wants rather than new wants giving rise to new activities.[15]

We might begin to see the import of Marshall's comment by noting the circumstances under which the use of hypothetical, rather than categorical imperatives, *would* support a claim to the ethical neutrality of a social scientific theory. This would be the case only if: i) the desires of the subjects under study *are* actually given as data for scientific investigation, without the theorist himself passing any value-judgement on the intrinsic worth of the desires, and ii) the description of the "means" or courses of action asserted by the theory as necessary to securing the subjects' ends, that is, to satisfying the given desires, must themselves be purely "factual" or empirical judgements, rather than value-laden. However, the validation of ii) requires, amongst other factors, that the subjects' wants are not themselves the product of the activities which the social scientist designates as a means to the fulfillment of the wants. If they are, then the assumption that those wants are *given* as data for investigation is a logically incoherent one. In effect, under such circumstances, it would not be possible to satisfy condition ii) without violating

15 MARSHALL: *Principles of Economics*, p. 89.

condition i). But the fact that the standard model is subject to just such a conundrum can be shown to be a direct implication of the genealogical situation affirmed in the preceding quotation from Marshall, the empirical truth of which assertion, furthermore, is well-attested. It is critical, then, to gain an understanding of what Marshall means by "activities giving rise to wants".

We may proceed, here, by way of illustration. For our purposes the most useful example is provided by the economic "activities" consisting in the instrumental, deliberative reasoning and choices of consumers. Suppose, for instance, that we are accounting for the consumer behaviour of what Marshall calls the historical "savage" or "uncivilized" contemporary man, those whom he classifies as "having no pride or delight in the growth of their faculties".[16] The character of such men is, for Marshall, comprised of such unVictorian qualities as idleness, capriciousness, incontinence, self-indulgence, and extravagance. Consequently, their consumption preferences will express a pattern of impulsive, ill-ordered desires issuing in the purchase of "ephemeral luxuries" or leading to the indulgence of "sensuous craving".[17] Not surprisingly, Marshall identifies such "unwholesome" commodities as alcohol, tobacco, and "fashionable dress" as typifying the purchases of these men of inferior virtue. As a case in point, he suggests we look at ... "that part of the English working classes who have no pride or delight in the growth of their faculties and activities, and spend on drink whatever surplus their wages afford over the bare necessities of a squalid life".[18]

In marked contrast, Marshall also categorized the buying pattern of the rational economic man of our standard model whose firm, "active-minded"[19] character disposed him to methodical deliberation resulting in well-ordered, consistent wants. But the critical point lies in the response to the question whether such wants have as their object a distinctive class of commodities. For we find that the high-grade mental activities involved in the careful deliberative reasoning of the rational consumer *determine what kind of goods he will desire*. In general, the rational agent, as characterized by Marshall, will want commodity-bundles which exercise and develop the higher faculties. As examples of such commodities, Marshall mentions artistic and pro-

16 *Ibid.*, p. 90.
17 *Ibid.*, p. 89.
18 *Ibid.*, p. 90.
19 *Ibid.*, p. 88, note.

fessional services, expansive house room, and distinguished clothing.[20] Or from the opposite perspective, Marshall admonishes that the rational consumer will avoid "food and drink that gratify the appetite and afford no strength, and of ways of living that are unwholesome physically and morally".[21]

Although the suitability of Marshall's examples might be well questioned, it seems to me that historical observation bears out the empirical truth of his main point concerning "new activities giving rise to new wants". Economic processes, including the deliberative calculations of the rational consumer, are a *cause* of economic wants in the form of desires for certain *kinds* of consumption. But the normative implications of this relationship are of the first order of importance as the neo-classical "welfare" principle of "consumer sovereignty" with its attendant claim to ethical neutrality has been rendered incoherent. In particular, the economic system represented by neo-classical theory cannot be vindicated on value-free "hypothetical" grounds – that whatever be the wants of individual consumers that are given, the activities of the system will be maximally conducive to their satisfaction. *For these very activities systematically determine the nature of the wants.*

It is significant that Marshall himself would probably not have been disturbed by the revelation of this theoretical anomaly. Again, as far as he was concerned, the ultimate justification of an economic system was not, as his followers have maintained, provided by the efficiency with which its characteristic processes led to the satisfaction of given consumer wants. Rather, in the final analysis, economic processes were to be appraised by their contribution to the development of the moral virtues of that ideal character which were sketched above in the person of *homo economicus*. Insofar as the activities in both the demand and the supply sectors of the economic system demanded the individual aquisitiveness, the calculatedness, the self-restraint – in short, the rationality – of *homo economicus*, to that extent the system was vindicated.[22] Admittedly, in violation of the contemporary doctrine of consumer sovereignty, a progression in the alliance of economic processes with the appropriate character virtues brings about re-orderings of preferences and new types of consumer wants. But, appealing to a sanguine conviction in

20 *Ibid.*, pp. 86-89.

21 *Ibid.*, p. 689.

22 In support, see *ibid.*, Book III, Chap. 1, sec. 2, p. 85; Book III, Chap. II, sec. 4; and Book VI, Chap. XIII, sec. 1.

moral evolution, Marshall contends that such a consequence is to be considered a "new step upwards" in mankind's "development".[23] As far as this patriarch of neo-classical economics is concerned, far from believing, in company with his present day followers, that *de facto* consumer tastes are to be held "sovereign", to be taken "as data" in determining the "welfare" produced by an economic system, we find him recommending that such systems take on the capacity for radically *modifying* the prevailing kind of consumer wants – otherwise their potential contribution to higher levels of human good would be seriously curtailed.

In anticipation of an impending objection, it will be useful to clarify further this criticism of the "givenness" of consumer wants and its connection with the neo-classical principle of consumer sovereignty. We may agree that from an *empirical* point of view consumers remain "sovereign" in that, unless the cost of production is recovered on the market by effective demand, the producer is at risk of producing himself out of the market. However, there is also an essential normative dimension to the concept of consumer sovereignty. In particular, from an ethical point of view the doctrine asserts two central beliefs: a) the individual consumer himself, rather than some external "authority", ought to be the judge of his own sources of satisfaction – hence, consumer desires and preference-orderings should be taken as "given" by the economic theorist; and b) the final end or goal which ultimately justifies all economic activity, including production, is that of the maximal satisfaction of the given desires of individual consumers. But our analysis challenges the coherence of this understanding within neo-classical theory and the market processes it represents. Most particularly, we have argued, following Marshall, that that the kind of deliberative activities designated in neo-classical theory for the maximization of individual consumer satisfaction are themselves a determinant of kinds of consumer wants, typically involving a transformation of the current kind of wants. Accordingly, in contravention of the normative claim of the doctrine of consumer sovereignty, given consumer tastes are not accepted as "sovereign", are not "taken as data" in the determination of the "welfare" delivered by the private market system. Of course, it is worth observing that the empirical and normative senses of consumer sovereignty remain consistent with each other: even if the economic activities represented by the standard model do bring about changes in the kind and pattern of consumer tastes, unless entrepreneurs monitor and cater to the ful-

23 *Ibid.*, p. 89.

fillment of these transformations of material desires, the firms they manage will not survive.

In the light of the above analysis, we may conclude that Marshall's demand theory provides perhaps the most telling substantiation of the origin of rational choice theory in normative theory-construction both informed and regulated by moral commitments. Nor, in my judgement, are the ethical presuppositions of his demand theory so much archaic obfuscation of whatever sound "factual content", and, therefore, genuinely scientific knowledge of economic behaviour his theory does offer. Marshall's approach to theory-construction is no idiosyncratic aberration from scientific rationality. Even the austerely "formal" contemporary versions of the standard model are perspicaciously interpreted as tacitly embedding a prescriptive element recommending the moral ideals not only of a particular form of maximizing behaviour, but also of the character of the rational agent engaged in the behaviour. Moreover, as I have argued elsewhere[24], such "value-laden" theory-construction can remain within the rules of a "liberalized" empiricist method, yet adequately serve scientific aims such as the explanation and prediction of actual behaviour. Such a perspective is validated through an understanding of the manner in which an originally normative theory can be *converted* into a descriptive science of actual behaviour through the application of institutional constraints to the motivations of individual agents.

It is instructive here to appreciate that earlier commentators on the founding constructions of the standard model of rational choice clearly recognized its essentially ethical frame. Indeed, critical reaction to the normative picture of economic man within the model and the moral attitudes he encapsulates was vehemently expressed. Weber,[25] for one, saw in *homo economicus* a personification of the capitalist spirit of "worldly asceticism". For Weber, the deliberate, self-controlled calculations of the ideal economic man of neoclassical price theory were underwritten by what he called the "rationalistic economic ethic" of capitalist economic systems,[26] which ethic commanded the repression of immediate personal enjoyment in order to maximize mate-

24 See B. HODGSON: *Economics as Moral Science*, Berlin/New York (Springer) 2001, especially chaps. 14 and 15.

25 See M. WEBER: *The Protestant Ethic and the Spirit of Capitalism*, trans. by Talcott Parsons, New York (Charles Scribner's Sons) 1958, Part I, Chap. II, and his *General Economic History*, New York (Collier Books) 1961, Chap. 30.

26 M. WEBER: *General Economic History*, p. 260.

rial wealth. As Weber put it... "the *summum bonum* of this ethic [is] the earning of more and more money with the strict avoidance of all spontaneous enjoyment of life."[27] According to Weber, this systematization or rationalization of economic conduct was morally supported, indeed commanded, by the religious ethos of Protestant Calvinism. Granted, more recent interpretations have typically agreed with the orthodox interpretation in its assertion of the ethical neutrality of the standard model. But there have been notable exceptions. Schumpeter, for instance, characterized the repressive notion of rational economic action outlined in Marshall as due to "mid-Victorian morality seasoned by Benthamism".[28] In a more general normative vein, according to such critics as Weisskopf, Marcuse, and Scitovsky, the systematic impulse control distinctive of neo-classical economics is *not* conducive to the general well-being of the individual, nor to the long survival of different societies.[29] Building on recent psychoanalytic theories[30], they claim that the methodical, regular repression of random or spontaneous desire only induces mental disorder for the individual and eventual anarchic rebellion for the institutions which foster such repression.

We need at this point to clarify a basic methodological issue that pervades any discussion of rational choice theory. In what sense does the distinction between the descriptive-explanatory dimension of the standard model and the prescriptive-normative dimension bear on our analysis. This distinction is certainly of one of fundamental significance, although reasons of space preclude an extensive consideration of its myriad ramifications here. But it will be appropriate for the specific intent of this paper to say at least the following:

From its inception, economic science has been charged with the dual task of constructing theories of human behaviour that possess both explanatory power and normative force. Not surprisingly, such a symbiosis has been notoriously difficult to sustain without impugning the scientific integrity of

27 WEBER: *The Protestant Ethic and the Spirit of Capitalism*, p. 53.

28 J. SCHUMPETER: *Ten Great Economists: From Marx to Keynes*, London (George Allen and Unwin) 1952, p. 104.

29 See W. A. WEISSKOPF: *Economics and Alienation*, New York (Dutton) 1971; H. MARCUSE: *One Dimensional Man*, Boston (Beacon Press) 1964; T. SCITOVSKY: *The Joyless Economy: An Inquiry into Human Satisfaction and Consumer Dissatisfaction*, Oxford (Oxford University Press) 1976.

30 See, for example, A. H. MASLOW: *Motivation and Personality*, 2nd ed., New York (Harper and Row) 1970.

economics. In identifying the difference between explanatory and normative versions of the standard model, it would be self-defeating to note a distinction between how rational agents act and how they ought to act, since a rational person, by definition, acts as he ought to act. Of course, there is a significant factual/explanatory issue: If we consider the axioms of the standard model as norms specifying how a rational agent ought to act in order to maximize his utility from the consumption of commodity-bundles, to what extent do they describe the norms actually followed by real-life consumers such that the norms of the standard model have significant explanatory power for actual behaviour? In answering this question for the case of rational choice theories, there are two related special conditions that it is critical to recognize. First, interpreted as normative rules, the axioms of the standard model do not depend on them having explanatory power, nor fail without such power. Admittedly, their normative significance would require the rules to satisfy the meta-normative postulate that "ought implies can": it must be empirically possible for real-life agents to at least *approximate* the satisfaction of the rules in their actual behaviour. But as long as this meta-normative postulate is satisfied, the axioms of the standard model remain significant standards of rationality specifying prescriptions as to how agents ought to behave, whether or not they currently do so behave. Secondly, let us assume that the norms of the standard model are *not* generally followed in actual economic behaviour. Even such descriptive-explanatory "failure" need not be received by the neo-classical theorist as decisive or *final.* For to develop a point made above, he has the option to intentionally promote the validation of the explanatory import of the axioms of the standard model by contributing to the establishment of the institutional causes – the official legislation and informal conventions – compelling or encouraging motivation to engage in activity in conformity with the axioms, while preventing or discouraging contrary inclinations. Hence, with respect to informal cultural determinants, commercial advertisements, political propaganda, the teaching of the "hidden curriculum" of formal education, the social ethic embedded in doctrines of religious denominations, and so on, have concurred in producing the individualistic, acquisitive, and calculative patterns of motivation among individual economic actors necessary to make them economic men – that is, to move them to follow the rules of rational choice set forth by the standard model. Extensive documentation of this empirical issue is beyond the scope of this paper. However, to ramify a reference above, the evidence which Weber invoked to establish a causal connection between the theological ethics of Protestant Calvinism and the "possessive individualism" required to motivate the choices of the rational agents represented in neo-classical economics provides some documentation of such an institutional-motivational nexus. Most significantly, once such conversion procedures are successfully enacted, behaviour which was initially in violation of the norms of the standard model would increasingly come to approximate compliance with these norms; accordingly, the standard model would then also acquire extensive "explanatory power" for the explanation and prediction of actual behaviour. In a certain sense, the principles of economic theory can be "made true".

III. Mechanical Maximizers and the Dissipation of Autonomy

To return to Marshall: It will come as no surprise that Marshall concludes that the kind of economic system which best expresses the virtues of *homo economicus* is the capitalist free enterprise variety. Here, whether labourer, entrepreneur, or consumer, we encounter one rational type expressing the moral excellences of "possessive individualism", self-control, and deliberateness distinctive of *homo economicus*. It appears that for Marshall an eminently desirable juncture has been reached – the congruence of maximally efficient economic processes with the behaviour of ideally virtuous agents. Nor should this connection be viewed as one of accidental coincidence. For these very economic processes are *constituted* by the deliberate choices of rational economic men.

Or so it seems. The conundrum of moral valuation reaches further. For Marshall's theory of demand was historically integrated with the development of a general theory of exchange of deeper and darker implications. Under the influence of other pioneers in the construction of neo-classical theory – Jevons, Walras, Edgeworth and Pareto – Marshall's *Principles* never consistently parted company with a reductive mechanistic reconstruction of economics that continues to be of immense theoretical and practical significance. As Jevons tersely put this development, economic theory in general is to be conceived as the "mechanics of utility and self-interest".[31] In one of the ear-

31 W. S. JEVONS: *The Theory of Political Economy*, 4th ed., London (MacMillan) 1924 (1st ed. 1871), p. 21.

liest and most consequential physicalist modellings of a human science, the principles governing individual behaviour in a market system were to be construed as special versions of the deterministic *extremal* laws governing the motion of an object in any natural system. As it was empirically necessitated for light rays to take least time passing between two points, and for physical systems to react to particular changes by restoring exact equilibrium at maximum/minimum values, so it was necessary for economic subjects to expend least effort in moving towards their natural end-states of maximum utility or conscious pleasure, or, in exchange, to reciprocate the utility transfer of another subject by restoring a precise equilibrium of mutually optimal utility. Indeed, in terms of general explanatory categories, for our economic mechanists, teleology itself is ontologically vacuous: what appears to an economic subject as full-fledged purposive deliberation and the intentional pursuit of conscious ends-in-view, is *only* appearance, that is accurately understood as the causally necessitated effect of the antecedent psychic forces to which he is subject – in particular, his sensations of pleasure and pain. Nor need one strain at interpretation here or engage in tendentious hermeneutics. As Edgeworth himself bluntly characterized this research programme in his *Mathematical Psychics*, and it is to be remembered that he is here in the process of actually constructing what was to become the canonical theory of exchange, not just philosophically commenting on it:

> *at least the conception of Man as a pleasure machine* may justify the employment of mechanical terms and mathematical reasoning in social science.[32]

But economic men need not worry. Although pleasure machines, or what we might call mechanical maximizers, they nevertheless remain, both in individual choice and market exchange, maximizers: unless irregular perturbating factors, like governmental price constraints, disturb the self-equilibrating mechanisms of the market system, the laws of motion of economic processes will necessarily bring individual consumers and entrepreneurs to maximal utilities and profits, and the social aggregate to the mutual advantage of Pareto optimality. What is in operation here might be instructively labeled the "super invisible hand". Although it does really appear to the consciousness of the individual economic subject that he is purposively endorsing his own

32 F. Y. EDGEWORTH: *Mathematical Psychics* (1881), London (London School of Economics) 1932, p. 15.

valued end of maximal satisfaction from the use of material goods, and deliberately choosing that action from among his alternatives that will serve this end, such telic, deliberative conscious processes are "epiphenomenal" in the sense that they exist, but have no causal bearing on what end-states obtain – such states are in fact caused by an underlying mechanics of pleasure and pain which, albeit uncontrolled by the agent, nevertheless, in invisible hand fashion, bring about effects that are benevolent for both the individual and society. As the sadly neglected Thorstein Veblen characterized the neo-classical reduction of a teleological explanatory system to a mechanistic one, the economic subject is now to be conceived as… "a lightning calculator of pleasures and pains, who oscillates like a homogeneous globule of desire for happiness under the influence of stimuli that move him about the area, but leave him intact".[33]

At first sight, Marshall's variant of economic man might appear to provide a coherent exception to our mechanical maximizer. In exercising his higher faculties in the dispassionate, calculated form of reasoning that generates more distinguished types and patterns of desire, surely Marshall's economic man is pre-eminently engaged in purposive deliberation. Such a reading of Marshall's theory of demand would, however, be misleading. Although his theoretical *cum* moralistic language often enough strains against such an interpretation, in general, his theory-construction remains within the framework of the neo-classical pleasure machine. More specifically, the structure of the productive processes of competitive capitalism induce a self-controlled, calculative form of instrumental reasoning or "deliberative" activity among the producers or consumers who are to survive within competitive markets, which activities in turn induce higher kinds of wants. Put in terms of ethical categories, the moral virtue in terms of the "firmness of character" informing the instrumental reasoning of economic man with expressive rationality is at best a regressive mutation of such rationality. There is no clear self-determined commitment to his own character development for such a subject, just a major evolution in his moral (or amoral?) self-identity brought about by the sort of reasoning processes requisite to surviving, let alone thriving, within an environment of competitive capitalism. In short, the virtue expressed by Marshall's economic man is a distorted image of autonomous virtue.

33 T. VEBLEN: "Why is Economics not an Evolutionary Science", in his *The Place of Science in Modern Civilization and Other Essays*, New York (Russell and Russell) 1961, p. 73.

On this matter, Marshall plays his ideological hand in rather cunning fashion, or rather, he gives with his left hand what he takes with his right. Although initially expressing his commitment to the standard doctrine of consumer sovereignty within market capitalism with his avowal that "consumption is the end of production",[34] and that "all wholesome enjoyments, whether luxurious or not, are legitimate ends of action, both public and private",[35] he subsequently exhibits an inclination to *evaluate* the worth of given tastes from the point of view of whether or not the purchasing pattern to which they give rise contributes to the efficiency of the *productive processes* in the consumer's society. It is on this basis that Marshall endorses the usefulness of the concept, central to classical economic theory,[36] of *productive* consumption, which he defines as the "use of wealth in the production of wealth, and it should properly include not all the consumption of productive workers, but only that which is necessary for their efficiency".[37] And, not surprisingly, when he spells out the kind of consumption which is to be classified as efficient, it is seen to exclude the spontaneous purchasing of goods that afford "immediate and transitory enjoyment",[38] and displays a lack of "wisdom, forethought and unselfishness"[39] on the part of uneconomic man. Rather, the efficient consumption he recommends calls upon the virtues of impulse-control and methodical calculatedness of the economic man who recognizes...

> that the true interest of a country is generally advanced by the subordinating of the desire for transient luxuries to those more solid and lasting resources which will assist industry in its future work, and will in various ways tend to make life larger.[40]

Of course, these structural features of the market value programme presuppose that it is production, not consumption, that is driving market capitalism – *pace* the official fantasy of consumer sovereignty, normatively construed.

---

34 MARSHALL: *Principles of Economics*, p. 67.

35 *Ibid.*, p. 66.

36 See especially, ADAM SMITH: *An Inquiry into the Nature and Causes of the Wealth of Nations* (1776), Ed. E. Cannan, New York (The Modern Library) 1937, Book II, Chap. III.

37 MARSHALL: *Principles of Economics*, p. 67.

38 *Ibid.*, p. 65.

39 *Ibid.*, p. 69.

40 *Ibid.*, p. 66.

In fact, the mechanistic mutation of expressive rationality within Marshall's demand theory is not unexpected as the original conception of the freedom of economic man within neo-classical theory lent itself to similar dissipation. Granted, such a regressive development seems dramatically surprising since, at first sight, *homo economicus* appears to be an embodiment of some of the foremost liberal values of the Enlightenment – viz., an independent, self-controlled, dispassionate, choosing power. However, whatever freedom is expressed by the "information processing" of the neo-classical subject is entirely ephemeral. As Jevons and Edgeworth anticipated, the orderly, calculative activities definitive of economic man can be *replaced* by the algorithmic decision-procedures of machine processing, since the former are essentially equivalent to the latter. Not surprisingly, then, the Marshallian dissipation of authentic autonomy of choice finds a legacy in its present offspring: the contemporary standard model of rational choice has preserved the reductive mechanistic understanding of "choice" initiated in the nineteenth century. As Martin Hollis acutely describes the kind of action-choices accessible to the current version of neo-classical pleasure machines:

> the act of choice [is] so like a gate in a basic logic circuit, switched one way or the other by the demands of the self-contained programme. Building on the thought we are tempted to regard the rational individual actor as a set of preferences and a programme for arriving at instrumental choices consistent over a series. [41]

Indeed, as Philip Mirowski has convincingly documented in his important recent book, *Machine Dreams: Economics Becomes a Cyborg Science*,[42] neo-classical economics is now ominously acknowledging its mechanistic intent by explicitly patterning its theory-construction concerning rational choice on cybernetic models.

The normative myopia of the displacement of human agency that comes with the standard model's ontology of the human subject as a mechanical maximizer is deeply significant. Basically, in identifying individual agents with an ordered set of preferences and a calculational capacity for maximizing the expected utility derivable from the set, the standard model camouflages our very real capability for rationally appraising preference ordering

41 M. HOLLIS: *The Cunning of Reason*, Cambridge (Cambridge University Press) 1987, p. 25.

42 P. MIROWSKI: *Machine Dreams: Economics Becomes a Cyborg Science*, Cambridge (Cambridge University Press) 2001.

themselves, including a moral ranking of alternative rankings of action choices, or, equivalently, for assessing the rationality of the objects of our preferences, the ends of actions, including final ends.

Moreover, even if the "autonomy" advertised in the self-restrained calculatedness of the neo-classical subject did not naturally lend itself to dissolution, it arrests recognition of a more authentic dimension of human freedom. I refer to the one signalled by the above quotation from Weber when he comments that the "rationalistic economic ethic" of neo-classical theory and the market activity it represents eschew "all spontaneous enjoyment of life". The consistent impulse-control characteristic of neo-classical instrumental reasoning is practiced with the repression of spontaneity of immediate affect. However, as the Canadian philosopher and psychoanalyst, John Russon, has recently well reminded us, such immediate spontaneity, as found, for instance, in erotic relations, is a form of expressive freedom that characteristically both moves us to an empathic bonding with others, and releases the mutual creativity to be found in such relatedness.[43] Let me suggest that such self-transcending is also a requisite ground for the type of innovative reshapings of productive systems taking place in the communal networking of managers in the new globalized "knowledge economy". However, this kind of inter-personal creative spontaneity will require that economic actors escape the ontological prison represented by neo-classical theory, apprehend their essential connectedness, not separateness, in terms of their ontological identity as persons, and thereby become capable of conceiving other agents as something other than classical market beings – that is, as something other than competitive rivals.

IV. Market Mechanics and the Displacement of Justice

Mention of the inter-personal or social context of economic agency brings to mind what is perhaps the most critical of the moral values embedded within an economy – that of moral justice. Of particular significance are the principles of distributive justice that specify a fair allocation of the material bene-

43 See J. RUSSON: *Human Experience: Philosophy, Neurosis, and the Elements of Everyday Life*, Albany (State University of New York Press) 2003, especially chaps. 5 and 6.

fits and burdens among the members of a particular community. It is here that we are confronted with the foremost impasse that continues to challenge us concerning the relation between neo-classical economic theory, the capitalist market activities it represents, and human well-being.

On the one hand, it is a basic observation of contemporary political economy that neo-classical theory continues the ethico-scientific tradition of the Invisible Hand and seeks to provide a more rigorous clarification of its moral import. Put in summary terms, neo-classical general equilibrium theory implies that if individual producers and consumers are left free to act in a solely self-regarding fashion to maximize their own profits and utilities in a perfectly competitive market, then, as an unintended consequence, the common good or social utility will be "Pareto maximized". More, precisely, "common good" is here defined in classical Utilitarian fashion as the satisfaction of the totality or aggregate of given individual consumer desires but as consistent with a Paretian distributive constraint – namely, any movement from such a "Pareto-optimal" state will make at least one consumer worse off in terms of the satisfaction of his *de facto* wants. It is in this light that the economist Tjalling Koopmans remarks that:

> the idea that perfect competition in some sense achieves efficiency in the maximization of individual satisfaction runs through the whole of classical and neo-classical literature.[44]

We may agree, moreover, that the Pareto-efficient production of an array of goods that did reflect the free choices of individuals acting on their strongest preferences would, other things being equal, constitute a socially desirable consequence of substantial moral force. In this sense, the freedom of free markets would be the handmaiden of the common good. However, such consequentialist reasoning is far from the whole moral story. Serious questions of ethical fairness or distributive justice have traditionally haunted consequentialist conclusions in moral thought. And the situation for a capitalist market economy as conceived by orthodox economics is no exception to this rule. It is arguable, furthermore, that neo-classical economic theory only reinforces the "knots" of the problem. Why? To begin with, general equilibrium theory only demonstrates that there will be a *set* of Pareto-optimal equilibria each member of which is generated by different distributions of "original

44 T. J. KOOPMANS: *Three Essays on The State of Economic Science*, New York (McGraw-Hill) 1957, p. 41.

endowments" – i.e. allocation of ownership of factors of production across the individual members of a particular society. Hence, a final moral appraisal of the various possible Pareto-optimal social outcomes cannot be made unless and until a defensible criterion of fairness is provided to determine an ethically acceptable initial distribution of factor endowments, and, thus, the comparative moral worth of the distinct Pareto-optimal consequences to which different distributions lead. But what could such a well-founded principle of distributive justice be?

If neo-classical economists were to have recourse to the history of Western moral philosophy to answer this question, they would do well to review the Aristotelian tradition wherein justice, in its root meaning, is correctly understood as a *virtue*, that is, a dispositional trait of human character wherein each individual is inclined to render under each other individual what is due him. As Aristotle comments:

> We see that all men mean by justice that state of character which makes people disposed to do what is just and makes them act justly and wish for what is just.[45]

A good deal is at stake philosophically in determining the content of the dispositions of justice as they seem rooted in the provenance of pure reason itself. In particular, criteria of justice express the extension of the first principle of rationality, namely, consistency, to the domain of practical judgement. Most critically, the imperatives of justice do not permit an individual to make exceptions in his own favour. This practical consistency or impartiality rule is most compelling when interpreted as an extension of our basic intuitive repugnance to avowing a formal contradiction (X is M and X is not M) to practical contexts bearing on an avower – for example, I should be allocated good B in circumstances C but not another person, P, in similar circumstances. Barring exceptive conditions, from the point of view of justice, persons as persons are moral equals. Aristotle, characteristically, was the first to get to the precise heart of the matter with his general view that, according to the meaning of justice equals should be treated equally and unequals unequally but only in proportion to their relevant difference. The relevant difference, for Aristotle, had to be one of merit or desert.

---

45 ARISTOTLE: *Nicomachean Ethics*, trans. by David Ross, rev. by J. L. Ackrill and J. O. Urmson, Oxford (Oxford University Press) 1980, p. 106.

Libertarian advocates of laissez-faire markets are sensitive to this constraint but, as we shall see, they respond in an incoherent way. For they invoke the view, as the prospectus to this conference puts it, that "the economic and the ethical coincide without any need of promotion by moral intent or action". More particularly, they claim, in terms of the principles of neo-classical theory, that if the natural mechanisms of an unconstrained market are left to run their course, then all workers (indeed all factor services) are considered to be treated in an impartial manner in that unequal returns in income for the service of different kinds of workers will be in exact proportion to the unequal desert of such workers as calculated by the value of their marginal product – i.e. the increase in the revenue from total output from the addition of one worker of that type. Hence, it is further argued that unfettered market mechanisms reward participants in productive activity in a measure equal to the proportion of the product for which their own selves and their capacities are responsible. Understandably, such a standpoint has spawned a potent rejoinder: An individual's contribution to the social product will be a function of his original endowment in external resources and productive talents; however, it is generally arbitrary to assign moral responsibility for such assets to such individuals as they are usually due to social contingencies or genetic inheritance beyond the capabilities of these individuals to control. In upshot, the conclusion is drawn that awarding unequal shares according to unequal product is not to comply with an adequate principle of moral desert, but simply morally arbitrary.

Not that the philosophical-economic dialectic at the heart of this controversy ceases at this point. For libertarian marketeers regularly invoke a "fall-back" argument in response to the preceding objection. (We may refer to this reply as the "master argument" for laissez-faire capitalism.) And it is here that the mechanistic reductionism internal to mainstream economics plays its most significant hand in both theory and practice. In effect, the classical Invisible Hand is replayed in neo-classical guise to close the gap between the arbitrary and the ethical. In particular, recourse is taken to an argument concerning *incentives* to ethically legitimate the unplanned consequences of "self-regulating" market mechanisms. Apparently rational men would assent to radically unequal ownership of initial resources within such a laissez-faire market order since the incentives for the highly talented to use private assets in innovatively efficient ways would produce such abundant goods that, either a) in Pareto superior terms, everyone's material well-being would be higher than in alternative forms of economic organization, or, b) at least, in "maximin" terms, if you were to be one of the worst off, you could expect to be better off than your counterparts within different economic systems. In sum, a *displacement thesis* is endorsed, namely, a re-positioning of the traditional ideal of justice from the Aristotelian conception of the moral virtue of agents participating in the politico-economic order to the agreement of rational self-interested individuals to the "social contract" or rules defining the institutional structure of the competitive capitalist order. Undertaking measures to retain the egalitarian Aristotelian viewpoint would, it is further contended, frustrate the incentive rationale of the master argument. Thus, in the straightforward words of the economist D. M. Winch:

> If such attempts are made to superimpose equity on the competitive equilibrium, then its efficiency is jeopardized. If income transfers are achieved by progressive taxation, then the marginal conditions of optimality that follow from the motivational assumptions of the competitive model are violated.[46]

However, independently of the question of its philosophical soundness, which can be severely questioned, is there factual backing for the displacement thesis? What exactly *is* the hard empirical evidence concerning the causal connection between laissez-faire capitalism and material well-being? In fact, on this question, we can be sympathetic with libertarian economists and philosophers who stress that we should be especially sensitive to the theory-practice nexus concerning the bearing of economic theory on social policy formation, as otherwise we may be subject to the self-deception of wishful thinking. So cautioned, suppose we were to seek a more precise operational handle on the question at hand in attempting to ascertain whether Pareto superior or maximin results are enhanced in direct proportion as an economy moves in the direction of a less externally regulated, "pure" private market system. Fortunately, the implementation of political legislation within the economic order during the last twenty-five in my own country, Canada, provides an instructive "social laboratory" for answering this critical question. During this period, the Canadian economy moved substantially towards

46 D. M. WINCH: *Analytical Welfare Economics*, Harmondswoth (Penguin Books) 1971, p. 99. It is worth noting that certain philosophers, of both libertarian and liberal persuasion, follow suit in endorsing the incentive rationale. For instance, in the terms of Thomas Nagel… "As acquisitive individuals they must force their socially conscientious selves to permit talent-dependent rewards as the unavoidable price of productivity, efficiency, and growth." (T. NAGEL: *Equality and Partiality*, Oxford (Oxford University Press) 1991, p. 115).

a more laissez-faire system with such measures as the privatization of public corporations, de-regulation of transportation and resource industries, the lowering of rates of corporate taxation, the removal of legal constraints on foreign investments, the creation of more severe criteria for the provision of social welfare benefits, etc. Such structural developments in the market system were certainly followed by significant economic growth in the goods and services to be distributed among the Canadian public: for instance, between 1981 and 2004, the value of the GDP per capita increased by over 48%.[47] However, whatever the empirical consequences of such radical freeing of free markets for economic productivity and growth, the consequences for the justice of unconstrained competitive capitalism as premised on the displacement thesis of the master argument were starkly embarrassing. Although the economic pie did get dramatically larger, the distribution of the slices to Canadian families was far from morally praiseworthy according to either Pareto superior or maximin standards. In showing this, we shall examine economic data from *Statistics Canada* for both income and wealth or net worth.

With respect to the former category, and focusing on quintile (20%) measures between 1981-2004, the share of adjusted market income of the top quintile households increased 4.9%, from 40.4% to 45.3%, whereas the share of the lowest quintile decreased by .35%, from 4.44% to 4.09%.[48] The ratio of the top to bottom quintiles was 11.03 in 2004, that is, the top 20% earned eleven times the bottom 20%, and during the 1981-2004 period this ratio increased by 22.3% from 9.01.[49] Nor can such an increase in economic inequality be licensed along maximin or Rawlsian "difference principle" lines that the increase led to the greatest benefit of the least advantaged.[50] Evidence from *Statistics Canada* confirms that there has been no "trickle down" beneficence from the disparity. There was negligible improvement in the percentage of the population moving above a level of after-tax low income ("the poverty line"): 11.6% were below this level in 1981 compared to 11.2% in 2004 – where the level in constant dollars was $27,000 for a family of four

47 *Statistics Canada*: "National Accounts", reported in A. SHARPE and J.-F. ARSENAULT: *Living Standards Domain of the Canadian Index of Wellbeing*, Ottawa (Centre for Study of Living Standards) October 2006, p. 19 n.

48 *Ibid.*, p. 46.

49 *Ibid.*, p. 47.

50 See J. RAWLS: *A Theory of Justice*, Harvard, Mass. (Harvard University Press) 1971, sec. 75 , p. 83, and sec. 46, p. 302.

persons in a medium sized city.[51] Similar results were found for the "poverty gap", the average amount needed by a low income family to rise above the poverty line – from $6,300 in 1981 to $6,500 in 2004 in constant dollars.[52] Data for wealth or net worth (personal assets minus personal debts) is available from *Statistics Canada* for the period 1970-1999, and, unsurprisingly, reveals the same sad story. Between 1970 and 1999, 75% of the wealth increase in constant dollars went to the top quintile, whereas the average wealth of the bottom quintile actually *declined* by almost $2000 leaving them in absolute debt of more than $5100.[53] Admittedly, it remains possible that other empirical case studies would provide dissimilar data than that found for Canada in recent decades. So, strictly, according to the canons of inductive logic, on the basis of the evidence supplied, we should explicitly limit our claim to have discredited "trickle down" arguments for legitimating market capitalist inequality to the Canadian context as specified. However, as the Canadian "social experiment" in the radical liberalization of the competitive market order is such a classic one, and the officially accumulated economic data so telling, we may conclude that our factual report has at least warranted an initial skepticism concerning the soundness of the trickle down thesis, such that investigations determining the validity of generalizing from the Canadian findings to other national economies is clearly a welcome project for further social scientific research. Of course, some of these inquiries are already underway.[54]

From a moral point of view, it is evident that the consequentialist claims of the displacement thesis have been strongly disconfirmed, at least for the Canadian situation. Not only is it empirically false that everyone's well-being improved, but the worst off were made even worse off. In decision-theoretic terms, let me suggest that the decision rule that has been actually satisfied by the radical liberalization of market relations in Canada might be usefully

---

51 *Statistics Canada*: "Survey of Household Spending", p. 53. A medium sized city is considered in the data to be one with a population between 100,000 and 500,000.

52 *Ibid.*, p. 53.

53 *Ibid.*, p. 63.

54 See, for example, E. SAEZ: "Income and Wealth Concentration in Historical and Economic Perspective", prepared for the *Berkeley Symposium on Poverty, the Distribution of Income, and Public Policy*, February, 2004, for the view that there is an increasing concentration of income and wealth among a small proportion of the population in the United States and the United Kingdom.

called a "bivalent maximax principle" – i.e. a "dual" maximization at both ends of the prosperity spectrum: maximization of the advantage of the best off while simultaneously maximizing the disadvantage of the worst off. No doubt, in Kantian language, laissez-faire marketeers may reply that it was certainly their intention in supporting the de-regulation of the economy to act *from* the familiar duty that one ought to relieve the distress of those in material need, even though, unintentionally, they acted *in accord* with the contrary maximax rule. But, then, it is always a lesson worth learning that the road to hell is often paved with the best of intentions. Of course, there is method in this moral madness.

In order to identify the method in the madness, we need to further our understanding of the mechanistic framework of classical and neo-classical thought. We have found that the principles of neo-classical market theory and the market practices it represents require a displacement of a subject's commitment to distributive justice as a matter of personal virtue, or an overriding of his natural intuition to sense the primitive meaning of justice in terms of practical consistency, that is, of understanding and treating other persons, in Kantian terms, as equal-ends-in-themselves. However, within the historically favoured conception of the economic agent as a "rational" pleasure machine, these dissolutions of personal virtue reappear as unintended strengths of the laissez-faire market system as a whole, *considered as a similar machine*, as a self-regulating, self-equilibrating, mechanical maximizer of aggregate utility output given factor service input. Moreover, if one were to reductively model the deliberative action of human subjects on the physical motion of objects, as neo-classical theory does, then the equilibrium of the whole system would only follow on the self-adjustment of its integrated parts. Hence, and most critically, if the market system is to deliver its optimal social order in the "spontaneous" manner claimed for it by libertarian theorists,[55] then the variable return to the factor input of labour must be a matter of "automatic" self-adjustment, not external design. Consequently, if according to some traditional egalitarian conception of moral justice, the return to this factor were adjudged unfair, there would be no coherent way of *integrating* redistributive

55 The foremost libertarian advocate of the desirability of the "spontaneous order" of a de-centralized market economy, is, of course, F. A. von Hayek. See, for example, his "The Errors of Constructivism", in: F. A. von HAYEK: *New Studies in Philosophy, Politics, Economics, and the History of Ideas,* Chicago (University of Chicago Press) 1978, chap. 1.

justice within the allocative efficiency guaranteed by the motions of the market machine. It is then unsurprising that recourse is taken to re-locating the core meaning of justice from that of individual virtue to that of assent to the expected hedonic consequences of the unconstrained mechanisms of the overall market structure. Within this reductionist framework, as John Maynard Keynes pointed out, our conception of social relations is held captive by one of the epoch-ruling paradigms of modern society, that is:

> the theory of the economic juggernaut ... that wages should be settled by economic pressure, otherwise called hard facts, and that our vast machine should crash along, with regard only to its equilibrium as a whole, and without attention to the chance consequences of the journey to individual groups.[56]

Of course, Keynes' shrewd comment on the advocacy of the instruments of self-equilibrating economies should give us moral pause here, namely, that its "faith in 'automatic adjustments' is an essential emblem and idol of those who sit in the top tier of the machine".[57] No doubt, those sitting among the most advantaged would re-affirm some version of the master argument to the effect that the natural mechanics of markets are the most effective way of ameliorating the lot of those in the bottom tier of the machine. We have, however, adduced empirical grounds to be significantly sceptical of such optimism. We may, moreover, amplify the theoretical basis of our reservations concerning such market utopianism.

We have grounded the primitive egalitarian sense of economic justice in the principle of practical consistency, of conceiving and interacting with other persons *qua* persons as equal ends-in themselves. The price, in epistemic logic, of forfeiting conceptual consistency as one's first principle of rationality, is unsurprisingly large: unless similar things are conceived similarly it would not be possible to make coherent predications about objects in general. Granted, we do retain the logical space to identify relevant differences between objects in order to make disparate judgements about them, including moral judgements legitimizing unequal distributions of material goods among persons due to morally relevant differences among them. But nothing like the retention of consistent reasoning by the noting of logically compelling exceptive conditions underwrites the moral reasoning embedded

56 J. M. KEYNES: "The Economic Consequences of Mr. Churchill", (1925) in: D. MOGGRIDGE (Ed.): *The Collected Writings of John Maynard Keynes*, London (MacMillan) 1972, Vol. IX, p. 223.

57 *Ibid.*, p. 224.

in the master argument of neo-classical theory and its application to social policy. Rather, the first principle of *economic* rationality within the classical and neo-classical framework – that whatever one's competitive position in economic relations, one should seek maximal self-regarding gain at least cost – simply overrides the preservation of consistency in matters of distributive justice by identifying morally relevant differences between persons.

V. The Incoherence of "Automatic Ethics"

Let me return to the perceptive content of the conference prospectus to probe further the method or artful agenda in the theses of market mechanics. Again, as the prospectus phrased one of the main positions in the history of economics... "the economic and the ethical coincide without any need for promotion by moral intent or action". Or to generalize another of the descriptions of this position in the prospectus which we mentioned earlier... "if economic agents act so as to maximize private utility or profit, they will automatically realize ethical principles". Surely, both of these hypotheses bespeak the most profound anomaly. In summary terms, if the hypotheses were true, and to the extent that we were to accede to a system of human interaction co-extensive with private market relations, then we could finally secure an ethics whose realization required no exercise of rational will. Nevertheless, although philosophically dramatic, such a conclusion can be seen to be one of logical entailment, not conceptual anomaly, for the preferred mechanistic mode of concept formation we have observed to be endemic to orthodox economic theory. As we outlined above, within such a theoretical framework, the valuations and choices of an individual subject are not, despite appearances to the subject, the actual effects of purposive deliberation about ends-in-view, but are in fact caused by an underlying mechanics of prior pleasure and pain. With respect to the social order in general, the normative provisions of the market machine as construed by neo-classical theory have been seen to be quite remarkable – again, as long as we don't think too thoroughly about questions of moral justice. The self-regulating mechanisms of an unconstrained private market system will necessarily result in maximal utilities and profits for individual consumers and entrepreneurs, and the common good of Pareto optimality. The ethico-political ideal promised by Adam Smith's "simple system of natural liberty" of a natural harmony of each with all will have been put in place. Not only orthodox economists have been impressed by such a prospect. Among the pivotal features of recent social thought is the fact that influential libertarian philosophers such as Robert Nozick, David Gauthier, and Jan Narveson, have premised their own moral and political theory on a rather uncritical acceptance of the normative implications of neo-classical general equilibrium theory.[58] Thus we find Gauthier arguing that the findings of neo-classical economics demonstrate that a perfectly competitive market society is politically ideal, indeed that such a social order would not even require moral constraints since, claims Gauthier, "the co-incidence of utility maximization and [Pareto] optimization in free interaction removes both the need and the rationale for the constraints that morality provides".[59]

---

58 See, for instance, R. NOZICK: *Anarchy, State, and Utopia*, New York (Basic Books) 1974, especially chap. 7; D. GAUTHIER: *Morals by Agreement*, Oxford (Oxford University Press) 1986; and J. NARVESON: "The Invisible Hand", *Journal of Business Ethics*, Vol. 46 (2003), pp. 201-212.

59 D. GAUTHIER: *Morals by Agreement*, p. 93. It would be instructive here to comment briefly on the viewpoint of the foremost Anglo-American libertarian philosopher, Robert Nozick, as set forth in his *Anarchy, State and Utopia*. In this work, Nozick provides a robust defence of the individual liberty embedded in capitalist market relations. However, there are grounds to be deeply skeptical of his fundamental perspective on market liberty and its relation to distributive justice. Basically, Nozick espouses the sense of liberty continuous with both classical and neo-classical economic thought – that is, the "negative" sense of liberty wherein the economic actor is free from external control in acting as he chooses, as long as such choosing does not preclude the right of others to so act. However, Nozick fails to address adequately the traditional criticism of such a conception of liberty within politico-economic philosophy: Insofar as an individual agent within a capitalist market economy has insubstantial original endowments in either external capital or internal talent, he will *ipso facto* have little access to the "positive liberty" of moral autonomy, of the freedom to be self-determining for his material well-being or to be in control of the quality of his economic life. And it should be observed that combined with his entitlements theory of distributive justice, Nozick's conception of liberty is ultimately indifferent to a Rawlsian raising of the economic position of the worst off in society. As long as historically there has been justice in the initial acquisition of holdings, and justice in the subsequent transfer of holdings – especially through voluntary exchange in free private markets – even the desperate impoverishment of the economically least advantaged would be just.

It should be noted, furthermore, that the reductionist programme of orthodox economics, in devising mechanistic theories of choice and exchange, entrenches the utopian character of the social ethos claimed for a laissez-faire market order in an especially significant way. In assimilating the kinds of equilibrating deliberations appropriate to a choice theory to the "automatic mechanisms" of physical systems, the entire economy is typically viewed as a system of "natural" or "impersonal" market forces. The economist Mark Blaug, for instance, suggests that Adam Smith's "invisible hand" be identified with the "automatic equilibrating mechanisms" postulated by neo-classical theories of producer and consumer behaviour.[60] As we have noted, within such mechanistic construals of social systems, causal processes are not understood as irreducibly and effectively dependent on deliberate, autonomous control – that is, conscious, intentional human deliberation and practical reasoning. *A fortiori*, the laws connecting antecedent states with subsequent behaviour are considered to be as permanently or timelessly applicable as the laws of physical science; hence, these laws are understood to govern behaviour which can be deemed inevitable or *unalterable*. Accordingly, mechanistic analyses of rational choice have led to a radically conservative moral attitude towards mainstream economic theory in general. For let us agree, as argued, that neo-classical theory does have a particular ethical system embedded within it. Then it will be the case that the neo-classical reading of economic behaviour *qua* automatic processes will suggest no need, indeed will preclude the possibility of an *alternative* moral basis for such behaviour than the one already (albeit unadmittedly) present in neo-classical theory. For it would be *pointless* to prescribe a different form of behaviour; after all, ought implies can, and the empirical possibility of such behaviour is precluded by the implied claim of the mechanistic view that the scientific laws constituting neo-classical theory are applicable to *any* antecedent setting of economic behaviour. Not surprisingly, such an ethical standpoint has also been applied as an apologia for political quietism. Indeed, an assumption of allegedly scientific grounds for political passivity engendered by the type of necessity claimed for economic laws has a long history in the application of economic theory in general. Such was the case, for example, in the acceptance of Adam Smith's generalizations invoking economic "naturalism". As Eric Roll describes the impact of Smith's economic theory... "this theory gave to the conduct of the prospective leaders of economic life (i.e. the indus-

60 M. BLAUG: *Economic Theory in Retrospect*, 5th ed., p. 57.

trial capitalists) an impact of inevitability".[61] Nor was this interpretation of the implications the theory of little practical import. For, as Roll further remarks... "among the forces which freed English foreign trade from regulations, which removed prohibitions...Adam Smith's work occupies a prominent place".[62] In moving to present historical circumstances, let me propose in a similar vein that among the cultural determinants of the acceptance of the "structural adjustments" deemed necessary to bring the economic systems of underdeveloped countries into the economic order of an increasingly globalized market capitalism, is the assumption that such adjustments are only accelerating what is empirically necessitated for the long run, or the "end of history",[63] in any event.

In sum, the anomaly of an "automatic ethics" promises not only the best of all possible social worlds, but also, for the end of history, the only world. The reasoning underlying the anomaly is, however, severely fallacious from both a moral and epistemic point of view. With respect to the former perspective, the belief that moral principles can be satisfied independently of irreducible practical deliberation and intentional choice is a logical non-starter. The very conceptual consistency of authentic moral agency, of doing what one ought, requires an *ontology of options*, a capability for a subject to reason towards an alternative to an anticipated course of events, and for such practical reasoning to make a real difference to what obtains in the world. Even if, contrary to actual fact, there were sufficient empirical evidence supporting the implication of classical and neo-classical theory-construction that, by some undesigned providence of nature, the market mechanics of utility and self-interest did lead to some collective bliss state for all economic subjects, such a state would be without genuine moral significance. Kant put the classic philosophical position as well as anyone:

> We cannot say anything in nature *ought to be* other than in what in all these time-relations it actually is. When we have the course of nature alone in view,

61 ERIC ROLL: *A History of Economic Thought*, 4th ed., London (Faber and Faber) 1973, p. 150.

62 *Ibid.*, p. 149.

63 The phrase is that of FRANCIS FUKUYAMA from his *The End of History and the Last Man*, New York (Penguin) 1992, wherein the historical inevitability of a final globalized market capitalism is argued.

> '*ought*' has no meaning whatsoever. It is just as absurd to ask what ought to happen in the natural world as to ask what properties a circle ought to have.[64]

In short, not only is the moral world appropriated by the classical and neo-classical tradition in economic thought not the only moral world, it is not a moral world.[65]

When we investigate the epistemological perspective, the dissolution of the anomaly may be completed and, fortunately, in so doing, we may recover a credible prospect for moral valuation in economic theory-construction. Basically, the neo-classical conservative errs because he misconceives the meaning of the phrase: "behaviour which is compatible with the scientific laws of human behaviour". Granted, it is true that if the antecedent conditions of an economic (or any other) law are satisfied, then the behaviour predicted

---

64 I. KANT: *Critique of Pure Reason*, (1781; 1787), trans. by Norman Kemp Smith, London (MacMillan) 1929, B575, p. 473.

65 It has been suggested to me that by distinguishing between different concepts of moral judgement, we might harmonize one, but not both, of the concepts with "automatic processes". I agree that this stratagem seems to be a promising one. In particular, we might usefully distinguish a concept concerning the moral "ought" and one concerning the moral "good". With respect to the ought, there would remain an inescapable antithesis to an "automatic ethics". Again, there must be a real ontology of options wherein the deliberations of individual agents make an irreducible difference to which option obtains in the world. And reductive mechanistic conceptions of human action characteristically obfuscate, if not preclude, the efficacy of such "intentionalist" reasoning – such is the case with contemporary variations on Edgeworth's understanding of the economic actor as a "pleasure machine". On the other hand, at least *prima facie*, one could agree that even the "automatic processes" of individual pleasure machines could, once aggregated at the macro level, be morally evaluated as to whether or not they (unintentionally) brought about the "common good", interpreted, for example, in terms of a Pareto optimal or maximin standard of the "social utility" or aggregated satisfaction of individual material desires. However, I remain reluctant to place the latter type of evaluation in the category of moral judgement *tout court*, since such social utility, as mechanistically interpreted, would not be the outcome of the *irreducible* deliberations of agents pursuing conscious ends-in-view – with respect to this see section III above. And it is instructive to remember here that the "good" is what *ought* to be desired, not simply what *is* actually desired; hence, the anomaly of classifying a mechanistic ought within the category of moral judgement would recur for a mechanistically produced "good".

in the consequent is causally necessitated – no alternative behaviour is possible, it being incompatible with the implications of the law. Nevertheless, it *is* possible by means of the practical deliberations of economic agents, that the satisfaction of the antecedent conditions *be avoided*, and, thus, the behaviour which otherwise would have been necessitated, *had* such conditions been fulfilled, need not take place. And if alternative behaviour does occur, it might well be in conformity with *different* moral values than those exhibited by behaviour in accord with the hypotheses of neo-classical economics.

VI. Conclusion

In the above, we have sought to provide a philosophical basis for constructing economics as a full-fledged moral science of a defensible sort – that is, one whose moral commitments are of a deliberative, fallible, open-ended kind. There remains, however, the large question as to the level and type of reform required to inform a market system and its theoretical modeling with ethical integrity. Towards this end, it is to be observed that the prevailing expectation of recent theoretical analysis *cum* political policy formation is based on the trust that a moderately mitigated market capitalism can sufficiently mitigate economic men such that their actions can reclaim consistency with sound moral principles. I remain sceptical. In terms of the analysis of this paper, the retrieval of a more authentic sense of autonomy enacting expressive rationality would require the transformation of the character of *homo economicus* from the self-centered, self-controlled subject of neo-classical theory to one engaged in mutual care and spontaneous creativity with others. Similarly, the recovery of a legitimate sense of justice in terms of the virtue of individual persons disposed to treat other persons as equal ends-in-themselves, would demand that economic actors become capable of conceiving other human beings as something other than Hobbesian market beings – that is, as something other than competitors to be feared. However, both of these reforms in the ethical ideals of conventional economics in theory and practice would be anything but moderate; they would require that we release ourselves from neo-classical market theory's atomistic shackles in recognizing the internal relatedness of persons *qua* persons. And such a "paradigm shift" would be irreducibly alien to this theory's ontology of self-regarding mechanical maximizers and its conception of the common good as an aggregate of the independent utilities of these micro-units. In other words, the necessary reforms would have to be deep structural ones in which our competitive capitalist order and its theoretical representation would lose their essential identity. But nor, given the current historical realities, do I believe that the foundational adjustments required have much chance of empirical realization for a considerable period of time. I wish I could have been more a messenger of hope in this paper. But then naively grounded hope is a recipe for despair.

References

ARISTOTLE: *Nicomachean Ethics*, trans. by David Ross, rev. by J. I. Ackrill and J. O. Urmson, Oxford (Oxford University Press) 1980.

BENTHAM, J.: *An Introduction to the Principles of Morals and Legislation* (1789), London (University of London) 1970.

BLAUG, M.: *Economic Theory in Retrospect*, 5th ed., Cambridge (Cambridge University Press) 1996.

BRAYBROOKE, D.: "Economics and Rational Choice", in: P. EDWARDS (Ed.): *The Encyclopedia of Philosophy*, New York (MacMillan and Free Press) 1967, Vol. 2, pp. 454-58.

CALDWELL, B.: *Beyond Positivism: Economic Methodology in the Twentieth Century*, London (Allen and Unwin) 1982.

EDGEWORTH, F. Y.: *Mathematical Psychics* (1881), London (London School of Economics) 1932.

EPICTETUS: *Moral Discourses and Fragments*, London (Dent) 1910.

FUKUYAMA, F.: *The End of History and the Last Man*, New York (Penguin) 1992.

GAUTHIER, D.: *Morals by Agreement*, Oxford (Oxford University Press) 1986.

HAYEK, F. A. von: *New Studies in Philosophy, Politics, Economics, and the History of Ideas*, Chicago (University of Chicago Press) 1978.

HODGSON, B.: *Economics as Moral Science*, Berlin and New York (Springer-Verlag) 2001.

HOLLIS, M.: *The Cunning of Reason*, Cambridge (Cambridge University Press) 1987.

JEVONS, W. S.: *The Theory of Political Economy*, 4th ed., London (MacMillan) 1924 (1st ed. 1871).

KANT, I.: *Critique of Pure Reason* (1781; 1787), trans. by Norman Kemp Smith, London (MacMillan) 1929.

KEYNES, J. M.: "The Economic Consequences of Mr. Churchill" (1925), in: D. MOGGRIDGE (Ed.): *The Collected Writings of John Maynard Keynes*, Vol. IX, London (MacMillan) 1972.

KERSTETTER, S.: *Rags and Riches: Wealth Inequality in Canada*, Ottawa (Canadian Centre for Policy Alternatives) 2002.

KOOPMANS, T.: *Three Essays on the State of Economic Science*, New York (McGraw-Hill) 1961.

LAKATOS, I.: "History of Science and its Rational Reconstruction", in: R. C. BUCK, R. S. COHEN (Eds.): *Boston Studies in the Philosophy of Science*, Vol. VIII, Dordrecht, Holland (D. Reidl) 1971.

MARCUSE, H.: *One Dimensional Man*, Boston (Beacon Press) 1964.

MARSHALL, A.: *Principles of Economics*, 9th Variorum ed. (1st. ed. 1890), Vol. 1, London (MacMillan) 1953.

MASLOW, A. H.: *Motivation and Personality*, 2nd ed., New York (Harper and Row) 1970.

MIROWSKI, P.: *Machine Dreams: Economics Becomes a Cyborg Science*, Cambridge (Cambridge University Press) 2001.

NAGEL, T.: *Equality and Partiality*, New York (Oxford University Press) 1991.

NARVESON, J.: "The Invisible Hand", *Journal of Business Ethics*, 46 (2003), pp. 210-212.

NOZICK, R.: *Anarchy, State and Utopia*, New York (Basic Books) 1974.

RAWLS, J.: *A Theory of Justice*, Cambridge, Mass. (Harvard University Press) 1971.

ROBBINS, L.: *An Essay on the Nature and Significance of Economic Science*, 2nd. ed. London (MacMillan) 1953.

RUSSON, J.: *Human Experience: Philosophy, Neurosis, and the Elements of Everyday Life*, Albany (State University of New York Press) 2003.

SAEZ, E.: "Income and Wealth Concentration in a Historical and International Perspective", prepared for the *Berkeley Symposium on Poverty, the Distribution of Income, and Public Policy*", February, 2004.

SCHUMPETER, J.: *Ten Great Economists*: *From Marx to Keynes*, London: George Allen and Unwin, 1952.

SCITOVSKY, T.: *The Joyless Economy*: *An Inquiry into Human Satisfaction and Consumer Dissatisfaction*, Oxford (Oxford University Press) 1976.

SHARPE, A., ARSENAULT, JEAN-FRANCOIS: *Living Standards Domain of the Canadian Index of Wellbeing*, Ottawa (Centre for the Study of Living Standards) October, 2006.

SMITH, ADAM: *An Inquiry into the Nature and Causes of the Wealth of Nations* (1776), ed. E. Cannan, New York (The Modern Library) 1937.

VEBLEN, T: "Why is Economics not an Evolutionary Science", in: T. VEBLEN: *The Place of Science in Modern Civilization and Other Essays*, New York (The Modern Library) 1937.

WEBER, M.: *The Protestant Ethic and the Spirit of Capitalism*, trans. by T. Parsons, New York (Charles Scribner's Sons) 1958.

WEBER, M: *General Economic History*, New York (Collier Books) 1961.

WEISSKOPF, W. A.: *Economics and Alienation*, New York (Dutton) 1971.

WINCH, D. M.: *Analytical Welfare Economics*, Harmondsworth (Penguin Books) 1971.

Chapter 5

Why Act Morally? Economic and Philosophical Reasons

HANSRUDI LENZ

Everybody who ascribes a material steering function to moral norms has to give some reasons why *rational individuals* actually obey these norms. This is a quite natural question to start with, especially for economists. Recently, the philosophers Stemmer (2000, 2001, 2002, 2003, 2004), Hoerster (2003) and Bayertz (2004) have tackled this not so new problem. Stemmer uses the hypothetical figure of a Rational Sceptic, i.e. an individual with purely selfish preferences who is not interested in the well-being of others except to the extent that this behaviour would restrict his own acts. A moral norm is rationally justified if and only if a Rational Sceptic could be convinced. It has to be shown that norm-abiding is in the self-interest of the Rational Sceptic. In this paper I argue that there are good arguments that the Rational Sceptic or the Amoralist should not be our natural reference point for a rational justification program of moral norms. Philosophers should make use of recent empirical results mainly from experimental economics and game theory because these studies show that a combination of altruistic and selfish concerns motivates human beings (Fehr/Fischbacher 2003). The reference individual who has to be convinced by arguments that obeying moral norms is in his best interest should be an individual characterized in line with current empirical research about the nature of human altruism and egotism. Thereafter, human beings can best be described as conditional co-operators.

Philosophers can benefit from empirical evidence about the nature of human altruism or egotism, whereas economists or psychologists stand to benefit from crucial questions arising from the philosophical discourse. For example, where exactly are the boundaries and limits of human norm-abiding behaviour in interactions between different ethnic groups? What are the obstacles for the evolution of a truly universal morality? The paper argues that exactly because human nature is neither truly altruistic nor truly egotistic there is a need for moral norms, otherwise they would be superfluous.

I. Introduction: the Rational Sceptic as a Reference Subject?

Can moral norms in addition to legal norms take over a complementary function with respect to cooperation between economic actors, thereby reducing conflicts of interests resulting for instance from incentives for managers to report untruthfully in financial statements or cheat customers? In the wake of some accounting scandals like Enron or WorldCom there is in the field of accounting and auditing an ongoing discussion on whether moral norms can fulfil such a supplementary function (Lenz 2005; Staubus 2005; Duska 2005; Rockness/Rockness 2005). Generally, business ethics are hotly debated in theory and practice (see Crane/Matten 2004 for an extensive overview).

Moral norms concern interactions of fundamental importance for the functioning of a society; they serve to protect the interests of other human beings (or animals?), regularly cause internal senses of guilt and shame by the offender and – in the case of offences against moral norms – anger and moral outrage by the other members of a moral community. Furthermore, moral norms place the members of the moral community under an obligation and can be sufficiently generalized (Lenz 2005). However, everybody who ascribes a material steering function to moral norms has to give some reasons why *rational individuals* actually obey these norms. This is a quite natural question to start with, especially for economists. Recently, the philosophers Stemmer (2000, 2001, 2002, 2003, 2004), Hoerster (2003) and Bayertz (2004) have tackled this not so new problem. Stemmer (2000, 2001, 2002) uses the hypothetical figure of a *Rational Sceptic*, i.e. an individual with purely selfish preferences who is not interested in the well-being of others except to the extent that this behaviour would restrict his own acts. Others are regarded as means towards ends, i.e. in a purely instrumental manner. A moral norm is rationally justified if, and only if, a Rational Sceptic could be convinced; that means it has to be shown that norm-abiding is in the self-interest of the Rational Sceptic. Bayertz (2004) calls his hypothetical reasoning counterpart an Amoralist who exhibits the same traits as the Rational Sceptic, but in contrast to Stemmer he considers later on in his argumentation that there is no stringent need to use the Amoralist as the ultimate litmus-test. Hoerster (2003) also argues that moral norms should be based on individual interests, but from the beginning takes on a more pragmatic view, i.e. the Amoralist is not the natural reference point. According to Hoerster it is sufficient if a majority comprised of individuals with normal traits accepts moral norms grounded on their (normal) interests.

In this study I argue that indeed there are good arguments that the Rational Sceptic or the Amoralist should not be our natural reference individual for a rational justification program of moral norms. That needlessly limits the scope of the argumentation and the results. Certainly, moral norms should be grounded in the interests of rational individuals. But in characterizing our individuals, philosophers should make use of recent empirical results mainly from experimental economics and game theory because these studies show that a combination of altruistic and selfish concerns motivates human beings (Fehr/Fischbacher 2003, p. 788; 2004a). The reference individual who has to be convinced by arguments that obeying moral norms is in his best interest should be an individual characterized in line with current empirical research. This individual has some feelings of sympathy for the well-being of others, dislikes unfair intentions and outcomes, but reacts also to the increasing costs of altruistic acts or non-cooperative behaviour of others. In particular, this individual uses non-selfishly motivated punishment to discipline non-cooperative members of the community (Fehr/Fischbacher 2004a,b; Gürerk et al. 2006). In the long run it also has to be shown that partially altruistic behaviour is an evolutionarily viable strategy. In this sense, this behaviour is rational, perhaps more rational than the behaviour of a Rational Sceptic only interested in his own (narrowly defined) well-being.

Philosophers can benefit from empirical evidence about the nature of human altruism or egotism, whereas economists or psychologists stand to benefit from fundamental questions arising from the philosophical discourse. For example, where exactly are the boundaries and limits of human norm-abiding behaviour in interactions between different ethnic groups? What are the obstacles for the evolution of a truly universal morality? What role does the philosophical discourse play in an empirical theory of morality?

The paper is organized as follows: Section II gives an explanation of the term "moral norm". Section III discusses if moral norms can be justified under the assumption that a Rational Sceptic, i.e. a purely selfishly-oriented individual, has to be convinced. Section IV shows some evidence mainly from experimental economics that human behaviour is driven by selfish *and* altruistic motives. Subsequently, the implications for the justification of moral norms based on rational individuals are discussed. The function of emotional feelings in this context is also clarified. Section V concludes and summarizes the results.

II. Moral Norms

Norms are normative statements which demand or proscribe specific acts from the norm addressees. They are intended to restrict the set of permissible acts of the norm addressee. Moral norms are a subset of social norms (Hausmann/McPherson 1996, pp. 53 et seq.). There is an apparent need for uniform behaviour in a society and therefore norm-deviant behaviour will be sanctioned with social pressure. *Moral norms* as a subset of social norms relate to interactions of fundamental importance for the functioning of society. Moral norms (Stemmer 2000; Hoerster 2003; Bayertz 2004; Ott 2006):

- relate to interactions of major importance for the functioning of societies, they define a "good cooperative being" (Tugendhat 1993, p. 58);
- serve to protect the interests of other human beings, i.e. concern also non-egotistic (altruistic) motives (unselfishness);
- relate to – in a narrower sense – the survival and physical integrity of others;
- in the case of deviant behaviour, regularly cause internal senses of shame and guilt by the norm offender and external senses of anger and outrage by other members of the moral community;
- have an obligatory character; and
- are sufficiently generalizable, ideally they are universally accepted and enforced; therefore moral norms are categorical statements.

The required behaviour can conflict with the self-interests of the norm addressee. Some philosophers see moral behaviour essentially as unselfish (benevolent) behaviour which is of use for other beings (Bayertz 2004, p. 40), e.g. an adult man who does without a life-jacket and gives it to a child or woman on a sinking ship. If somebody acts according to moral norms, her or his behaviour is guided by a *sense of duty*. He or she is doing a certain act "X" due to a sense or feeling of duty even if this behaviour contradicts the person's immediate self-interest. "*Duties*" are obligating and suppress (short-sighted) self-interest. The crucial function of "*feelings*" is to cause senses of guilt and shame by the offender and anger by members of the moral community. Therefore, they place specific artificial (man-made) internal and external sanctions on the offender. The obligation to obey moral norms is therefore "*a must contingent upon legitimate sanctions*" (Stemmer 2001, p. 833; 2003). A "morally justified must" can be differentiated from an "extortionate must" due to the fact that sanctions by the former are contractually legitimate. For example, "I'm participating in an extortionate robbery for good reasons because I fear for my life, but I'm not obliged to do so". We should be able to distinguish between an extortionate regime and a legitimate system (Stemmer 2003, p. 68). The term "duty" refers only to the latter.

A moral proposition has the following structure (see Kutschera 1973, pp. 11-72):

$$\forall x\, M(x) \wedge S(x) \wedge B(x) \rightarrow O(Y(x)) \qquad \{or\ P(Y(x))\ or\ F(Y(x))\}$$

For all x holds: if x is a human being with a certain degree of consciousness (or member of a specific moral community, M) and if x is in certain class of situations S, e.g. a communication or trading situation, and if certain application conditions B are given for x which govern, for example, certain justified exceptions to the norm, then it is obligatory that x does action Y (or it is permissible to do Y or it is forbidden to do Y). B, as the specified part of a ceteris paribus clause, expresses the conditionality of human acts (Ott 2006, pp. 474 et seq.). One of the most important questions in ethics is "who is a member of the moral community?" Is the morality restricted to a specific ethnic group or is it a really cosmopolitan morality? I will come back to this point later. Different specific moralities can be formulated by means of restrictions of M.

We should differentiate between the *norm addressee* and the *norm representative*. The latter is a person who has adopted the norm as his/her own because this person prefers the required behaviour of the norm addressee (Hoerster 2003, p. 46). A norm is *efficient* because external sanctions prevent norm-offending and/or because the norm has been internalized by the norm addressee (Hoerster 2003, p. 48).

III. Justification of Moral Norms by Means of Rational Agreements

We can generally differentiate between *objective* and *subjective* justifications of moral norms. The first program (*cognitivism*) tries to justify moral norms in an objectively valid way independent of individual self-interests, e.g. the Kantian tradition. The second program (*non-cognitivism*) argues that moral norms can be argued for and accepted by individuals if it can be demonstrated that compliance with certain moral norms is in the best self-interest of the individual (Pauer-Studer 2003, pp. 164-167; Morscher 2006, with respect to cognitivism and non-cognitivism). Only the latter point of view is compatible with basic assumptions of (traditional) economic theories, e.g. the famous opportunistic and (mainly) materially-minded *Homo Oeconomicus* (Güth/Kliemt 2003). In short, as Suchanek (2001, p. 141) writes, "Economic ethics answers the question why one should be moral: because it is advantageous for oneself." Justifications can contain empirical premises, firstly, to avoid the risk of asking the impossible and, secondly, to characterize the interests of an average or majority individual adequately. The latter aspect will be discussed later on.

The fundamental problem is "Why should somebody act in a moral way, if this behaviour is harmful to his self-interest?" The best world for a moral opportunist would be a world in which all other members except for the moral opportunist obey moral norms, so he or she can act as a free-rider taking the opportunities presented by cheating and lying without paying the costs, e.g. being cheated by others. Let us assume a rational moral opportunist could choose between the following alternatives:

1. All except me should obey moral norms;
2. All should obey moral norms;
3. No-one should obey moral norms;
4. No-one except me should obey moral norms.

Faced with this decision, he or she would have the following preferences: 1 > 2 > 3 > 4 (Ott 2006, p. 479; Bayertz 2004, pp. 141-155). The resulting *free rider problem* immediately causes an *enforcement problem* in a population comprised of rational self-interested individuals. In such a world, the enforcement problem is only solved if the "*Rational Sceptic*" (Stemmer 2003) or the "*Amoralist*" (Bayertz 2004) (perhaps even with "bad preferences", i.e. to torture other people) has to be convinced that it is in his self-interest to obey moral norms. For a (traditional) economist for whom the HOM-model is a cornerstone of economic theory, it seems quite natural to agree to this position. HOM stands for: H = Homo, i.e. the theories are based on a position of methodological individualism; O = opportunistic, i.e. man acts opportunistically, for example to gain an advantage by cheating or lying even at the expense of others; and M = individuals are (mainly) material or monetary orientated (Güth/Kliemt 2003, p. 316). The moral opportunist can be roughly equated with the well-known Homo Oeconomicus.

Faced with this enforcement problem, some philosophers have recently argued that moral norms should be justified with recourse to individual self-interests (e.g. Stemmer 2003, Hoerster 2003, Bayertz 2004). The Rational Sceptic, the Amoralist – with or without "bad preferences" – has to be convinced that obeying moral norms is in his/her best long-term self-interest. Only if this is the case are moral norms justified. This program tries to reconcile morality and rationality. However, as philosophers, they drive this justification program to the limits and, in contrast to economists, they try to explore in detail some difficulties and limitations of such an argumentation. For example, Stemmer (2003) argues from a contractual point of view: moral norms, he argues, are the results of "contractual agreements" between rational individuals. Morality is created intentionally by rational individuals by means of "contractual" agreements. Because such a contract was never signed in reality, it is a *rational reconstruction of a hypothetical contract.* Members of a moral community agree hypothetically ex ante upon certain moral norms including internal and external moral sanctions because observing the rules is ex ante mutually beneficial.

We can use David Hume's classic example of two farmers who make promises to help each other in a game-theory reconstruction as an example of such a hypothetical contract. Hume uses an example to analyze what would happen if there were no duty of keeping promises,

> Your corn is ripe to-day; mine will be so tomorrow. It is profitable for us both, that I should labour with you to-day, and that you should aid me to-morrow. I have no kindness for you, and know you have as little for me. I will not, therefore, take any pains upon your account; and should I labour with you upon my account, in expectation of a return, I know I should be disappointed, and that I should in vain depend upon your gratitude. Here then I leave you to labour alone: You treat me in the same manner. The seasons change; and both of us lose our harvest for want of mutual confidence and security. (Hume 1740/2000, Sect. V, Of the Obligation of Promises).

In Fig. 1 this situation is reconstructed as a trust game, a one-sided variant of the prisoner's dilemma game (Lahno 1997; Kreps 1990).

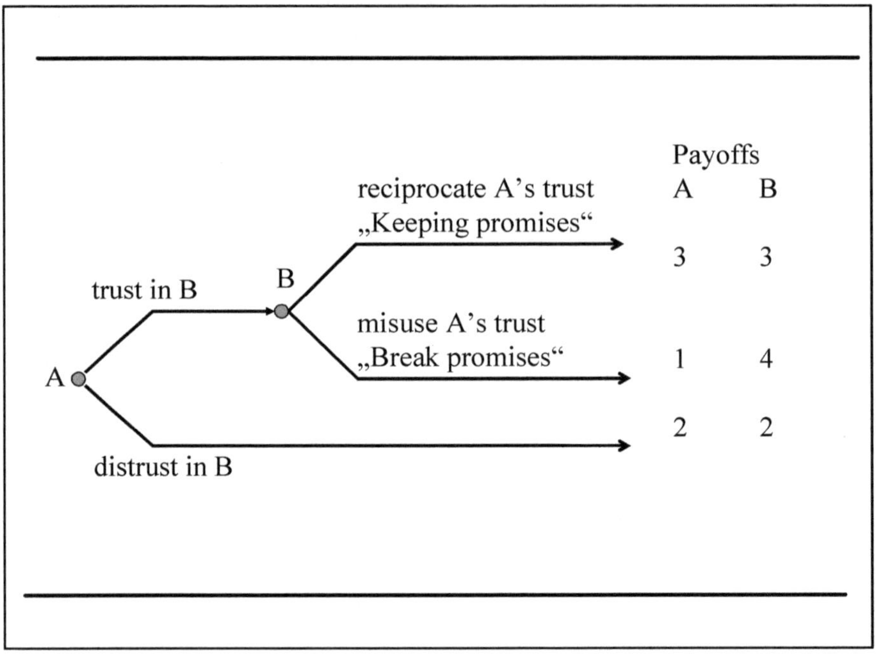

Fig. 1: The Trust Game

If there is a sufficient probability of a recurrence of that game and a credible threat that A, in case of an abuse of trust by B, will never trust B in the future, then A can rationally trust B because it is in the interest of B to reciprocate A's trust (Kreps 1990). But it should be mentioned that moral norms as normative statements like "Keep one's promise!" are superfluous in a strictly rational world. At most we need the norm "Be rational". Only because player A knows that it pays off for player B to reciprocate player A's advance performance, player A can trust B, not because A believes that B accepts a certain moral norm. In a purely economic view, a promise is only "cheap talk". Only if individuals with limited rationality are tempted to break a promise to gain a short-term advantage at the expense of long-term benefits can internalized moral norms fulfil the function of an "internal guard" against such (irrational) temptations. So, in my view strictly rational justification programs lead us into a *conceptual contradiction* (Bayertz 2004, p. 160) to central elements of the term "moral norms" (as explained in Section II). If obedience of a norm is in my own best rational interest and I am a rational enlightened person, why should I need a moral norm as a standard of behaviour? Does it then make sense to talk about "acting from a sense of duty" (connected with sanctions in case of breach), if self-interest alone ensures the obedience of norms? Norm-deviant behaviour would then be irrational. In such a world of mutual and repeated transactions, enlightened rational egotists calculate their interests without emotions and act accordingly. Only from an external viewpoint does it appear that such persons follow certain norms ("as-if compliance"). In a nutshell: the norm is rationally justified but that means also that the norm as such is unnecessary. Emotions like guilt and shame are useless as well.

One of the *problems* of this methodology, e.g. the rational reconstruction of a hypothetical contract, is "why should a Rational Sceptic agree to the establishment of internal sanctions (senses of guilt and shame)?" A completely informed and perfectly rational person needs no self-bonding because he always chooses to obey moral norms if this maximizes his self-interest. Furthermore, equipped with moral emotions he/she would not be able to expropriate the trust of others in unique situations ("golden opportunities") with high pay-offs. Let us go back a step to a one-shot trust game like that in Fig. 1. This game can be solved by establishing ex ante an informal system of sanctions (Stemmer 2000). Therefore, B's payoffs decrease and the abuse of trust is therefore no longer advantageous to B. But why should a Rational Sceptic ex ante agree to accept such a system of sanctions? He gives up a potential benefit, i.e. abuse of trust in a one-off situation with high payoffs. Bayertz argues as follows:

> Why should an Amoralist abandon this option? Why should he strictly and irrevocably abnegate the opportunity offered by prudent misuses of moral norms. From the viewpoint of a solely self-interested person, the decision for an irrevocable self-bonding is not rationally obligatory (2004, p. 175).

The problem becomes more complex if we think about individuals with restricted possibilities to exercise sanctions or about members of future generations. "How moral behaviour in such situations can also be "calculated" in the long-term is completely incomprehensible" (Bayertz 2004, p. 175).

Furthermore, the empirical development of the system of internal sanctions remains opaque. Going back to socio-biological, neuro-biological and cultural theories of the development of emotions seems far more promising. It is highly counter-intuitive to think of informal sanctions like guilt and shame as the results of a rational reconstruction of a hypothetical contract. To understand the empirical evolution of such a system of moral sanctions we should use socio-biological and cultural theories of the evolution of norms and internal sanctions. Another problem arises because an external sanction imposes costs but creates no direct utility for the person who exercises the sanctions. Therefore, why is it rational to exercise a sanction? Punishment of a norm-offender via social disesteem by third parties who are not directly affected by the violation of a moral norm has to be justified. In contrast, in repeated non-anonymous interactions a person can establish a reputation with respect to sanctions. This can deter potential opportunists who try to exploit a trust game-like situation (Fehr/Fischbacher 2003).

In particular, the above mentioned *unique situations* ("golden opportunities") where secret wrongdoing is possible without detection are the ultimate "stress-test" for an ethical justification program based solely on individual rationality. In the end, the Rational Sceptic cannot be convinced with respect to such situations (Steinfath 2003; Schaber 2003; Roughley 2003). Even Stemmer (2000, p. 190) considers with respect to such situations: "If the moral sanctions are powerless, then the rational obligation is also necessarily powerless."

Further limits of norm justifications based on rational individual self-interest are:

(i) We have to assume interacting individuals capable of strategic rationality, good knowledge of future situations and with approximately the same power (Stemmer 2000).

(ii) The justification of norms protecting unborn children, handicapped human beings, members of future communities is not possible. As a result the moral community is highly selective, e.g. the moral norms are not strictly universal. On the question "who is a member of the moral community?" Stemmer (2000, p. 261) concludes: "… those who as a result of a severe deformation by birth are not capable of a reasonable life are not members of the moral community, just as a foetus or small children up to a certain age are also not members of the community". Members of future generations are also not included. The consequence is that a morality based solely on rationality is in some sense only a "weak" morality (Stemmer 2000, p. 286) and a behaviour which benefits other beings is determined to a large degree by "moral-free" factors like compassion or altruism. "A human attitude is far more than just behaving morally" (Stemmer 2000, p. 287).

(iii) The intuitive pre-understanding of moral norms ("protection of weaker human-beings") cannot be captured within such a justification program.

In the next section we will present some empirical evidence about the nature of human altruism and egotism. The aim is to draw some conclusions with respect to our philosophical justification problem thereby avoiding to derive "Ought" from "Is". Then, our hypothetical dialogue partner isn't anymore the Rational Sceptic, instead of that we argue with a person who is characterized through the biological and cultural evolution as contingent co-operator.

IV. From Homo Oeconomicus to Homo Reciprocans to Homo Moralis?

Due to the difficulties of arguing exclusively from the position of a Rational Sceptic, it seems promising to install some empirical elements in our justification program. Recent experimental evidence (Fehr/Falk 2002; Falk 2003; Güth et al. 2003; Güth/Kliemt 2003; Fehr/Renninger 2004) shows that at least to some extent and under some conditions the Homo Oeconomicus is more adequately described as a *Homo Reciprocans*, perhaps partly even as a *Homo Moralis*. In the following, I try to argue that the Rational Sceptic is no longer our natural reference subject, i.e. the starting point for our hypothetical argumentation. Instead, we argue with an individual equipped with at least a minimal sense for the interests of other beings. Moral argumentation then tries to enhance this biologically- and culturally-rooted capability of humans. Furthermore, the functions of moral-emotional dispositions (senses of guilt and shame) can be clarified with the help of evolutionary biology (Frank 1988; Föhr/Lenz 1992; Frank 2004).

With respect to the above mentioned *one-shot sequential trust game* (see Fig. 1), Fehr/Fischbacher (2003, p. 786) summarize that, despite the incentive to cheat, more than 50 % of the respondents behave cooperatively and the degree of cooperation increases with the investment of the first player. Punishment and rewarding play a decisive role and can force even selfish players to cooperate. "Like altruistic punishment, the presence of altruistic rewarding has also been documented in many different countries, in populations with varying demographic characteristics and under stake levels approaching 2-3 months' income (Fehr/Fischbacher 2003, p. 786). In these experiments interactions among kin, repeated encounters, and reputation formation have been ruled out (Fehr/Fischbacher 2003, p. 785). This is important from a philosophical point of view because these results could cautiously be interpreted as weak evidence for a potential universal moral attitude. Similar evidence exists from *public good experiments* that are played only once. Here, "subjects typically contribute between 40 and 60% of their endowment, although selfish individuals are predicted to contribute nothing" (Fehr/Fischbacher 2003, p. 786). This is the good news; the bad news is that "cooperation is, however, rarely stable and deteriorates to rather low levels if the game is played repeatedly (and anonymously) for ten rounds" (Fehr/Fischbacher 2003, p. 786). Altruistic punishment of non-cooperators, however, can sustain cooperation by deterring potential non-cooperators. Fehr/Fischbacher (2004a) show that the establishment of a costly punishment opportunity in a finitely repeated public good experiments with anonymous interactions effectively disciplines free riders. Even in one-shot prisoner dilemma games with a "neutral" third-party who has the possibility to sanction defectors a majority of third-parties punishes defectors (Fehr/Fischbacher 2004b). Self-interest cannot explain this behaviour because the involved players remain anonymous and there are no future interactions between the players. Fehr/Fischbacher (2004a, p. 186) conclude that "there is a strong social norm behind the desire to punish". The evidence is interpreted in favour of a "norm of conditional cooperation" and, in general, "non-selfishly motivated punishment constitutes a powerful device for the enforcement of social norms and human cooperation" (Fehr/ Fischbacher 2004a, p. 189). In a recent study, Gürerk et al. (2006) show experimentally that in a repeated anonymous public goods game the participants freely prefer in the long run a world in which it is possible to sanction free riders. In the end, a nearly perfect contribution to the public good can be achieved. Further evidence of altruistic behaviour stems from experimental ultimatum and dictator games (Fehr/Fischbacher 2003).

Let us discuss in more detail a simple example taken from Falk et al. (2000) and Falk (2003) which characterizes some features of the Homo Reciprocans. The experiment, based on the "moonlighting game" (Abbink et al. 2000), shows that behaviour is driven by the perceived fairness (or unfairness) of intentions and outcomes and can be described as follows (Falk et al. 2000, p. 6; see also Figure 2):

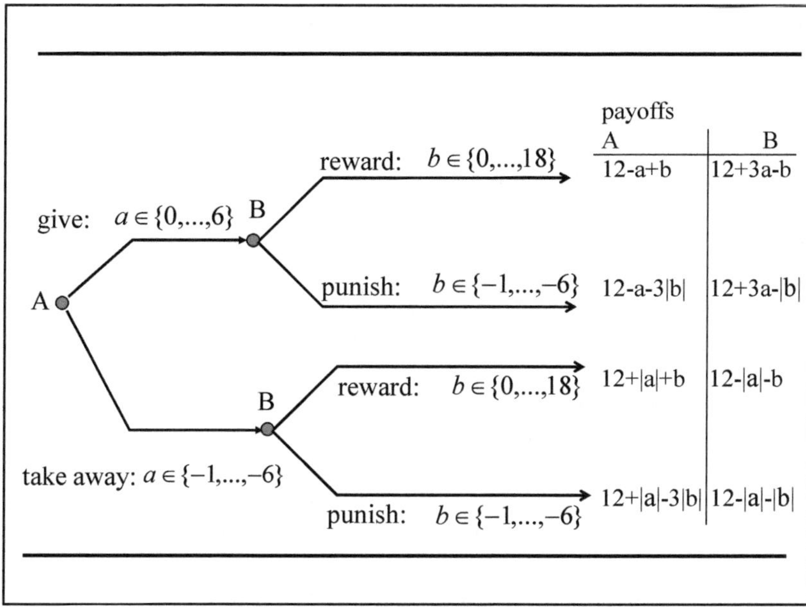

Fig. 2: The Homo Reciprocans Game
(Moonlighting Game, Abbink et al. 2000)

"The 'moonlighting game' is a two-player sequential move game that consists of two stages. At the beginning of the game, both players are endowed with 12 points. At the *first stage*, player A chooses an action $a \in \{-6,-5,...,5,6\}$. If A chooses $a \geq 0$, he gives player B a tokens while if he chooses $a < 0$, he takes away $|a|$ tokens from B. In the case of $a \geq 0$, the experimenter triples a so that B receives $3a$. If $a < 0$ A reaps $|a|$ and player B loses $|a|$. After player B observes a, she can choose an action $b \in \{-6,-5,...,17,18\}$ at the second stage, where $b \geq 0$ is a reward and $b < 0$ is a sanction. A reward transfers one point from B to A. A sanction costs B exactly $|b|$ but reduces A's income by $3b$. After B's decision, final outcomes are determined. Since As can give and take while Bs can reward or sanction, this game allows for both, positively and negatively behaviour."

The experiment was conducted in two treatment conditions. In the Intention-treatment (I-treatment) A himself determines a, whereas in the No-intention treatment (NI-treatment) A's move was determined by a random device in which the probabilities resembled a "human choice distribution". To this extent, the consequences for the Bs were exactly the same as in the Intention treatment.

If all players are rational and selfish, the Homo Oeconomicus prediction would be as follows (Falk et al. 2000, p. 9): "In both treatments B will always choose $b = 0$, i.e., she will neither punish nor reward, because any other choice is costly. Therefore in the I-treatment, player A will choose $a = -6$ because he only loses if he chooses $a > 0$ and has nothing to fear if $a < 0$. In the NI-treatment, player A's move is determined by a random device."

However, if behaviour is motivated by people's desire to be fair or if they dislike unfair intentions and/or outcomes, then the prediction would be that in the I-treatment b increases with a. In the NI-treatment b also increases with a but less than in the I-treatment (Falk et al. 2000, p. 10). For the Homo Reciprocans giving is a friendly and efficiency-increasing measure which increases the joint payoffs, e.g. if $a = 6$ then the joint payoffs are 12-6 + 12 + (3 x 6) = 36. The experimental results confirm the fairness predictions.

Falk (2003, p. 144) concludes that a *majority* of human beings reward fair behaviour and punish unfair behaviour even if the latter is associated with costs. It should be mentioned here that the literature distinguishes between reciprocity and "*strong reciprocity*". "Strong reciprocity is a combination of altruistic rewarding, which is a predisposition to reward others for cooperative, norm-abiding behaviours, and altruistic punishment which is a propensity to impose sanctions on the others for norm violations. Strong reciprocators bear the cost of rewarding or punishing even it they gain no individual economic benefit whatsoever from their acts" (Fehr/Fischbacher 2003, p. 785). Strong reciprocators reward and punish even in anonymous one-shot interactions. Therefore, strong reciprocators could play a decisive role in the enforcement of moral norms.

What are the motives for rewarding and punishing in the above experiment? Retaliation and revenge feelings, anger and resentment by B? Such deep-rooted, perhaps innate and non-controllable feelings could explain why B punishes A despite some costs. A norm offender will therefore be penalized. A anticipates this, especially if B has a reputation of this nature or if B can credibly signal his/her disposition to sanction, and therefore A does not take away from B. With respect to the non-reciprocity of awards, feelings of shame and guilt could be risked, whereas otherwise reciprocity could positively lead to feelings of gladness and gratitude. An important function of culture is to strengthen cooperative behaviour. The learning of moral norms is encouraged by emotions which assist and stabilize norm-compliant behaviour (Föhr/Lenz 1992, pp. 153 et seq.). A person may realize that in the long-term it pays off to impose penalties despite some costs. But even in this case, the person may be tempted to avoid these costs. A disposition in favour of anger and resentment may help to control this impulse (Föhr/Lenz 1992, p. 149). Frank (1988, 2004) attributes precisely this function to positive and negative emotions. Human beings with a stable disposition to be fair can successfully survive in the long run if they are able to identify people who are emotionally predisposed to cooperate. Frank (2004, pp. 28-44) gives some evidence that cooperators can find one another. In Frank (1988) it is argued that the resulting equilibrium must entail a mixed population of cooperators and defectors. "In any population consisting of only cooperators, no-one would be vigilant, and opportunities would thus abound for defectors. In a mixed population, cooperators can survive only by being sufficiently vigilant and skilled in their efforts to avoid good mimics" (Frank 2004, p. 11). More recently Fehr/Renninger (2004) and Fehr/Fischbacher (2003) discuss the possible mechanism of the gene-culture coevolution of human altruism and especially the interaction between selfish and strongly reciprocal individuals. They also point out that cultural forces, e.g. learning and socialization, have a significant influence on human altruism (Fehr/Fischbacher 2003, p. 790).

Are there additional motives or reasons for rewarding and punishing in the above example? According to the philosopher Hoerster (2003, p. 201) a further motive could be a *conscious mental attitude of fairness*, an attitude which a person has deliberately chosen under rational conditions. If the person has been educated accordingly, then he or she could later rationally adhere to this attitude. The mental attitude of fairness could be described as follows, "I will not be unfair and I will not exploit the situation of a cooperative undertaking to my additional personal benefit at the cost of others". According to Hoerster, this ideal of a fair and righteous life could lead to the acceptance of moral norms. "I accept moral norms because they help to realize my ideal of a fair life. In this sense the moral norms are based on my interests and are therefore rationally justified" (Hoerster 2003, p. 204). Indeed, the above discussed evidence from experimental economics shows that a remarkable portion of individuals can be characterized exactly in this way (Fehr/Falk 2002; Fehr/Fischbacher 2003; Fehr/Fischbacher 2004a; Falk/Renninger 2004; Gürerk et al. 2006). There are, therefore, at least some empirical arguments in favour of the rationality of this mental attitude of fairness.

However, with respect to the justification of moral norms, the philosopher Bayertz (2004) points out that if there are strong empirical arguments in favour of human altruism or moral feelings then moral norms as *normative statements* would be redundant. We need (additional) moral norms exactly because human beings are not moral by nature (Bayertz 2004, p. 212). The argument from Bayertz should be formulated more precisely as follows. Moral norms are only pointless if all humans are either perfect selfish rationalists (as we have seen in Section II) or perfect unselfish altruists. It is exactly because the empirical truth lies between these extremes that moral norms can fulfil a specified function. They remind not so perfect, sometimes shortsighted, rationalists who are tempted to break a norm that it may be wise in the long run to obey that norm. Also, they remind not so perfect altruists in a situation of moral temptation which could compromise their personal integrity or the fairness attitude of their (endangered) moral feelings. This could help to trigger the "right" behaviour which is in accordance with their moral feelings. To use a metaphor: moral norms are like road signs which give hints for imperfect human-beings.

A severe argument is that central moral feelings such as sympathy or fairness for others are maybe restricted to friends, relatives or members of the same ethnic group. Insofar as this is the case, the resulting morality is only a particular ethic and not a truly universal one (Bayertz 2004, pp. 212 et seq.). Whereas some experiments (ultimatum, dictator and trust games) show that human altruism can be found even in the absence of kin or group relations, others support the hypothesis that in stable groups with the possibility to sanction, the degree of cooperation is remarkably higher than in groups with changing members from round to round without sanctions (Fehr/Fischbacher 2003; Fehr/Renninger 2004). At the moment, it must be said that based on empirical grounds the exact scope of moral feelings is an open question and at "the ultimate level, the evolution and role of altruistic rewarding for cooperation in larger groups remains in the dark" (Fehr/Fischbacher 2003, p. 790). It follows from a philosophical viewpoint that we have to transcend the limits of our 'moral nature' and must create a 'man-made moral institution'" (Bayertz 2004, p. 213; with reference to David Hume). A particular morality, i.e.

moral norms which are valid only for members of a specific group of human beings, leads to unacceptable results especially in conjunction with social and political inequality between different groups (see for details Bayertz 2004, pp. 218-220). For philosophical reasons the truly moral viewpoint is characterized by its universalism.

Bayertz points out that in the end we have no stringent argument to convince our Rational Sceptic or Amoralist (Bayertz 2004, p. 245), but that does not mean that we have no convincing answers at all to our question "Why act morally?" We have good arguments despite being unable to win with arguments against an Amoralist because a precondition would be that the other side has to accept some normative premises (Bayertz 2004, p. 249; see also Tugendhat 1993, pp. 89, 93), for example the interests of others should be reasons to consider in moral deliberations. If the Amoralist denies taking on the *moral point of view* and if there remains a gap between morality and selfish-rationality, then the last argument against the Amoralist is (Bayertz 2004, p. 259) "You should act morally because otherwise you have to put up with sanctions". A further argument against the Amoralist is that he or she is not able to defend publicly his or her position which can be described as follows "All others except me should act morally".

To some extent empirical arguments from research on altruistic behaviour is helpful because this research could be used to define an individual endowed with, for example, fairness (or other morally relevant) preferences as a realistic starting point. Obviously it would be easier to argue in favour of the acceptance of moral norms with the Homo Reciprocans instead of the Homo Oeconomicus (or Rational Sceptic). The following drafted and stylized example tries to demonstrate this point:

Let us assume a simple situation like the *ultimatum game* or *dictator game* where *distributive justice* is in question. In an ultimatum game person A decides about the distribution of a certain amount X, say 100 €, between A and another person B. B can accept or reject the proposed distribution. If B accepts, then the amount X is distributed according the proposal from A; if B rejects the proposal, then both get nothing. In a world populated with Homo Oeconomici or Rational Scepticists, A would propose 99 € for A and 1 € for B and B would accept this proposal because 1 € is better than nothing. However, most people call this distribution unfair anyway. In the dictator game B has no possibility to accept or reject the proposal from A, i.e. A acts like a dictator. That means a purely self-regarding player A takes all and B gets nothing. I see no way to convince a Homo Oeconomicus that he/she should share the amount nearly equally between A and B in these games, i.e. to accept the norm DisJus "*Share goods between actors according to a standard which measures their relative merits*" (a norm which can be traced back to Platon and Aristotle, see Stemmer 2000, pp. 223-225; Tugendhat 1993, pp. 366-369; additionally, we can consider the relative wealth positions and the relative needs of A and B). Only because the fear of a rejected proposal a self-interested player may propose a fair distribution in the ultimatum game but this argument does not apply in the dictator game. Because in an ultimatum or dictator game neither A nor B can take credit for earning the amount X, the norm calls for an equal sharing between A and B (see for an analogue example Tugendhat 1993, p. 373). However, if we assume an individual which has *some* feelings of sympathy for the well-being of others and dislikes unfair intentions and outcomes, the remaining task is to demonstrate that obeying DisJus and acting accordingly is in harmony with the interest of our reference individual. For instance, if the reference individual is in the position of A (the proposer) in the ultimatum or dictator game, we can point out that an unequal distribution harms the well-being of B and leads to negative feelings by A himself. So, there may be good chance to come to the conclusion that the norm DisJus is in the (rational) interest of A, i.e. that A accepts and approves the norm DisJus. That said it should be mentioned that the justification of moral norms does not mean that moral norms can be logically derived from premises. I refer only to a process of *plausible deliberative reasoning* which can lead to a non-coercive agreement. If the moral norm DisJus is justified then the sanctioning of norm offenders is legitimate.

The remaining problem is "How far-ranging are the fairness preferences with respect to the members of the relevant community?" Are they really universal as required under the moral point of view? In my opinion this should be a question for further empirical research in which the players in experimental games come from different ethnic groups. Some obstacles of this approach should also be mentioned. It may be questioned that there is enough strong and convincing evidence to characterize precisely the nature of human beings as conditional cooperators? Furthermore, the specific content of moral norms has to be developed in detail under such an approach.

V. Summary and Conclusions

Empirical reasons stemming from experimental economics should be carefully considered in a justification programme for moral norms because they give us a good starting point for our argumentation. For example, we can rely on individuals with at least a minimum sense of moral feelings like fairness or sympathy. There is no need to convince a purely selfish Rational Sceptic. The latter position, i.e. a moral norm is justified if and only if a Rational Sceptic accepts the norm without coercion, leads into a *conceptual contradiction* because for these actors moral norms – as defined in Section II – are senseless. If obedience to a norm is in my own best rational interest and I am a rationally enlightened person, why should I need a moral norm as a standard of behaviour? In contrast, philosophers should make use of recent empirical results mainly from experimental economics and game theory because these studies show that a combination of altruistic and selfish concerns motivates human beings (Fehr/Fischbacher 2003). The reference individual who has to be convinced by arguments that obeying moral norms is in his best interest should be an individual characterized in line with current empirical research. This individual has some feelings of sympathy for the well-being of others, dislikes unfair intentions and outcomes, but reacts also to the increasing costs of altruistic acts or the non-cooperative behaviour of others. It can best be described as a *conditional cooperator* (Fehr/Fischbacher 2004a). In the long run it also has to be shown that partially altruistic behaviour is an evolutionarily viable strategy. In this sense, this behaviour is rational, perhaps more rational than the behaviour of a Rational-Sceptic only interested in his own (narrowly defined) well-being.

Furthermore, empirical arguments show that obeying moral norms regularly may be wise, at least in smaller and stable groups characterized by repeated and non-anonymous interactions. In these situations, there are some benefits for moral individuals in the shape of reputation formation and signalling. There is no permanent contradiction between morality and rationality. Even in non-stable groups with anonymous interactions cooperate behaviour can be induced if a minority of strong reciprocators punish non-cooperative behaviour of group members. However, up to now we have no convincing empirical insights that a *truly universal* (minimum) morality for all human beings has been established by means of gene-culture co-evolution. If this were the case, then philosophical efforts to justify moral norms would be superfluous. Because the way in which altruistic cooperation has been developed and how it works in larger groups or societies remains an open question, there also remains a need to transcend empiricism and to enter the philosophical and normative sphere for justification and persuasion purposes. Such a justification endeavour provides no definitive answers but only tentative deliberative reasons for universal moral norms.

Philosophers can benefit from empirical evidence about the nature of human altruism or egotism, whereas economists or psychologists stand to benefit from central questions arising from the philosophical discourse. For example, where exactly are the boundaries and limits of human norm-abiding behaviour in interactions between different ethnic groups? What are the obstacles for the evolution of a truly universal morality? What are the normative implications of the experimental results with respect to indirect reciprocity (Nowak/Sigmund 2005) or punishing of non-cooperative behaviour? Exactly because human nature is neither truly altruistic nor truly egotistic there is a need for moral norms, otherwise they would be superfluous.

References

ABBINK, K., IRLENBUSCH, B., RENNER, E.: "The moonlighting game. An experimental study on reciprocity and retribution", *Journal of Economic Behaviour & Organization*, 42 (2000), pp. 265-277.

BAYERTZ, K.: *Warum überhaupt moralisch sein?*, München (C. H. Beck) 2004.

CRANE, A., MATTEN, D.: *Business Ethics*, Oxford (Oxford University Press) 2004.

DUSKA, R.: "The Good Auditor – Skeptic or Wealth Accumulator? Ethical Lessons Learned from the Arthur Andersen Debacle", *Journal of Business Ethics*, 57 (2005), pp. 17-29.

FALK, A.: „Homo Oeconomicus versus Homo Reciprocans: Ansätze für ein neues wirtschaftspolitisches Leitbild?", *Perspektiven der Wirtschaftspolitik*, 4 (2003), pp. 141-172.

FALK, A., FEHR, E., FISCHBACHER, U.: "Testing Theories of Fairness – Intentions Matter", Working Paper No. 63, Institute for Empirical Research in Economics, University of Zurich (2000).

FEHR, E., FALK, A.: "Psychological foundations of incentives", *European Economic Review*, 46 (2002), pp. 687-724.

FEHR, E., FISCHBACHER, U.: "The nature of human altruism", *Nature*, 425 (October 2003), pp. 785-791.

FEHR, E., FISCHBACHER, U.: "Social norms and human cooperation", *Trends in Cognitive Science*, 8 (2004a), pp. 185-190.

FEHR, E., FISCHBACHER, U.: "Third-party punishment and social norms", *Evolution and Human Behavior*, 25 (2004b), pp. 63-87.

FEHR, E., RENNINGER, S.-V.: „Das Samariter-Paradox", *Gehirn & Geist*, No. 1 (2004), pp. 34-41.

FÖHR, S., LENZ, H.: „Unternehmenskultur und ökonomische Theorie", in: W. H. STAELE, P. CONRAD (Eds.): *Managementforschung 2*, Berlin/New York (Walter de Gruyter) 1992, pp. 111-162.

FRANK, R. H.: *Passions Within Reasons. The Strategic Role of the Emotions*, New York (W. W. Norton) 1988.

FRANK, R. H.: *What Price the Moral High Ground?*, Princeton/Oxford (Princeton University Press) 2004.

GÜRERK, Ö., IRLENBUSCH, B., ROCKENBACH, B.: "The Competitive Advantage of Sanctioning Institutions", *Science*, 312 (2006), pp. 108-111.

GÜTH, W., KLIEMT, H.: „Experimentelle Ökonomik: Modell-Platonismus in neuem Gewande?", in: M. HELD ET AL. (Eds.): *Normative und institutionelle Grundfragen der Ökonomik*, Jahrbuch 2, Marburg (Metropolis) 2003, pp. 315-342.

GÜTH, W., KLIEMT, H., NAPEL, S.: „Wie Du mir, so ich Dir! Evolutionäre Modellierungen", in: M. HELD ET AL. (Eds.): *Normative und institutionelle Grundfragen der Ökonomik*, Jahrbuch 2, Marburg (Metropolis) 2003, pp. 113-140.

HAUSMAN, D. M., MCPHERSON, M. S.: *Economic analysis and moral philosophy*, Cambridge (Cambridge University Press) 1996.

HOERSTER, N.: *Ethik und Interesse*, Stuttgart (Reclam) 2003.

HUME, D.: *A Treatise of Human Nature*, ed. by D. F. Norton and M. J. Norton, Oxford (Oxford University Press) 1740/2000.

KREPS, D.: "Corporate Culture and Economic Theory", in: J. E. ALT, K. A. SHEPSLE (Eds.): *Perspectives on Positive Political Economy*, Cambridge et al. (Cambridge University Press) 1990, pp. 90-143.

KUTSCHERA, FRANZ V.: *Einführung in die Logik der Normen, Werte und Entscheidungen*, Freiburg/München (Karl Alber) 1973.

LAHNO, B.: „Über den quasi-naturrechtlichen Charakter der Pflicht, Versprechen zu halten", in: R. HEGSELMANN, H. KLIEMT (Eds.): *Moral und Interesse*, München (Oldenbourg) 1997, pp. 47-64.

LENZ, H.: „Bilanzpolitik, Bilanzfälschung und Bilanzprüfung – eine moralökononomische Analyse von Interessenkonflikten", in: D. AUFDERHEIDE, M. DABROWSKI (Eds.): *Corporate Governance und Korruption*, Volkswirtschaftliche Schriften, Heft 544, Berlin (Springer) 2005, pp. 219-252.

MORSCHER, E.: „Kognitivismus/Nonkognitivismus“, in: M. DÜWELL ET AL. (Eds.): *Handbuch Ethik*, 2. ed., Stuttgart/Weimar (J. B. Metzler) 2006, pp. 36-48.

NOWAK, M. A., SIGMUND, K.: “Evolution of indirect reciprocity”, *Nature*, 437 (2005), pp. 1291-1298.

OTT, K.: „Prinzip/Maxime/Norm/Regel“, in: M. DÜWEL ET AL. (Eds.): *Handbuch Ethik*, 2. ed., Stuttgart/Weimar (J. B. Metzler) 2006, pp. 474-480.

PAUER-STUDER, H.: *Einführung in die Ethik*, Wien (UTB WUV Facultas) 2003.

ROCKNESS, H., ROCKNESS, J.: “Legislated Ethics: From Enron to Sarbanes-Oxley, the Impact on Corporate America”, *Journal of Business Ethics*, 57 (2005), pp. 31-54.

ROUGHLEY, N.: „Normbegriff und Normbegründung im moralphilosophischen Kontraktualismus“, in: A. LEIST (Ed.): *Moral als Vertrag?,* Berlin (Walter de Gruyter) 2003, pp. 213-244.

SCHABER, P.: „Die Pflichten des Skeptikers. Eine Kritik an Peter Stemmers moralischem Kontraktualismus“, in: A. LEIST (Ed.): *Moral als Vertrag?,* Berlin (Walter de Gruyter) 2003, pp. 199-212.

STAUBUS, G. J.: “Ethics Failures in Corporate Financial Reporting”, *Journal of Business Ethics*, 57 (2005), pp. 5-15.

STEMMER, P.: *Handeln zugunsten anderer. Eine moralphilosophische Untersuchung*, Berlin/New York (Walter de Gruyter) 2000.

STEMMER, P.: „Der Begriff der moralischen Pflicht“, *Deutsche Zeitschrift für Philosophie*, 49 (2001), pp. 831-855.

STEMMER, P.: „Moralischer Kontraktualismus“, *Zeitschrift für philosophische Forschung*, 56 (2002), pp. 1-21.

STEMMER, P.: „Der Begriff der moralischen Pflicht“, in: A. LEIST (Ed.): *Moral als Vertrag?*, Berlin (Walter de Gruyter) 2003, pp. 37-70.

STEMMER, P.: „Die Rechtfertigung moralischer Normen“, *Zeitschrift für philosophische Forschung*, 58 (2004), pp. 483-504.

STEINFATH, H.: „Wir und Ich. Überlegungen zur Begründung moralischer Normen“, in: A. LEIST: *Moral als Vertrag?,* Berlin (Walter de Gruyter) 2003, pp. 71-96.

SUCHANEK, A.: *Ökonomische Ethik*, Tübingen (UTB J.C.B. Mohr) 2001.

TUGENDHAT, E.: *Vorlesungen über Ethik*, Frankfurt a.M. (Suhrkamp) 1993.

Chapter 6

Business Ethics and the Rhetoric of Reaction

ALEXANDER BRINK

I. Introduction

1. Strategic Aspects of Business Ethics

The past years have nurtured the hope that business ethics would become increasingly a field of application and research for management.[1] This development was certainly spurred on by several international corporate scandals

1 Numerous articles dealing with the ethical issues of management have recently appeared, cf. BRINK/TIBERIUS (2005), CIULLA/PRICE/MURPHY (2006), GÖBEL (2006), MAAK/PLESS (2006), and KÜPPER (2006).

as well as the concern that false management theories might be held (jointly) responsible for such bad managerial praxis (cf. Ghoshal 2005 as well as Ghoshal/Moran 1996). In regard to the strategic aspects of business ethics, the 1980s saw the establishment of diverse fields of research in the German-speaking world. In broad terms, one can identify two major camps. The first practices a business ethics which, in certain circumstances, *correctively* intervenes in corporate strategy. For this reason, some speak here of a *corrective business ethics* (cf. e.g. Büscher 1995 and Ulrich 2004). Advocates of such an approach argue for a type of business ethics which can be traced back to the theories of Horst Steinmann. The second faction argues that ethics should be integrated into the economic paradigm. Advocates of this stance often face the critique that their approach is merely *functional*: that ethics is used as the "lubricant" for economics. For this reason such an approach is called *functional business ethics* (cf. e.g. Büscher 1995 and Ulrich 2004).

The theoretical basis, or the act of deciding to which group one belongs, has had major consequences: On the corrective side, it is not uncommon for measures such as ethics committees or codes of ethics to be suggested to management. Here, one seeks to guarantee moral conduct in possible conflict situations via a code of ethics, for example. In certain cases, this may then lead to the situational limitation of the profit principle. And thus ethics becomes a corrective for exceptional cases. Yet in recent times, representatives of American management science (such as R. Edward Freeman and Michael E. Porter) have been arguing increasingly for a functionalization of ethics. In other words, what they are seeking is the systematic integration of ethics into the economic paradigm. In this respect, they agree with the second camp – that of a functional business ethics.

In the following paper, I would like to show (via a long-term and, in part, even evolutionary perspective) how both positions are in fact compatible. In simplified terms, and based on the current situation,[2] one can in principle represent this as a two-stage process: In the first stage, economics is enriched with the functionalization of ethics. This then allows at least for an easier (though admittedly not effortless) implementation of a corrective (and extending up to an integrative) approach. Massive resistance from economists (as is still experienced today) should then no longer be expected. As such, we are dealing here, on the one hand, with a systematic or analytical compatibil-

2 Cf. also note 5.

ity; but on the other hand, we have an evolutionary as well as a historical perspective.

2. Hirschman's Importance for Business Ethics

If one understands morality as encompassing all of a society's accepted behavioral norms (those stabilized by tradition) or as those norms which are actually in effect and enforceable (when necessary) within a group or organization, then morality always possesses an ontological and phylogenetic line of development, i.e. one which is closely tied to the history of being and the history of humanity. Thus morality is to be seen as a matrix of behavioral rules, standards and ideas of meaning which become visible in the 'lived-out' or articulated economic, social, political and cultural order of a particular society or societal group. However, if moral convictions are to gain traction in a society, they must be justified and must finally assert themselves in daily practice. Yet any further development or change of a moral conviction is connected with the need to *overcome inertial tendencies and resistance.*

It is precisely at this point that I would like to pick up the argument. Using the insights developed by A. O. Hirschman, I would like to show how one must first expose the rhetoric of those critics of change (referred to below as *conservatives* or *reactionaries*) in order then to implement that which is new (representatives of this approach are referred to below as *progressives*). Such an 'unmasking' works particularly well when one can defuse the arguments of the reactionaries – which is precisely what one achieves by *strategically integrating ethics into economics.* This is not to say that ethics should be 'sold off' to economics, but rather that one must first take note of the theoretical bases of management, accept them, and then (through the very process of functionalization) make ethics a genuine component of economics. Then in a further step, corrective approaches (and above all integrative approaches) can be better implemented – which can then occur with less reactionary opposition. In the following discussion, Hirschman's theory and research results should provide us with the necessary instruments for this task.

Hirschman uses 'reaction' in a mechanical sense. He criticizes "belief in the forward march of history" (Hirschman 1991, p. 9) and therefore also strives to avoid politically defaming reactionaries as people who struggle against (positive) change. Reactionary thought has "[n]o derogatory meaning" (ibid., p. 8), but can rather be used in thoroughly progressive and innovative ways. The 'new' is not always better than the 'old'; that which is proven and conservative can also be sensible. Hence the passing of time does not automatically imply a positive effect – and therefore a 'return' is not necessarily anti-progressive. Thus 'reactionary' and 'progressive' must first be viewed as neutral terms. Here one must also bear in mind that such a slice in time – even though it may have been influenced by trends or tradition – is always already the historical result of a previous conflict between action and reaction.[3]

Hirschman published *The Rhetoric of Reaction* in 1991. In this work he examines three basic forms of reactionary thought: the *perversity thesis,* the *futility thesis* and the *jeopardy thesis.* According to the perversity thesis, intended goals are transformed into their opposites. The futility thesis argues that the setting of goals is useless since history runs its own course independent of those goals. The jeopardy thesis claims to preserve what already exists since change might substantially endanger that which has already been achieved.

Hirschman explains his theses against the background of important events in world history and exposes them as the pure rhetoric of a reaction to progressive attacks. Yet he merely seeks to engage here in a "'cool' examination of surface phenomena: discourse, arguments, rhetoric, historically and analytically considered" (ibid., p. x). I hope to show in this paper that Hirschman's ideas can be interpreted not only *historically* from the perspective of the *political sciences,* but that his theses also bear importance for the strategic interplay between the academic disciplines. Thus not only do they explain developments ex post, they are also able to produce recommendations for future positions and conduct. Over the last few decades, numerous sciences have diversified so far as to lead to the existence of completely new interdisciplinary or transdisciplinary sciences. However, this has often not been a consciously directed process. Hirschman himself influenced this transdisciplinary field, and placed the economic sciences into a larger, particularly political context.

---

3 One might also categorize the reaction to a reaction as a reaction, but also as a renewed action. Even that which is supposedly conservative certainly does not originate from some pre-existent conceptual "primeval soup", but is rather in turn the result of a historical conflict thus always already the result of differing positions between conservatives and progressives. In this respect, this approach also bears importance for evolutionary economics.

The importance of Hirschman's ideas for the strategic interplay between the academic disciplines can be seen quite clearly in the example of *German business ethics* which, as an interdisciplinary science, itself represents (in a manner of speaking) on the one hand 'the progressive' within the conservative field of economic sciences (both economics as well as management sciences), and philosophy on the other hand. While Anglo-American research into business ethics has largely taken account of Hirschman's work (though it has probably done so unconsciously), German research into business ethics has ignored Hirschman (probably also unconsciously, but with far-reaching consequences nevertheless).

Economic history has shown that one of the founders of political economy, Adam Smith, never separated economics and ethics, even when many would later attribute such a division to him. His work led namely to what was, in his time, a strongly debated division with economics on the one side and philosophy on the other (cf. Smith 1759 and 1776). Thus in this respect, Hirschman represents an excellent starting point for the following investigation, not only on the basis of his rhetoric of reaction, but also due to his personal interest in a science which crosses boundaries.

An *interpretation* of these three basic forms from the perspective of *business ethics* first requires that one define Hirschman's own observational level. In doing so, one notes that in reference to his three theses, Hirschman describes a phenomenon at the meta-level and, in regard to historical analysis, a phenomenon at the macrolevel (cf. Enderle 1991). Reactionary thought, and its secondary analytical character, support the following statement: *Hirschman's rather politico-scientific remarks, which are initially analyzed meta-scientifically within the framework of the three topoi before subsequently being illustrated at a macrolevel, can in fact be reconstructed within business ethics.* This will be displayed below with reference to Hirschman's three theses (Section 3). Finally, implications will be drawn for business ethics in general (Section 4.1) and for management theory in particular (Section 4.2). However, I would first like to show the ways in which business ethics, as a progressive stream, is exposed to reactionary tendencies (Section 2).

II. Reactionary Tendencies in Response to the Business Ethics Movement

1. Business Ethics as a Progressive Stream

Business ethics is an emergent and interdisciplinary science which must assert and defend itself in the conservative environment of the established sciences. For this reason its proponents find it important to recognize the rhetoric of their critics and prepare (when needed) a progressive strategy of defense based on opposing topoi. Specifically, the development of schools of business ethics in the 1980s and 1990s in Germany was strongly focused on methodology and theory – in contrast to pragmatic and application-oriented business ethics in Anglo-American countries (as mentioned above). This intensively reflexive character provided the ideal target for conservative thinking. Business ethics was then forced to place stress on the 'other' or the 'critical' and thus distance itself from pure economic sciences and philosophy (cf. Breuer et al. 2003). From the very beginning (and in contrast to its development in Anglo-American countries) it exposed itself to a reactionary critique and now offered an interesting field of thematic interpretations when dealing with the formal analysis of typical argumentative constructs in the sciences (cf. Reese-Schäfer 2006, p. 143), here: business ethics. Thus Hirschman's theses are interesting for scientists who wish to establish a structural order in what appears at first to be a confusing field of analysis (cf. ibid., p. 143).

If one understands these topoi in an Aristotelian sense, then the goal of the argument is already known to those arguing: hence a topos here is always the (strategically and favorably positioned) location (cf. Primavesi 1998, p. 1264) which is valid both for dialectic and rhetorical purposes. Yet what Hirschman now attempts is the unmasking of the art of persuasive argumentation itself, thus undermining the force of its validity. This idea can be transferred to scientific argumentation and delivers interesting attempts at explanation.

In his book, *The Rhetoric of Reaction,* Hirschman provides the soil for the development and (above all) effective implementation of new boundary-crossing disciplines, such as business ethics. The volume was published at a time when business ethics in Germany found itself at a particularly decisive stage.[4] Yet it neglected the essential questions: If business ethics remains primarily theoretical and methodological, how can it position itself between two academic disciplines in order to be able to establish itself as that which is 'new' in a rather conservative environment? How can business ethics prepare itself for possible objections on the part of individual scientific disciplines, and how can it defend its independence?

Business ethics has been subject to numerous accusations from economic theorists and philosophers. This also explains the difficult position of business ethics in Germany. Here, at the very beginning, we lost ourselves in theoretical discussions on the *place of morality* and the *relationship between ethics and economics* instead of attempting to refute these externally imported topoi. However, it is astounding that it is precisely in the market-oriented U.S. that the business ethics movement should be so strongly represented – though this may well be grounded in their strong focus on application.

2. Economics as Reaction

In the *Aristotelian trias,* politics, economics and ethics formed a single unit. If we leave politics aside for a moment, let us assume that ethics and economics are now separate academic fields devoted to differing theories, methods, models and fields of application. Let us further assume that we can speak of such a division since the days of Adam Smith. *Pure economics,* in which the concentration on the neoclassics can be described as *mainstream economics,* reinforces (in Ulrich's words) the *two world theory:* i.e. of economic and non-economic worlds.

At this point, what is important is the assumption that business ethics should be made compatible first and foremost with economics rather than philosophy. To this extent, in the following discussion business ethics will also be understood as 'new' in relation to the *economic sciences.* While this is much the same for the relation to philosophy, it is not nearly so clear since philosophy has become more extensively differentiated than has economics. There is no single, clear philosophical position from which one can argue

4 In the field of management science, one could think back to the so-called "Schneider Controversy" (SCHNEIDER 1990, 1991) or perhaps to the development of particular schools (around the approaches taken by HORST STEINMANN, KARL HOMANN and PETER ULRICH).

rationally, rather we have countless differing positions and well-founded paradigms, so that an argument against business ethics from a philosophical discipline is more diffuse than the voice of (pure) economics.[5] For this reason, the progressive character of business ethics also becomes clearer when contrasted against the background of economic history.

However, Hirschman simply stresses the *economic dimension of politics* – which he cannot avoid due to his macropolitical method of observation. I would like to reverse this approach by observing the mesolevel (i.e. the corporate level) in order that the *political dimension of economics* should then come to the fore. We are dealing here with a setting of political economy. In this way, the object under investigation and the perspective are swapped. Companies form the object of investigation, and the perspective from which we observe them is a political one. Once in this context, companies then appear not only as moral actors, but also with a controlling or guiding, political function, as Josef Wieland and others have argued in Germany (cf. Wieland 2000 and 2005 as well as Steinmann/Scherer 1997 and 1998). In the context of such an approach, the aim is then to show that the topoi developed by Hirschman on the basis of Marshall's stage theory in the *development of citizenship* also possess mesoethical relevance (cf. Marshall 1965).

Conservative *mainstream economists* have used reactionary arguments to attack the attempt to reunite ethics with economics (or at least to strengthen the voice of the progressives). This can be displayed (at least in outline) on all three levels, in parallel to Hirschman's work at the macrolevel.

3. Marshall's Stage Theory

Drawing upon T. H. Marshall's stage theory in the "development of citizenship", Hirschman points to three developmental stages: (1) civil rights (human rights such as freedom of speech, ideological and religious freedom as well as equality before the law), (2) political rights (participation in political power through the right to vote) and (3) social and economic rights (the establishment of a welfare state). The three corresponding political events of progressive, political initiative – which have occurred in the "more enligh-

5 Though please note that the following analysis simply seeks to investigate that phase since the 1980s. However, one could certainly take a larger field of view beginning for example with Aristotle and tracing the various cycles of action and reaction.

tened human societies" (Hirschman 1991, p. 1), and which he uses as examples within the framework of his "three-century scheme" – are: (1) the French Revolution in the eighteenth century, (2) the development of American political suffrage in the nineteenth century, and (3) the development of the welfare state in the twentieth century (cf. ibid., p. 2). Hirschman shows that each of these phases were exposed to massive reactionary critique to these successive forward thrusts (cf. ibid., p. 3ff.). His topoi are therefore argumentative models as a reaction to particular progressive claims or events.

If we extend this process beyond Hirschman, we can reconstruct the expansion and achievement of individual civil rights, political rights and social rights at the corporate mesolevel. The history of workers' interests and workers' rights could be interpreted as (1) the liberation of workers from paternalism (= achievement of individual civil rights), (2) the democratization of companies (= achievement of political rights), and (3) the social or economic valuation of employees (= the achievement of social and economic rights).

The efforts at justification made by pure economics can be understood at a meta-level as a reaction to business ethics. Seen through the eyes of ethics, on each of Marshall's three developmental stages one could now display their own action and reaction mechanisms in Hirschman's sense. In the following sections I would like to use the example of the perversity thesis in Marshall's sense of *stage theory* and the example of the futility and jeopardy theses bringing the three topoi into play *in aggregate* against business ethics.

III. Hirschman's Theses and their Relevance for Business Ethics

1. Perversity Thesis

The perversity thesis deals with the perverted results of action and states that the goals of revolutionaries are, in the end, perverted into their opposite. This normally occurs via "a chain of unintended consequences" (Hirschman 1991, p. 11). All intentional activity which seeks to improve the political, social or economic order only leads *de facto* to a deterioration of the status quo (cf. ibid., p. 7). Accordingly, the argument against business ethics here would read: *Business ethics attempts to bring more morality into the business world, but in effect it only serves to make it more immoral.*

Hirschman refers here to Adam Smith, who has also taken on a central role in the German business ethics approaches through the work of Peter Ulrich and Karl Homann, though he is interpreted differently by these authors (cf. e.g. Ulrich 1998, Mayer-Faje/Ulrich 1991 as well as Homann 1994). Anglo-American literature also hosts an intensive debate on the importance of Smith's work for business ethics (cf. Bishop 1995, Pack 1997 and Wilson 1989). For Smith, the unintended results of the pursuit of personal interests or self-interests – through the invisible hand – still led to a general increase in wealth (cf. Smith 1776). Hirschman now transfers this argument to Marshall's three phases: The French Revolution led to fewer *individual* and *bourgeois civil rights,* leading instead to terror and war; the expansion of suffrage led to fewer *political rights,* leading instead to limitations; and the welfare state led to fewer *social* and *economic rights,* leading instead to less employment and thus to a worsening of the socioeconomic situation for the individual.

If one were now to swap from the political level to the level of the strategic interplay between the academic disciplines, then, for the discussion on business ethics, this would mean that:

(1) *Ethics does not lead to greater individual civil rights – as some progressive business ethicists argue – but rather perverts its intention into its opposite: it limits civil rights.* Economists repeatedly argue, for example, that codes of ethics limit the available scope of possibilities and conduct and fail to generate any new formative options. The introduction of ethics ombudsmen (let alone ethics committees in line with the Anglo-American model) or whistle-blowing mechanisms for the prevention of corruption are felt to be patronizing (especially among continental managers). Many economic leaders see such ethical measures as limits upon their freedom of decision.

(2) *Ethics does not lead to more democracy – as some progressive business ethicists argue – but rather perverts its intention into its opposite: it robs companies of democracy.* Here too, the central accusation, leveled particularly at ethical codes with set and organized content, is that they anticipate a result arising from discourse. Even if perfect guidelines were to be decided upon in a stakeholder dialogue, these would simply become a given for future generations. One could argue that codetermination actually fails to represent any participatory co-"determination" of these rules and guidelines in the true sense, but is rather a corporate, political construct which only tries to pass itself off

as a democratic process. In the end, the important decisions have already be made either in the guidelines or beforehand (e.g. in negotiations between management boards and union representatives).

(3) *Ethics does not lead to more social freedom in business – as some progressive business ethicists argue – but rather perverts its intention into its opposite: it declares that employees are incapable of managing their own affairs and robs them of the right.* Employees find themselves in a situation of learned helplessness, since they no longer need to think about their own values or the implications of their own behavior. This leads to a moral vacuum and the deterioration of the individual's own abilities of reflection. Citizens hardly have any possibilities left for acting out of a sense of duty, their ability for decision and self-determination is robbed by a set of standards and they are forced instead to act dutifully.

However, qualifications are called for here and we need a differentiated view: the perversity thesis is no "daring intellectual maneuver" (Hirschman 1991, p. 11), rather it can only really work successfully within a very narrow framework of deontological approaches. It is precisely these approaches which are concerned with the *purpose* of an act and thus its *intention* and *meaning*. According to the perversity thesis, it is this aspect which is converted into its exact opposite. Teleological ethics – which are common in business ethics – would have more of a chance here since they focus precisely upon the effects and side-effects of action. This is also one of the reasons why Mandeville's fable of the bees and Adam Smith's invisible hand are so often quoted in this context (cf. Mandeville 1714 and Smith 1776): what finally counts is the result and not the intention. The perversity thesis attacks precisely those ethics with distinct *contents*. For this reason, formal ethical processes are helpful since they only set down a rough framework for life together rather than establishing content-based instructions or standards – a charm which discourse ethics has, for example, due to its two-stage process (cf. Apel 1990 and 1997, Habermas 1991, French/Kimmell 2000 and Harpes/Kuhlmann 1997).

In the debate with economists, teleological approaches (which are in essence formally shaped) should be well-prepared for facing Hirschman's perversity thesis. The critique is directed especially against deontological and content-based ethical conceptions – this at least should be made clear in any qualification of the issue.

2. Futility Thesis

The futility thesis states that, in effect, revolutionaries seek their goals in vain. History will run its course without their initiative and will finally arrive at the same result – guided as by an invisible hand – on its own. Nothing can be changed in the course of history. "The futility thesis holds that attempts at social transformation will be unavailing, that they will simply fail to 'make a dent'." (Hirschman 1991, p. 7). Each attempt to affect change is "largely surface, facade, cosmetic, hence illusory" (ibid., p. 42). We could sum up the underlying motto here in the following way: *Business ethics fails to have any effect. Good and evil will appear in the course of history completely on their own.*

If necessary, the economic world will turn to ethics on its own when, for example, it recognizes that ethical management serves its economic goals. This can occur when critical stakeholder groups demand ethics, or abandon a business when such ethics are missing, or when stakeholder groups cash in their 'reputation pledge' and threaten to damage the reputation of a company. Thus ultimately, business ethics is not seen as really necessary: rather when such ethics are demanded they merely fulfill an 'alibi function'. In the end, this argument is not so important since it only calls on the mainstream economists to make use of ethics in a genuine and final way out of their own discipline.

Hirschman discusses at length that, in relation to the perversity thesis, the futility thesis is not a weakened form of the former, where positive and negative effects and side-effects neutralize each other. With the futility thesis, the actors' goal is "to change the unchangeable" (ibid., p. 72). While the perversity thesis sees the world as unstable and unstructured (so that every action leads to a wealth of effects and side-effects), in the context of the futility thesis the world presents as stable and structured (cf. ibid., p. 72f.).

Admittedly, while the comments made above about deontological ethics also apply to the futility thesis, teleological approaches also fail here since (according to the definition) even an implemented consideration of consequences and side-effects must fail to have any effect.

3. Jeopardy Thesis

The jeopardy thesis states that one must preserve the status quo since a change can substantially endanger that which has already been achieved – so that we effectively pay too dearly for reform programs (cf. Hirschman 1991, p. 7). "The older hard-won conquests or accomplishments cannot be taken for granted and would be placed in jeopardy by the new program" (ibid., p. 84). This is the standard accusation leveled against business ethics: *The purposeful implementation of ethics endangers those norms and standards which have already been achieved. It reduces economic profits or the generated shareholder value.*

If one examines the usual practice underway within the framework of 'corporate social responsibility' activities, then this critique can hardly be ignored. Many forms of social engagement, such as so-called 'corporate giving', provide a good example of instances where companies use money for social purposes (often without any consideration for the returns) and thus put additional strain on costs. This can jeopardize the very existence of a company. Specifically, ethics endangers individual civil rights, democratic rights and social rights because it is purchased at too high a price. According to the conservatives, economics should remain value-free; and this is an achievement that one should not relinquish. At the macrolevel, the central task of economic actors is to provide customers with goods and services, and at the mesolevel, to realize profits or value. However, as we will show, Freeman and Porter's management approach could weaken the arguments of the jeopardy thesis, since this approach actually supports profit objectives rather than endangering them.

IV. Consequences for the Development of Business Ethical Schools and Management Theories

1. Implications for the Development of Ethical Schools

According to our results thus far, if we follow Hirschman then the revolution announced by business ethics (the great revolutionary upheaval) is in reality just empty and hollow words (cf. Reese-Schäfer 2006, p. 153) and has either *perverted its meaning* (*perversity thesis*), served an already *ongoing tendency* (*futility thesis*) or *undermines that which already exists and everything we have already achieved* (*jeopardy thesis*). Thus for a mainstream economist, business ethics is at best utterly superfluous and, at worst, counter-productive.

However, once we have exposed these three topoi in the context of business ethics through such an analysis, then the rhetoric of reaction loses a good deal of its impressive power. This then weakens the argumentative strength of the conservatives (here: mainstream economists). "[R]eactionary rhetoric" (Hirschman 1991, p. 35) is thus exposed and can then be used against itself.

This analysis of Hirschman's *Rhetoric of Reaction* has (1) led to the identification of three topoi, (2) shown that they exist in reality at a macrolevel (three-century scheme) and (3) made clear through their identification as rhetorical figures that they lose their efficacy. Now, knowing this, one could (1) develop counter-topoi (cf. ibid., p. 166f.) or (2) further defuse the mentioned topoi by pursuing a progressive strategy (so to speak) which further weakens such forms of thought – now particularly well-known among progressives. However, a further possibility would be (3) to establish one's argument in such a way so that one would not be open to attack from these three topoi.

In business ethics, this perspective explains why the German *corrective approach* by Steinmann, for example, could not be implemented: ethics here intervenes in the economic process in a corrective sense and thus represented the primacy of ethics over economics (cf. esp. Steinmann/Löhr 1994a, 1994b). The perversity, futility and jeopardy theses become applicable here. Steinmann represents a clear progressive position which, with the help of these three topoi, is called into question. Even Ulrich's approach – an *integrative economic ethics* – can be viewed in the same way since he virtually demands a paradigm change when he speaks of the transformation of economic rationality and of integrative economic ethics (cf. esp. Ulrich 1993; 2001). In this way he attacks the very heart of economics. Here too, the perversity, futility and jeopardy theses would be relevant.

However, things appear differently when one considers Karl Homann's style of institutional ethics, which is not exposed to these three dangers precisely because of its process of functionalization (cf. esp. Homann/Blome-Drees 1992). Homann speaks the language of economics and explains his approach within the economic paradigm. He is in mainstream economists' element and like a 'first hit' or 'starter drug', they view him with incredible interest. This also explains the success he has achieved among economic scientists. The perversity, futility and (above all) jeopardy theses hardly get a grip.

The demands facing business ethics are clear: on the one hand, it must be provocative in order to be noticed; on the other hand, ethical development should occur out of the economic paradigm – in any case at first, since only in such a way can the perversity, futility and (above all) jeopardy theses remain ineffective, even though they are now weakened by Hirschman's insights. Once ethics has established itself within the economic paradigm, it will then become a genuine part of conservative ideas and conservative ways of thinking. Raising arguments against ethics would then hardly be possible – that is, without becoming self-contradictory or calling into question one's own discipline.

2. Implications for Management Theories

Since the late 1980s the conservative and reactionary paradigm of the shareholder value concept has dominated management theories in the U.S. and (since the mid-1990s) also continental Europe (cf. esp. Rappaport 1981 and 1999). The goal here is seen as growing corporate value and the alignment of management with the interests of shareholders. This concept is represented by most mainstream economists. Critique has come from management theorists such as R. Edward Freeman who, already in 1984 in his classic book *Strategic Management,* appealed for a revolutionary counter-concept: one could here in Hirschman's sense speak of a progressive countermovement (cf. esp. Freeman 1984).[6] Put simply, stakeholder management is brought into play as a progressive countermovement at the management level against mainstream economics, and the focus of management is extended to all stakeholder groups. However, it must be noted that the issue for Freeman was primarily the establishment of strategic and economic, rather than ethical or normative, goals. Only in his later publications (in hindsight, so to speak) did he first sketch out the normative importance of this approach (cf. Freeman 2004).[7] Stakeholder value aims at increasing value for stakeholder groups. The future of this approach at the management level lies in the integration of a stakeholder orientation into the concept of shareholder value, that is, in the value-oriented expansion of the importance of legitimate stakeholder interests. This example displays how well American management theorists have understood that one must first take up the economic standpoint in order for

6 There is a wealth of literature dealing with stakeholder theory. A good and current overview is provided by FREEMAN/VELAMURI (2006), FREEMAN/WICKS/PARMAR (2004) as well as CARROLL/BUCHHOLTZ (2003), pp. 67-92.

7 As have others such as DONALDSON/PRESTON (1995) or BRINK/EURICH (2006).

the concept to be compatible with economics. This then immunizes one against strong objections from the reactionary camp and is why Freeman has been so successful, over the last twenty years, in implementing his concept, precisely among economists. In this way Freeman has been able to immunize himself primarily against the jeopardy thesis, though also in part against the futility thesis.

A second example deals with the *efficient and effective implementation of ethics within the context of corporate social responsibility.*[8] As with a portfolio strategy, companies attempt to orient their corporate social responsibility activities with their core competencies in order to use them as value generators. The strongest representative here in the Anglo-American world is the management theorist M. E. Porter (cf. Porter 1987 and 1990 as well as Porter/Kramer 2003, but also e.g. Smith 1994). Within the context of his so-called *Corporate Philanthropy* he states that "there is a more truly strategic way to think about philanthropy" (Porter/Kramer 2003, p. 27). Strategic philanthropy assumes that a company can improve its competitive context through its social commitments. The competitive context is influenced by four elements: (1) context for strategy and rivalry, (2) demand conditions, (3) related and supporting industries and (4) factor conditions. These four elements are all compatible with economic theory. Corporate philanthropy gathers at precisely that point to improve these four influencing factors. Hence, in contrast to other philanthropic measures, the social benefit here is significantly increased. In this way, social achievements – which could neither be generated at the individual level through individual action nor at a governmental level with such efficiency and effectiveness – are now made possible. Management praxis provides countless best-in-class examples: DaimlerChrysler provides vehicles to those feeding the homeless in the U.S., banks could help finance Third World projects, pharmaceutical companies (such as Betapharm) provide healthcare counseling, and network companies like Cisco Systems maintain entire educational institutions (Cisco Networking Academy). In this way, the economic success of a company is secured and business ethics immunizes itself against a reactionary rhetoric in the form of the futility and jeopardy theses. This example also shows how strategically sensible it is in the development of theory to ensure compatibility with a discipline (here: economics). This also serves to reduce the prejudices and concerns raised by the conserva-

8 On corporate social responsibility see esp. CARROLL (1991 and 1999), CRANE/MATTEN (2004) as well as CARROLL/BUCHHOLTZ (2003), p. 29-65.

tive camp. Porter/Kramer (2003) consciously speak of a "false dichotomy" (ibid., p. 32), that "social and economic goals are not inherently conflicting but integrally connected" (ibid., p. 32). While Porter/Kramer focus upon one particular part of corporate social responsibility, namely philanthropy, one could consider extending the concept to all activities in the field of corporate social responsibility.

In Germany, the American concept (based on managerial science) has long been neglected. From a theoretically-supported German perspective, Homann's approach would be the most appropriate since he has shown that his topoi are stable and that he has taken Hirschman's insights into account. Andreas Suchanek further extends Homann's approach by leaving room for individual ethics (cf. Suchanek 2001 and 2005). Yet it needs to be investigated whether such an approach does not actually revive reactionary potential, since the integration of individual ethical aspects strengthens the perversity thesis. However, American managerial concepts, based on the insights of Freeman and Porter, appear very well-suited for carrying the contents of business ethics into the field of economics.

V. Concluding Remarks

As we saw in the last section, Hirschman failed to consider the mesolevel in his theories. Nor did he seek to gain any insights for business ethics. His view was primarily a political-economic one. Freeman and Porter's approaches (though only roughly sketched out here) have shown that companies as moral actors are compatible with economics in a business ethics way. Thus Hirschman's theses provide interesting perspectives for the future development and strategic orientation of business ethics. It has been noted that mainstream economists, as "'(r)eactionaries' have no monopoly on simplistic, peremptory, and intransigent rhetoric" (Hirschman 1991, p. 149). Similar models and theses could also be brought into play by business ethicists. In this way, one could in fact use the futility thesis to argue against economics: to argue that the primary goal of profit realization is actually in vain over the long term; or that (from the perspective of the perversity thesis) economic measures could even lead to a reduction in profits. As a result, in the end "they, along with their progressive counterparts, become simply extreme statements in a series of imaginary, highly polarized debates" (ibid., p. 167). However, the situation for reformers and progressives is becoming increasingly difficult since they must first deliver the arguments for change.

To date, Hirschman's models have not been considered seriously either in the Anglo-American or German-speaking fields of business ethics. If business ethics had attacked the conservative topoi from the very beginning, then it would have found itself in a much better position today, especially in Germany. However, the hope remains that business ethics will still have a future. Though if it wishes to do justice to these claims, then it must position itself sensibly, not just in regard to its content but also with a mind for the strategic interplay between the academic disciplines – and that means critically examining conservative objections. Economists such as Freeman and Porter have pointed us in new directions.

References

APEL, K.-O.: "Diskursethik als Verantwortungsethik und das Problem der ökonomischen Rationalität", in: B. BIERVERT, M. HELD, J. WIELAND (Eds.): *Sozialphilosophische Grundlagen ökonomischen Handelns*, Frankfurt (Suhrkamp) 1990, pp. 270-305.

APEL, K.-O.: "Institutionenethik oder Diskursethik als Verantwortungsethik? Das Problem der institutionellen Implementation moralischer Normen im Falle des Systems der Marktwirtschaft", in: J. P. HARPES, W. KUHLMANN (Eds.): *Zur Relevanz der Diskursethik. Anwendungsprobleme der Diskursethik in Wirtschaft und Politik*, Münster et al. (LIT Pup.) 1997 (= Ethik und Wirtschaft im Dialog, Vol. 9), pp. 167-209.

BISHOP, J. D.: "Adam Smith's Invisible Hand Argument", *Journal of Business Ethics*, 3 (1995), pp. 165-180.

BREUER, M., BRINK, A., SCHUMANN, O.: *Wirtschaftsethik als kritische Sozialwissenschaft*, Bern et al. (Haupt) 2003.

BRINK, A., EURICH, J.: "Recognition Based upon the Vitality Criterion: A Key to Sustainable Economic Success", *Journal of Business Ethics*, 2 (2006), pp. 155-164.

BRINK, A., TIBERIUS, V. A.: *Ethisches Management: Der wert(e)orientierte Führungskräfte-Kodex*, Bern et al. (Haupt) 2005.

BÜSCHER, M.: "Integrative Wirtschaftsethik: Grundkonzept und wirtschaftswissenschaftliche Forschungshorizonte", *Die Unternehmung*, 4 (1995), pp. 273-284.

CARROLL, A. B.: "The Pyramid of Corporate Social Responsibility: Toward the Moral Management of Organizational Stakeholders", *Business Horizons*, 4 (1991), pp. 39-48.

CARROLL, A. B.: "Corporate Social Responsibility. Evolution of a Definitional Construct", *Business and Society*, 3 (1999), pp. 268-295.

CARROLL, A. B., BUCHHOLTZ, A. K.: *Business and Society: Ethics and Stakeholder Management*, Cincinnati (Southwestern Pub.) 2003.

CIULLA, J. B., PRICE, T. L., MURPHY, S. E.: *The Quest for Moral Leaders. Essays on Leadership Ethics*, Northampton (Edward Elgar Pub.) 2006.

CRANE, A., MATTEN, D.: *Business Ethics: A European Perspective*, New York (Oxford University Press) 2004.

DONALDSON, T., PRESTON, L. E.: "The Stakeholder Theory of the Corporation", *Academy of Management Review*, 1 (1995), pp. 65-91.

ENDERLE, G.: "Zum Zusammenhang von Wirtschaftsethik, Unternehmensethik und Führungsethik", in: H. STEINMANN, A. LÖHR (Eds.): *Unternehmensethik*, Stuttgart (Schäffer-Poeschel) 1991, pp. 173-187.

FREEMAN, R. E.: *Strategic Management: A Stakeholder Approach*, Boston (Pitman) 1984.

FREEMAN, R. E.: "The Stakeholder Approach Revisited", *Zeitschrift für Wirtschafts- und Unternehmensethik*, 3 (2004), pp. 228-241.

FREEMAN, R. E., VELAMURI, S. R.: "A New Approach to CSR: Company Stakeholder Responsibility", in: A. KAKABADSE, M. MORSING (Eds.): *Corporate Social Responsibility*, New York (Palgrave Macmillan) 2006.

FREEMAN, R. E., WICKS, A. C., PARMAR, B.: "Stakeholder Theory and the 'Corporate Objective Revisited'", *Organization Science*, 15 (2004), pp. 364-369.

FRENCH, W., KIMMELL, ST.: "Business Ethics and Discourse Ethics: Germanic Roots with Intercultural Applications", in: P. KOSLOWSKI (Ed.): *Contemporary Economic Ethics and Business Ethics*, Berlin (Springer) 2000, pp. 193-209.

GHOSHAL, S.: "Bad Management Theories Are Destroying Good Management Practices", *Academy of Management Learning & Education*, 1 (2005), pp. 75-91.

GHOSHAL, S., MORAN, P.: "Bad for Practice: A Critique of the Transaction Cost Theory", *Academy of Management Review*, 1 (1996), pp. 13-47.

GÖBEL, E.: *Unternehmensethik*, Stuttgart (Lucius & Lucius) 2006.

HABERMAS, J.: *Erläuterungen zur Diskursethik*, Frankfurt (Suhrkamp) 1991.

HARPES, J. P., KUHLMANN, W. (1997) (Eds.): *Zur Relevanz der Diskursethik. Anwendungsprobleme der Diskursethik in Wirtschaft und Politik*, Münster et al. (LIT Pup.) 1997 (= Ethik und Wirtschaft im Dialog, Vol. 9).

HIRSCHMAN, A. O.: *The Rhetoric of Reaction: Perversity, Futility, Jeopardy*, Cambridge (Harvard University Press) 1991.

HOMANN, K.: "Marktwirtschaft und Unternehmensethik", in: FORUM FÜR PHILOSOPHIE BAD HOMBURG (Ed.): *Markt und Moral. Die Diskussion um die Unternehmensethik*, Bern et al. (Haupt) 1994, pp. 109-130.

HOMANN, K., BLOME-DREES, F.: *Wirtschafts- und Unternehmensethik*, Göttingen (UTB) 1992.

KÜPPER, H.-U.: *Unternehmensethik: Hintergründe, Konzepte, Anwendungsbereiche*, Stuttgart (Schäffer-Poeschel) 2006.

MAAK, T., PLESS, N. M.: *Responsible Leadership*, London (Routledge) 2006.

MANDEVILLE, B.: *The Fable of the Bees or Private Vices*, Publick Benefits, Indianapolis (Liberty Classics) 1714.

MARSHALL, T. H.: *Class, Citizenship and Social Development*, New York (Doubleday Anchor) 1965.

MAYER-FAJE, A., ULRICH, P. (Eds.): *Der andere Adam Smith – Beiträge zur Neubestimmung von Ökonomie als Politischer Ökonomie*, Bern et al. (Haupt) 1991 (= St. Galler Beiträge zur Wirtschaftsethik, Band 5).

PACK, SP. J.: "Adam Smith on the Virtues: A Partial Resolution of the Adam Smith Problem", *Journal of the History of Economic Thought*, 1 (1997), pp. 127-140.

PORTER, M. E.: "From Competitive Advantage to Corporate Strategy", *Harvard Business Review*, 3 (1987), pp. 43-59.

PORTER, M. E.: *The Competitive Advantage of Nations*, New York (Free Press) 1990.

PORTER, M. E., KRAMER, M. R.: "The Competitive Advantage of Corporate Philanthropy", in: HARVARD BUSINESS REVIEW (Ed.): *Harvard Business Review on Corporate Responsibility*, Boston (Little, Brown and Company) 2003, pp. 27-64.

PRIMAVESI, O.: "Artikel 'Topik, Topos'" in: J. RITTER, K. GRÜNDER (Eds.): *Historisches Wörterbuch der Philosophie*, (Bd. 10), Basel et al. (Schwabe & Co.) 1998, pp. 1263-1269.

RAPPAPORT, A.: "Selecting Strategies that Create Shareholder Value", *Harvard Business Review*, 3 (1981), pp. 139-149.

RAPPAPORT, A.: *Creating Shareholder Value: The New Standard for Business Performance*, New York (Free Press) ^{2}1999.

REESE-SCHÄFER, W.: "Albert Hirschmans Studie zur ‚Rhetorik der Reaktion'", in: I. PIES, M. LESCHKE (Eds.): *Albert Hirschmans grenzüberschreitende Ökonomie*, Tübingen (Mohr Siebeck) 2006, pp. 143-160.

SCHNEIDER, D.: "Unternehmensethik und Gewinnprinzip in der Betriebswirtschaftslehre", *Zeitschrift für betriebswirtschaftliche Forschung*, 10 (1990), pp. 869-891.

SCHNEIDER, D.: "Wird Betriebswirtschaftslehre durch Kritik an Unternehmensethik unverantwortlich?", *Zeitschrift für betriebswirtschaftliche Forschung*, 6 (1991), pp. 537-543.

SMITH, A.: *Theorie der ethischen Gefühle*, ed. and transl. by W. Eckstein, Hamburg (Meiner) 1759.

SMITH, A.: *Der Wohlstand der Nationen. Eine Untersuchung seiner Natur und seiner Ursachen*, ed. and transl. by H. C. Recktenwald, München (Beck) 1776.

SMITH, C. W.: "The New Corporate Philanthropy", *Harvard Business Review*, 3 (1994), pp. 105-116.

STEINMANN, H., LÖHR, A. (1994a): *Grundlagen der Unternehmensethik*, Stuttgart (Schäffer-Poeschel) 1994.

STEINMANN, H., LÖHR, A. (1994b): "Unternehmensethik – Ein republikanisches Programm in der Kritik", in: FORUM FÜR PHILOSOPHIE BAD HOMBURG (Ed.): *Markt und Moral. Die Diskussion um die Unternehmensethik*, Bern et al. (Haupt) 1994, pp. 145-180.

STEINMANN, H., SCHERER, A. G.: "Die multinationale Unternehmung als moralischer Akteur: Bemerkungen zu einigen normativen Grundlagenproblemen des interkulturellen Managements", in: N. BERGEMANN, A. L. J. SOURISSEAUX (Eds.): *Interkulturelles Management*, Heidelberg (Physica) 1997, pp. 23-53.

STEINMANN, H., SCHERER, A. G.: "Corporate Ethics and Global Business: Philosophical Considerations on Intercultural Management", in: B. KUMAR, H. STEINMANN (Eds.): *Ethics in International Management*, Berlin (De Gruyter) 1998, pp. 13-46.

SUCHANEK, A.: *Ökonomische Ethik*, Tübingen (Mohr Siebeck) 2001.

SUCHANEK, A.: "Moral als Managementaufgabe", in: A. BRINK, J. EURICH, C. GIERSCH (Eds.): *Anreiz versus Tugend? Merkmale moderner Unternehmensethik*, Hamburg (Dr. Kovac) 2005.

ULRICH, P.: *Transformation der ökonomischen Vernunft. Fortschrittsperspektiven der modernen Industriegesellschaft*, Bern et al. (Haupt) 1993.

ULRICH, P.: *Der kritische Adam Smith im Spannungsfeld zwischen sittlichem Gefühl und ethischer Vernunft*, St. Gallen (St. Gallen) 1998 (= Beiträge und Berichte, Vol. 40).

ULRICH, P.: *Integrative Wirtschaftsethik – Grundlagen einer lebensdienlichen Ökonomie*, Bern et al. (Haupt) 2001.

ULRICH, P.: "Sich im ethisch-politisch-ökonomischen Denken orientieren. Der St. Galler-Ansatz der integrativen Wirtschaftsethik", in: D. MIETH, O. SCHUMANN, P. ULRICH (Eds.): *Reflexionsfelder integrativer Wirtschaftsethik*, Tübingen (Francke) 2004, pp. 11-28.

WIELAND, J.: "An Institutional Approach to Business Ethics", in: P. KOSLOWSKI (Ed.): *Contemporary Economic Ethics and Business Ethics*, Berlin (Springer) 2000, pp. 245-255.

WIELAND, J.: "Corporate Governance, Values Management, and Standards – A European Perspective", *Business & Society*, 1 (2005), pp. 74-93.

WILSON, J. Q.: "Adam Smith on Business Ethics", *California Management Review*, 1 (1989), pp. 59-72.

Chapter 7

A Critical Perspective on Social Accounting – The Contribution of Discourse Philosophy

DIRK ULRICH GILBERT AND ANDREAS RASCHE

I. Context and Motivation

Since the turn of the century, social accounting has become one growth area in the field of business ethics (Gray 2002, 2001; O'Dwyer 2001; Rasche/Esser 2006; Unerman/Bennett 2004). Particularly in the international context there has been a proliferation of different concepts providing multinational corporations (MNCs) with ways to systematically assess and communicate their social and ethical performance (Donaldson 2003; Göbbels/Jonker 2003; Mathews 1997; McIntosh et al. 2003; Rasche/Esser 2007; Tulder/Kolk 2001). Especially so-called social accountability standards have gained momentum over the last couple of years. In her latest review, Leipziger (2003) identifies 32 tools that help firms to cope with the increasing demand for transparency and ethical performance measurement. Well-known examples of such standards are the Global Reporting Initiative (GRI), the Fair Labor Association (FLA), AccountAbility 1000 (AA 1000), and Social Accountability 8000 (SA 8000).

A closer look at the literature reveals that only limited attention has been given to the ethical qualities and basic normative assumptions of standards (Gilbert/Rasche 2007; Göbbels/Jonker 2003; Leipziger 2001). Gray (2002, 2001) even argues that the field of social accounting has yet to gain maturity and is still under-theorized. This criticism particularly applies to *international* social accountability standards because these tools need to theoretically justify a *common* moral basis to gain cross-cultural acceptance. Initiatives like SA 8000 or the GRI need to be based upon validity claims that provide a "moral point of view" stakeholder in different countries, with diverse norms and values, can agree to. For this reason, the universal applicability of these standards is often questioned and their guidelines regarded as means to impose Western norms on developing countries (Gilbert/Behnam/Rasche 2003). Notwithstanding these claims, a critical discussion of justification problems of accountability standards has not been part of the literature yet.

To overcome this drawback, we suggest to link critical theory (Hoy/McCarthy 1994; McCarthy 1991; Parker 2003; White 1980) and in particular *discourse ethics*, as developed by Jürgen Habermas (1990, 1996, 1999, 2004), with the literature on social accounting. We deem discourse ethics and its adaptation to economic theory (Schnebel 2000; Ulrich 1998) to be an appropriate framework to assess accountability standards for three reasons: First, Habermas's concept is a formal ethical approach developed for pluralistic societies that can no longer draw on a single moral authority and that differ on questions of value and the good life. Habermas has sought to redeem the notion of *universally* valid norms on the basis of a theory of discourse and language (Habermas 1996, 1999). Second, Habermas brings moral philosophy into the realm of political and social science. His approach develops a system of different forms of practical reason to validate moral and ethical choices, particularly those of how society and its institutions should be designed. He thus presents a framework of how to critically examine accountability standards and their underlying ethical presuppositions. Third, discourse ethics has received only limited attention in the English-speaking business ethics literature thus far. While a number of publications related to different fields of business like accounting (Chua/Degeling 1993; Laughlin 1987; Power/Laughlin 1996; Unerman/Bennett 2004), organization theory (Alvesson 1991; Burrell 1994; Froomkin 2003) or strategic management (Levy et al. 2003) are dealing with Habermasian ideas, the business ethics literature seems to be more or less unaffected (Hendry 1999; Lozano 2001; Reed 1999).

The objectives of this paper are twofold. First, we like to contribute to the discussion of SA 8000 in particular and social accountability standards in general, which, from our perspective, are still not adequately represented in the business ethics literature. We primarily focus on a critical evaluation of SA 8000 because this standard seems to be one of the most important initiatives when it comes to the institutionalization of business ethics. The standard is currently used by over 1.300 production facilities in 51 countries, whereas only 200 MNCs report in accordance with the GRI and 20 leading companies are participating in the FLA (all data as of October 2007). Besides, SA 8000 seems to be representative for other accountability standards as it provides a verification system for ethical performance and understandable guidelines to comply with (McIntosh et al. 2003; SAI 2005). Insights gained from a critical examination of SA 8000 can thus be applied to other initiatives. Second, we wish to highlight meaningful linkages between the current literature on social accounting practices (i.e. accountability standards) and discourse ethics. Based on the main lines of discourse ethics, we illustrate theoretical deficits and resulting practical problems of SA 8000 to be able to make suggestions to advance the standard and to learn more about how to further develop other internationally valid social accountability standards.

To address the mentioned research objectives the structure of this chapter is as follows. In the second section, we briefly discuss discourse theory and specify the route by which discursive agreements on different validity claims can be reached. The basic conception and main purpose of SA 8000 is presented in the third section. We then critically examine SA 8000 from a Habermasian perspective and discuss advantages and drawbacks of the initiative. In the last section, we introduce a discursively informed version of SA 8000 and argue that this framework represents an appropriate tool to institutionalize social accounting in MNCs. We close by outlining implications of our findings for other ethics initiatives and provide some clues for further conceptual and empirical research.

II. A Brief Introduction to Discourse Ethics

Habermas has developed *discourse ethics* trying to advance the goals of human emancipation, while maintaining an inclusive universalist moral framework. Discourse ethics proposes a morality of equal respect and solidaristic responsibility by outlining how to arrive at a universally accepted and acceptable moral and ethical consensus through discourse (Habermas 1990, 1996, 2004). The basic idea is that the universal validity of a moral norm cannot be justified in the mind of an isolated individual but only in a process of argumentation between individuals. Discourse ethics states that the sources of every moral consensus are contained in the formal pragmatic preconditions of speech and language, the *communicative action*, and are not drawn from particular religious convictions (Finlayson 2000; Habermas 1996).

1. Communicative Action – An Intersubjective Perspective on Rationality

By communicative action Habermas explains human rationality as a necessary outcome of the successful use of language. According to this, the potential for rationality and mutual understanding is inherent in communication itself because communicative rationality is "inscribed in the linguistic telos of mutual understanding and forms an ensemble of conditions that both enable and limit. Whoever makes use of a natural language in order to come to an understanding with an addressee about something in the world is required to take a performative attitude and commit herself to certain presuppositions" (Habermas 1996, p. 4).

Interpersonal communication and mutual understanding is at the heart of discourse ethics, and other participants are treated as genuine persons, not only as objects of manipulation. Often, however, individuals do not refer to communicative action as a means of coordinating their actions but to what Habermas (1990, p. 58) calls *strategic action*. According to this, an actor who acts strategically primarily seeks to manipulate and influence the behavior of another by means of threat of sanctions or the prospect of gratification and does not rely on the power of communicative understanding.

Although Habermas (1996, 1999) admits that most of corporations' actions are strategic in nature and firms in general simply follow price signals (and not mutual communication) to coordinate their activities, his concept can make a significant contribution to the field of business ethics. In line with Sen (1993) and Ulrich (1998), we believe that the normative preconditions for legitimate business activities should be considered as predominant and not subordinate to economic interests. Likewise, modern business ethics concepts are concerned with a critical reflection of the institutional framework of the economy which are expected to generate acceptable results from an ecological and human perspective (Crane/Matten 2004; Ulrich 1998; Unerman/Benett 2004). Habermas himself, in his recent *Studies in Political Theory* (Habermas 1999), points out that we need a critical evaluation of general rules in existing market frameworks. By proposing communicative action, he provides the appropriate means to analyse the normative logic of market economies. That is why communicative action should not be considered as an endeavour to limit (strategic) business activities from an outside perspective but as a possibility to critically reflect the normative preconditions of value-creation from *within* the economic system.

To understand how communicative action is possible, Habermas performs a pragmatic analysis of language and develops a theory of speech acts (Habermas 1990). Speech acts constitute the basic unit of analysis and are of different types (e.g. constative, regulative, expressive, etc.) to make different validity claims (e.g. claims to effectiveness, goodness, rightness, etc.). According to Habermas (1999, p. 40), all individuals taking part in a conversation share certain inescapable presuppositions of communication in order for argumentation to even begin. These rules ensure the equality of opportunity to offer speech acts and are collectively termed as the *discourse rules* of the *ideal speech situation* (Habermas 1996, p. 322).

Figure 1

Habermas's Rules for an Ideal Speech Situation

1. Logical Level

1.1 No speaker may contradict himself/herself

1.2 Every speaker who applies predicate F to object A must be prepared to apply F to all other objects resembling A in all relevant respects.

1.3 Different speakers may not use the same expression with different meanings

2. Dialectical Level of Procedures

2.1 Every speaker may assert only what she/he really believes.

2.2 A person who disputes a proposition or norm not under discussion must provide a reason for wanting to do so

3. Rhetorical Level of Processes

3.1 Every subject with the competence to speak and act is allowed to take part in the discourse

3.2 a) Everyone is allowed to question any assertion whatever

b) Everyone is allowed to introduce any assertion whatever into the discourse

c) Everyone is allowed to express his/her attitudes, desires, and needs

3.3 No speaker may be prevented, by internal or external coercion, from exercising his rights as laid down in (3.1) and (3.2)

These presuppositions are at the center of Habermas's concept of communicative action and set down the conditions of how individuals can try to reach mutual understanding. To show that these rules of argumentation are not mere conventions but rather inescapable presuppositions, Habermas refers to the notion of *performative contradiction*, in which every speaker is caught up when contesting the above mentioned rules of argumentation. The point is, that, in taking part in a process of argumentation, even the consistent opponent, has already accepted as valid the above mentioned rules of criticism, the rules of argumentation. Any subject capable of speech and action necessarily makes substantive normative presuppositions as soon as the subject engages in any form of argument with the intention of critically investigating certain hypothetical claims to validity (Habermas 1996, p. 322). By demonstrating the existence of performative contradictions, Habermas (1990, p. 95) demonstrates "[…] that if one is to argue at all, there are no substitutes. The fact that there are *no alternatives* to these rules of argumentation is what is being proved; the rules themselves are not being *justified*."

At this point, a particular advantage of Habermas's concept becomes clear: By strictly refering to the presuppositions of argumentation to justify his theory, he circumvents a *formal* deduction of norms and finally gives up an "ultimate justification" without damage to his theory. He rather describes practically existing possibilities and prerequisites to achieve argumentative understanding among human beings (Habermas 2001, p. 47). Discourse ethics does not attempt to *generate* and *justify* moral principles with universal validity but only provides a process of argumentation to *test* them (Phillips 2003, p. 110).

2. Fundamental Principles of Discourse Ethics

Because of the concept of communicative action, a general acceptance of any norm can only be obtained through a process of *dialogical* argumentation. Based on this assumption, discourse ethics provides a "*principle of universalization*" (U), which has to be considered as the fundamental guideline of moral reasoning.

- (U) "A norm is valid when the foreseeable consequences and side-effects of its general observance for the interests and value-orientations of *each individual* could be *jointly* accepted by *all* concerned without coercion" (Habermas 1999, p. 42).

The principle of universalization forms the cornerstone of Habermas's theory of moral validity and by introducing it he describes *how* normative claims can be justified in dialogues. As a rule of reasoning the principle of universalization is implied by the presuppositions of argumentation because, for Habermas, a prerequisite for reaching a consensus on generalizable maxims is that all participants in the discourse must speak honestly and comprehensibly and refer to the rules of the ideal speech situation (Habermas 1990, p. 120-121). As a moral principle (U) states that the amenability to consensus is a necessary and sufficient condition for the validity of a moral norm.

The principle of universalization specifies the type of argumentation and the route by which an agreement on conflicting normative claims can be reached and should not be confused with the "*principle of discourse ethics*" (D), which presupposes that norms exist that satisfy the conditions specified by (U). This principle of discourse ethics states:

- (D) "Only those norms can claim validity that could meet with the acceptance of all concerned in practical discourse" (Habermas 1999, p. 41).

A closer look at the principle of discourse ethics reveals that (D) makes reference to a procedure of argumentation, namely the *practical discourse* and the discursive redemption of normative validity claims. A discourse has to be understood as a process that follows the guidelines of the "ideal speech situation" to guarantee an open, unbiased, and truthful argumentation to ensure that all participants accept the force of the best argument (Habermas 1996; Unerman/Bennett 2004). Assuming that a practical discourse has been sufficiently well prosecuted, failure to reach a consensus on a conflicting norm indicates that this norm is not valid (Finlayson 2005). In other words, norms are *not deduced* from existing guidelines, but *brought into being* by consensus in a practical discourse.

Habermas recognises that the consequences of (U) and (D) and the theoretical archetype of the ideal speech situation are difficult to realise in practical discourses. However, for him this does not *in principle* preclude the possibility of these assumptions to usefully inform the conduct of dialogues (Unerman/Bennett 2004). Drawing upon discourse ethics, both principles (U) and (D) can be regarded as catalysts for a moral learning process in organizations which is guided by universal guidelines of communication extracted from the deep structures of argumentation.

3. Forms of Practical Reason – Differences in Validity Claims

Based on his understanding of communicative action and the principles of discourse ethics, Habermas (1996, p. 109) distinguishes various forms of practical reason and their corresponding types of discourse. This is because not every question at issue asks for a discussion of *universal moral* principles that need to be resolved in a discourse following the rules of the ideal speech situation. Habermas (1990, 1992, 1996, 1999) distinguishes between three forms of practical reason, viz. *pragmatic*, *ethical*, and *moral*, according to the validity claim to be redeemed.

Pragmatic reasoning occurs in situations where an actor is seeking advice to choose the means to a given end but does not critically evaluate the choice of these ends (Habermas 1996, p. 159). In the case of an argument about the right or wrong of such a decision we engage in *pragmatic discourses* in which the goal is to rationally justify the choice of technique or strategy (Habermas 1996, p. 159). Under such circumstances, the *ought* of the imperative derived is directly linked to an individual's own interest and an application of decision rules familiar to him or her (Reed 1999, p. 459), therefore the scope of the validity claim is *non-universal*. The goal of an *ethical discourse* is to critically evaluate the ends discussed in a pragmatic discourse. This form of practical reasoning involves value decisions by assessing what is "good for me" or "good for us" (Habermas 1996, p. 161). For Habermas the answer to the question of what is "good" or "bad" is always defined in terms of the specific identity and particular life history of the person or the group and hence cannot claim to be universal (Habermas 1999). Accordingly, an advice issued by an ethical discourse has only *relative* validity and is only binding upon an individual or the members of the relevant group (Finlayson 2005, p. 95).

Although the notion of ethical discourse plays an important role in Habermas's thought, discourse ethics primarily aims at explaining which role morality plays and how moral reasoning sets limits to ethics (Habermas 1996, 2001, 2004). It is a defining characteristic and a particular strength of discourse ethics to draw a clear distinction between ethical and moral reasoning (Habermas 1996). While the former investigates questions of the good life, the latter looks at generalizable norms and the procedures necessary for regulating conflicts between members from competing cultural traditions. According to this, ethical reasoning is a source of justification that always has to operate within the boundaries of moral justification (Habermas 2004). The default concept for the resolution of conflict is the *moral discourse* which refers to (U) as the principle of morality to find an agreement concerning the just resolution of an issue in the realm of norm-regulated action (Habermas 1999, p. 42; Reed 1999, pp. 461-462). A moral discourse leads to norms for a specific situation which are an expression of a rational consensus of all concerned parties that had to comply with the criteria of the ideal speech situation (Habermas 1993, pp. 54-60).

All three forms of practical reason represent complementary components of Habermas's theory and, of course, can overlap. As Reed (1999, p. 463) argues, the same issue may be treated either as a pragmatic, ethical or a moral question. Most scholars interested in discourse ethics, see the concept of three interrelated realms of reason as a major strength of the theory (Finlayson 2005; Reed 1999). As we shall see in the course of analysis, this distinction also provides some clues to critically evaluate the normative assumptions of SA 8000.

III. Certifying Workplace Conditions Through SA 8000

The New York-based NGO "Social Accountability International" (SAI) is the responsible institution for SA 8000. In 1996, SAI convened an international multi-stakeholder Advisory Board to develop and introduce SA 8000 as the first global certification standard obligating companies to accept social responsibility in certain areas and to prove compliance by allowing for independent audits.

1. Key Elements of SA 8000

Based on SAI's conviction that supranational standards can provide a basis for socially responsible actions of corporations, SA 8000 defines minimum requirements for workplace conditions that need to be met by corporations and their suppliers. SA 8000 is the first social accountability standard for retailers, brand companies, suppliers, and other organizations to maintain decent working conditions throughout the supply chain. The standard is applicable to a wide range of industry sectors and to any size of organization (Göbbels/Jonker 2003, p. 56; Jiang/Bansal 2003). There are two options how corporations can implement SA 8000 (SAI 2005): *certification in compliance with SA 8000* and participation in the *Corporate Involvement Program*:

1. *Certification in compliance with SA 8000*: corporations operating own production facilities can aim to have individual facilities certified in compliance with SA 8000 through audits conducted by SAI accredited certification bodies.
2. *Corporate Involvement Program (CIP):* The CIP helps companies, particularly retailers, brand companies, wholesalers, and sourcing agents to assure that goods are made under decent working conditions by seeking SA 8000 certification of their suppliers.

The decisive difference with regard to common ethics programs (like codes of conduct) is that successful implementation of SA 8000 is monitored by *external* auditors (certification bodies). Audits are supervised *and* certified in compliance with accepted, well-known, and understandable rules. Third party monitoring of standards is still very rare, although the last decade has witnessed an increased number of auditing bodies available to undertake these types of audits (Mamic 2005, p. 95). In an empirical study, Tulder/Kolk (2001) discover that it is included in only three of 138 companies.

Figure 1 depicts the overall framework of SA 8000 and reflects the two-tiered character of the initiative by distinguishing between a macro and a micro-level. On the macro-level one can find the catalogue of consensus-based standards comprising three elements that shall be specified below. The macro-level restricts actions on the micro-level where the certification process and audit is carried out in cooperation with affected stakeholders. A mutual consideration of both levels establishes an open dialogue around the initiative and thus drives the continuous improvement process.

Figure 2

Basic Conception of SA 8000 (Gilbert/Rasche 2007)

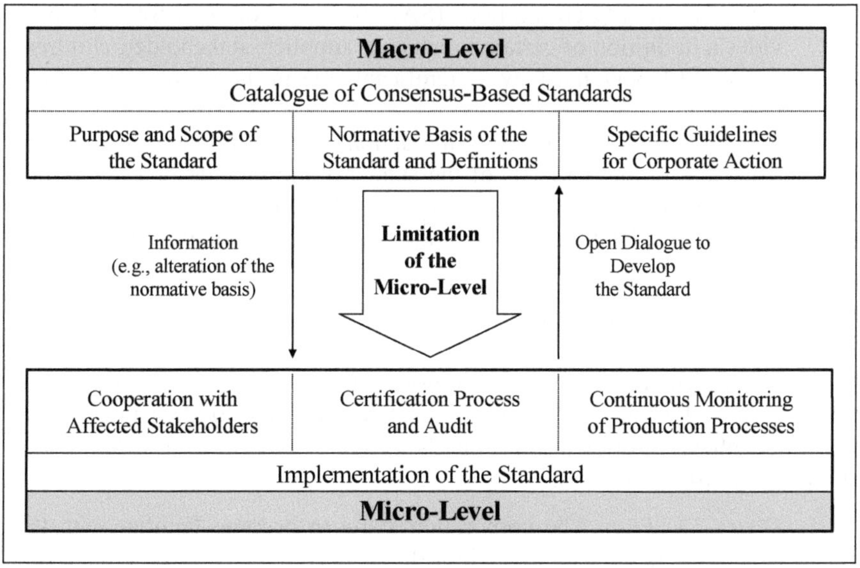

2. Macro-Level of SA 8000

On the macro-level one can find the specific contents of the standard consisting of (1) *purpose and scope of the standard,* (2) *normative basis of the stan-*

dard and definitions, and (3) *specific guidelines for corporate action* (SAI 2005):

1. *Purpose and scope of the standard*: Following SA 8000, corporations are under obligation to actively handle all areas of social accountability that can be controlled and influenced. The "controllable" area also includes suppliers. Certification is awarded only for a local production facility but not for the entire value chain of a company at a time. The guidelines have to be applied considering the respective geographical, societal, political, and economic situation of the corporation.
2. *Normative basis of the standard and definitions*: The normative basis emerges out of the claim that corporations have to meet all nationally and internationally valid laws. In addition, companies need to act in accordance to the United Nations Universal Declaration of Human Rights, the United Nations Convention on the Right of the Child, and a number of ILO-conventions (SAI 2005). In addition, SA 8000 provides a definition of certain terms (e.g. supplier, stakeholder, children, and child labor) that play a significant role in the scope of certification.
3. *Specific guidelines for corporate action*: These guidelines are derived from the normative basis of the standard and include precise regulations on a range of issues including child labour, forced labour, wages and benefits, health and safety, and the right to collective bargaining.

3. Micro-Level of SA 8000

Operative implementation on the micro-level takes place at the local production facilities. To foster implementation, SAI suggests dividing the process into four phases, following Deming's (2000) *Plan-Do-Check-Act model* (Leipziger 2001, pp. 60-63):

1. *Phase 1 – Plan*: The corporation starts to become familiar with the standard and chooses an auditor that is accredited by SAI. To uncover deviations from SA 8000, the production facility is asked to conduct a first self-assessment.
2. *Phase 2 – Do*: Necessary modifications of production processes and management systems are accomplished during this phase. The auditor analyzes the production processes and informs the company about

deviations from SA 8000. Pre-audits are conducted to document first improvements and interviews with affected employees are carried out by the auditor to evaluate working conditions.

3. *Phase 3 – Check*: The actual audit takes place once a production facility meets all demanded requirements. Auditor, production facility, and affected stakeholders (e.g. unions and employees) work together while the audit is conducted. In case of a successful certification, the production facility is awarded the SA 8000 seal for three years.
4. *Phase 4 – Act*: To guarantee compliance with the standard, auditors are allowed to make follow-up visits and are permitted to withdraw certification if the production process does not meet the requirements anymore. To increase the sustainability of the audit, top management and employees are responsible to periodically reassess the effectiveness of the auditing procedures. Independent stakeholders (e.g. unions or NGOs) act as monitoring institutions by reporting violations to the auditor or directly to SAI.

The description of the different phases demonstrates that corporations need to understand the reorganization of their production processes as an ongoing task and challenge: a challenge that is not completed once the certificate is awarded. SA 8000 tries to guarantee that standards are still met after the external auditor has left to ensure a continuous improvement of workplace conditions (Leipziger 2001, p. 59).

IV. Critical Analysis of SA 8000

1. Strengths of SA 8000

SA 8000 is currently one of the most developed and widely used social accounting standards for MNCs because it not only provides proper guidelines to improve working conditions but also is *auditable*. McIntosh et al. (2003, pp. 117-120) consider auditability as the major advantage and most important distinguishing feature of the standard. Regular audits help companies to ensure that they are respecting worker's rights and enable them to take responsibility for the *consequences* of their economic activities. In accordance with (U), the "foreseeable consequences and side-effects" of business operations come to the fore and due to independent auditing processes, working conditions become highly transparent. SA 8000 does not only ask for pragmatic discourses to enhance the *effectiveness* of production by improving workplace conditions, lowering the risk of liabilities, and increasing product quality (Gilbert 2003; McIntosh et al. 2003) but also fosters authentic *ethical* reflection on the *ends* of business practices. From a Habermasian perspective, the auditing process can be considered as an *ethical discourse* where the question of the *goodness* of production is critically discussed in collaboration with affected stakeholders. As stated by the principle of discourse ethics (D), in such a process of ethical reasoning *all* stakeholder feeling affected by SA 8000 are basically entitled to express their opinion to foster a reformulation of the proposed guidelines. SA 8000 should not be considered as just another fashion or trend in management (Abrahamson 1996), implemented solely to protect or even "polish" a firm's reputation but as an effort to advance stakeholder dialogues and to draw MNCs attention to the consequences of their cross-border operations.

2. Weaknesses of SA 8000

Despite the advantages of SA 8000, a closer assessment of the initiative, from a Habermasian perspective, reveals three problems: First, the norms contained in SA 8000 are based on an insufficient *justification.* Macro-level norms, contained in the "catalogue of consensus-based standards", claim to be *moral* and thus *universal* maxims for corporate behavior. Following the principle of universalization (U), norms can only be sufficiently justified to claim universal validity when all affected stakeholders jointly and freely accept the consequences and side effects of its general observance (Habermas 1999, p. 42). Taking a closer look at how these norms were developed, one needs to doubt that *all* affected stakeholders, not even all key stakeholders, were involved in the process of justifying the proposed principles. SAI (2005) states that the standard was developed by an international multi-stakeholder "Advisory Board" (Leipziger 2001; McIntosh et al. 2003). A closer look at the composition of the Advisory Board shows that the development process was dominated by experts from trade unions, businesses, and NGOs (Leipziger 2001; SAI 2005). Other key stakeholder groups, particularly suppliers, employees of production facilities, and consumers were not invited, although they are heavily affected by SA 8000.

In addition, the Advisory Board seems to be dominated by representatives from a small number of developed countries resulting in an imbalance between stakeholders from industrialized and less-developed nations. That is why, the standard is often considered to be just another initiative trying to impose Western standards on people from other cultural backgrounds (Gilbert 2003). The maxims included in the current version of SA 8000, which claim to be *moral* norms with *universal* validity, can only be considered as *ethical* norms with *relative* validity, reflecting the intentions and cultural backgrounds of the members of the Advisory Board. Against this background, a more profound justification of SA 8000 and a consensus on a catalogue of *moral* maxims on the macro-level would not only be an interesting academic endeavor but also a starting point to distinguish this initiative from other social accounting standards. It would boost the acceptance of SA 8000 mainly by reducing the likelihood of conflicts among stakeholders on the micro-level. Under conditions of scarce resources, firms must choose which initiatives they want to adopt and a solid normative-grounding provides a central criterion to make such a decision in favor of SA 8000.

Second, the standard does not provide any idea of *how* to design dialogues with affected stakeholders so far. In discourse ethics, normative validity cannot be understood as separate from the *argumentative procedures* used to resolve issues concerning the legitimacy of ethical and moral norms (Habermas 1996). Every validity claim to normative rightness depends upon a mutual understanding achieved by individuals in discourse. Although the current version of SA 8000 asks for stakeholder discourses to advance macro-level norms and to adapt the guidelines to the micro-level context, no clues are given *how* these dialogical processes are supposed to be organized. The only advice provided is that "[...] the company shall establish and maintain procedures to communicate regularly to all interested parties" (Leipziger 2001, p. 121). We argue that the absence of a structured idea about how to organize stakeholder dialogues presents a fundamental shortcoming of the current version of SA 8000. Many companies lack experience in designing stakeholder engagement processes (Belal 2002). Others have such processes in place but put an exclusive focus on key stakeholders like employees, customers, and shareholders while neglecting the legitimate interests of other parties (KPMG 2002, pp. 24-25). To be able to arrive at universally accepted maxims (macro-level) and to locally adapt these maxims (micro-level), a more developed concept of communication is needed.

Third, commitment to the standard often seems to be a result of coercion (and thus of *strategic action*) and does not reflect the idea of a voluntary participation. Indeed, (U) states that consensus on conflicting norms should be a result of an agreement reached without *coercion* (Habermas 1996, p. 42). When looking at the practice of MNCs, firms often place an obligation on their suppliers to comply with SA 8000. Then, the acceptance of the standard is not based on the integrity of the supplier but represents a response to external pressure and fear of sanctions in case of non-compliance. All of this results in an odd situation: suppliers try to formally comply with the standard, but do not alter their internal decision making procedures and production processes (Treviño et al. 1999, p. 135). From a discourse ethics perspective such an enforced certification can be termed as strategic action and therefore barely ensures legitimate actions. The application of the whole initiative should not be *limited* to such an understanding, at least from the viewpoint of discourse ethics, because MNCs simply "pass" the responsibility on to their suppliers by demanding certification. As a result of an empirical investigation of the development of codes of conduct, Mamic (2005, p. 86) reports that the influence from MNCs acts as the main determinant of the adoption of social accountability measures.

V. Introducing an Advanced Version of SA 8000

1. Macro-Level: Moral Discourses and a Catalogue of Discursively Legitimized Standards

As a response to the insufficient justification of norms and due to the fact that SA 8000 does not address the question of how to set up stakeholder dialogues, we propose to integrate the basic principles of discourse ethics (U) and (D) as well as the discourse rules (ideal speech situation) into the macro-level. SAI would have to supplement the current version of the standard by a *preamble* comprising (U) and (D) and the discourse rules of the ideal speech situation. This has particularly three advantages: First, the principle of universalization (U) provides an impartial moral point of view for SA 8000 to capture the practice of moral argument, particularly the process of universalization which is of utmost importance for a social accounting standard trying to assure humane workplaces *across cultures*. Second, the principle of discourse ethics (D) provides SA 8000 with a stronger stakeholder focus because it expresses the strict obligation that norms can and must be impartially justified in practical discourses where affected members of society have the opportunity to raise their voice. Third, an integration of the procedural principles of the ideal speech situation offers SAI and its stakeholders a more precise idea of how to design and maintain stakeholder dialogues between people from different cultural backgrounds. Although the archetype of the ideal speech situation is not fully realizable in practical communication, the discourse rules have a counterfactual potential to facilitate a greater degree of equity among stakeholders and to move away from a one-sided prioritization of economically powerful stakeholders (Unerman/Bennett 2004).

In more practical terms, the SAI Advisory Board has to initiate a practical discourse to critically evaluate the current normative basis of the standard and the specific guidelines for corporate action. As the present version of SA 8000 can only be referred to as a catalogue of *ethical* values with *relative* validity, SAI needs to initiate a *moral discourse* at the macro-level to be able to derive a catalogue of moral maxims with *universal* validity. SAI has to ensure that not only members of the Advisory Board have a voice in advancing the standard but also fringe stakeholders like suppliers, workers, and customers. As an outcome of such a debate norms that are not accepted in an unconstrained way have to be reformulated or eliminated from the standard whereas missing norms need to be included. We propose to label the result of this moral discourse a *catalogue of discursively legitimized standards*.

2. Micro-Level: Dealing with Cultural Diversity through Local Discourses

A discursive extension of the micro-level deals with cultural diversity and the local adaptation of the macro-level norms. According to Habermas's concept of different forms of practical reason, local discourses can be characterized as *ethical discourses* because they involve decisions on what is *good* for a specific group, community, or culture. As ethical norms always have to operate within the limits of moral justification, the macro-level restricts the activities of affected stakeholders at the micro-level. In practice, this means that the norm-catalogue proposed at the macro-level needs to be operationalized via ethical discourses on the micro-level since every norm shows room for interpretation and needs to be applied to a context (Derrida 1992). Because local production conditions differ widely, management and employees need to "fill the pre-given rules" with a contextualized interpretation. Within ethical discourses they need to develop a mutual understanding of how they interpret terms like "forced labor", "compensation", and "healthy work environments" in their specific local context.

A discursively extended certification process offers yet another advantage: once affected stakeholders have agreed on certain moral standards on the macro-level and their local specification on the micro-level, they are freed from a permanent *ethical* reflection of their operative business practices under discursive conditions. As long as the issue being discussed on the micro-level does not evoke an ethical conflict and therefore is only a question of *rational* choice, *pragmatic discourses* are the appropriate means to justify actions or even compliance regulations used for achieving certification. Pragmatic discourses are not supposed to refer to the assumptions of the ideal speech situation and thus allow for quick and efficient decision making.

VI. Conclusions and Need for Further Research

This paper first aimed at introducing SA 8000 as a means of social accounting in MNCs and at testing whether discourse ethics can successfully inform this concept to better answer the needs of SAI and its international stakeholders. When meaningfully based on discourse ethics, SA 8000 supports SAI, MNCs, suppliers, and other stakeholders to effectively communicate about conflicting issues to "live" social responsibility. The principles of discourse ethics and the discourse rules can be applied at the macro-level of SA 8000 (moral discourses to develop a legitimized norm-catalogue) and the micro-level (ethical discourses to resolve local conflicts). Furthermore, and maybe most important for a concept trying to offer guidance in the field of *international* business ethics: Based on the assumption of unavoidable presuppositions of argumentation, Habermas presents a general theory of justification with formal and processual characteristics that (a) allows for a sharp differentiation between ethical and moral validity and (b) can be found in and applied to *all* cultures. Whoever enters into a discussion with the serious intention of becoming convinced of something via dialogue has to accept that "[...] true propositions are resistant to spatially, socially, and temporally unconstrained attempts to refute them. What we hold to be true has to be defendable on the basis of good reasons not merely in a different context but in all possible contexts, that is, at any time and against anybody" (Habermas 1998, p. 367).

Another advantage we would like to highlight is the applicability of our remarks to other ethics initiatives in the international context. Among the myriad of so called "international corporate citizenship initiatives" (for an overview see Goodell 1999; McIntosh et al. 2003; Zadek et al. 1997), particularly the Global Reporting Initiative, AccountAbility 1000, the OECD Guidelines for Multinational Enterprises, and the UN Global Compact have attained a high degree of acceptance in the business community and a significant following. However, despite a common focus on stakeholder relations, in none of these initiatives one can find an elaborated concept of how to actually perform stakeholder dialogues and how to justify the normative basis. Although the UN Global Compact fosters stakeholder collaboration (Kell/Levin 2003) and AA 1000 operates under the leading principle of "stakeholder inclusivity" (Göbbels/Jonker 2003, p. 57; ISEA 1999), both standards do not provide sufficient discourse-oriented justification and assistance in establishing stakeholder engagement processes.

As stakeholder engagement is the core of every concept based on discourse ethics, we suggest including Habermasian ideas not only into SA 8000 but also the Global Reporting Initiative, AccountAbility 1000, the OECD Guidelines for Multinational Enterprises, and the UN Global Compact. We believe that the initiatives can benefit from Habermas's findings because he provides a sound justification for his concept of communicative action and the procedural discourse rules, both of which can be applied in the context of other standards. The framework provides a clear-cut guideline of how to design stakeholder dialogues to promote open and unbiased discourses. To distinguish between different forms of practical reason also offers the chance to bring the national voice of stakeholders into the global debate about universal norms and values.

Some implications for future research can be identified. First, the relation between international social accountability standards like SA 8000 or the Global Reporting Initiative and other spheres of democratic societies need to be investigated in more detail. This is to answer the question how such initiatives can be successfully linked to each other and to existing political institutions. Second, the Habermasian approach to advance SA 8000 is a purely normative theory and would benefit from empirical findings on the practicality of the concept. Empirical insights are especially required to learn more about how to apply the discourse guidelines to local contexts and how to integrate fringe stakeholders into practical discourses. Unerman/Bennett (2004) provide first empirical evidence and show that the regulative idea of an ideal discourse in a specific local context can be at least partially achieved. To extend this line of inquiry, we suggest empirical studies to investigate to what degree SAI's norm-development process (macro-level) and local stakeholder dialogues (micro-level) meet the proposed discursive framework. The results together with the presented arguments can effect the co-operation among SAI, auditing bodies, corporations, and other stakeholders. Third, more research seems to be necessary to address the cultural differences with regard to the implementation of ethics initiatives. Approaches to handle normative issues in business vary greatly across cultures (Watson/Weaver 2003, p. 77) and have an impact on the implementation of accountability standards.

References

ABRAHAMSON, E.: "Management Fashion", *Academy of Management Review*, 21 (1996), pp. 254-285.

BELAL, A. R.: "Stakeholder Accountability or Stakeholder Management: A Review of UK Firms' Social and Ethical Accounting, Auditing, and Reporting (SEAAR) Practices", *Corporate Social Responsibility and Environmental Management*, 9 (2002), pp. 8-25.

BURRELL, G.: "Modernism, Postmodernism and Organizational Analysis 4: The Contribution of Jürgen Habermas", *Organization Studies*, 15 (1994), pp. 1-19.

CHUA, W. F., DEGELING, P.: "Interrogating an Accounting-based Intervention on three Axes: Instrumental, Moral and Aesthetic", *Accounting, Organizations and Society*, 18 (1993), pp. 291-318.

CRANE, A., MATTEN, D.: *Business Ethics: A European Perspective,* Oxford et. al. (Oxford University Press) 2004.

DEMING, W. E.: *Out of the Crisis*, Cambridge, MA (MIT Press) 2000.

DERRIDA, J.: "Force of Law: The Mystical Foundation of Authority", in: D. CORNELL, M. ROSENFELD, D. G. CARLSON (Eds.): *Deconstruction and the Possibility of Justice*, New York, London (Routledge) 1992, pp. 3-67.

DONALDSON, T.: "Taking Ethics Seriously – A Mission Now More Possible", *Academy of Management Review*, 28 (2003), pp. 363-366.

FINLAYSON, J. G.: "Modernity and Morality in Habermas's Discourse Ethics", *Inquiry*, 43 (2000), pp. 319-340.

FINLAYSON, J. G.: *Habermas. A Very Short Introduction*, Oxford (Oxford University Press) 2005.

FROOMKIN, A. M.: "Habermas@Discourse.net: Towards a Critical Theory of Cyberspace", *Harvard Law Review*, 116 (2003), pp. 751-873.

GILBERT, D. U.: "Institutionalisierung von Unternehmensethik in internationalen Unternehmen", *Zeitschrift für Betriebswirtschaft*, 73 (2003), pp. 25-48.

GILBERT, D. U., BEHNAM, M., RASCHE, A.: *Assessing the Impact of Social Standards on Compliance and Integrity-Management in Organizations*, Paper presented at the Annual Meeting of the Academy of Management, Seattle 2003.

GILBERT, D. U., RASCHE, A.: "Discourse ethics and social accountability – The ethics of SA 8000", *Business Ethics Quarterly*, 17 (2007), pp. 187-216.

GÖBBELS, M., JONKER, J.: "AA1000 and SA8000 Compared: A Systematic Comparison of Contemporary Accountability Standards", *Managerial Auditing Journal*, 18 (2003), pp. 54-58.

GOODELL, E.: *Standards of Corporate Social Responsibility*, San Francisco (Social Venture Network) 1999.

GRAY, R.: "Thirty Years of Social Accounting, Reporting and Auditing: What (if anything) Have we Learnt?", *Business Ethics: A European Review*, 10 (2001), pp. 9-15.

GRAY, R.: "The Social Accounting Project and Accounting Organizations and Society Privileging Engagement, Imaginings, New Accountings and Pragmatism over Critique?", *Accounting, Organizations and Society*, 27 (2002), pp. 687-708.

HABERMAS, J.: *Moral Consciousness and Communicative Action*, Cambridge, MA (MIT Press) 1990.

HABERMAS, J.: *Postmetaphysical Thinking: Philosophical Essays*, Cambridge, MA (MIT Press) 1992.

HABERMAS, J.: *Justification and Application. Remarks on Discourse Ethics*, Cambridge, MA (MIT Press) 1993.

HABERMAS, J.: *Between Facts and Norms*, Cambridge, MA (Blackwell Publishing) 1996.

HABERMAS, J.: *On the Pragmatics of Communication*, Cambridge, MA (MIT Press) 1998.

HABERMAS, J.: *The Inclusion of the Other. Studies in Political Theory*, Cambridge, MA (Blackwell Publishing) 1999.

HABERMAS, J.: *Kommunikatives Handeln und dezentralisierte Vernunft*, Stuttgart (Reclam) 2001.

HABERMAS, J.: *Wahrheit und Rechtfertigung*, Frankfurt am Main (Suhrkamp) 2004.

HENDRY, J.: "Universalizability and Reciprocity in International Business Ethics", *Business Ethics Quarterly*, 9 (1999), pp. 405-420.

HOY, D. C., MCCARTHY, T.: *Critical Theory*, Cambridge, MA (Blackwell Publishing) 1994.

INSTITUTE FOR SOCIAL AND ETHICAL ACCOUNTABILITY (ISEA): *AA 1000 Framework – Standards, Guidelines and Professional Qualifications*, London (ISEA) 1999.

JIANG, R., BANSAL, P.: "Seeing the Need for ISO 1400", *Journal of Management Studies*, 40 (2003), pp. 1047-1067.

KELL, G., LEVIN, D.: "The Global Compact Network: An Historic Experiment in Learning and Action", *Business and Society Review*, 108 (2003), pp. 151-181.

KPMG: *International Survey of Corporate Sustainability Reporting 2002*, Maasland (Druckgroep Maasland) 2002.

LAUGHLIN, R. C.: "Accounting Systems in Organizational Contexts: A Case for Critical Theory", *Accounting, Organizations and Society*, 12 (1987), pp. 479-502.

LEIPZIGER, D.: *The Corporate Responsibility Code Book*, Sheffield (Greenleaf) 2003.

LEIPZIGER, D.: *SA 8000. The Definitive Guide to the New Social Standard*, London et al. (FT Prentice Hall) 2001.

LEVY, D. L., ALVESSON, M., WILLMOT, H.: "Critical Approaches to Strategic Management", in: M. ALVESSON, H. WILLMOT (Eds.): *Studying Management Critically*, London (Sage Publications) 2003, pp. 92-110.

LOZANO, J. F.: "Proposal for a Model for the Elaboration of Ethical Codes Based on Discourse Ethics", *Business Ethics: A European Review*, 10 (2001), pp. 157-162.

MAMIC, I.: "Managing Global Supply Chain: The Sports Footwear, Apparel and Retail Sectors", *Journal of Business Ethics*, 59 (2005), pp. 81-100.

MATHEWS, M. R.: "Twenty-five Years of Social and Environmental Accounting Research: is There a Silver Jubilee to Celebrate?", *Accounting, Auditing & Accountability Journal*, 10 (1997), pp. 481-531.

MCCARTHY, T.: *Ideals and Illusions: On Reconstruction and Deconstruction in Contemporary Critical Theory*, Cambridge, MA (MIT Press) 1991.

MCINTOSH, M., THOMAS, R., LEIPZIGER, D., COLEMAN, G.: *Living Corporate Citizenship – Strategic Routes to Socially Responsible Business*, London et al. (FT Prentice Hall) 2003.

O'DWYER, B.: "The Legitimacy of Accountant's Participation in Social and Ethical Accounting, Auditing and Reporting", *Business Ethics: A European Review*, 9 (2001), pp. 86-98.

PARKER, M.: "Business, Ethics and Business Ethics: Critical Theory and Negative Dialectics", in: M. ALVESSON, H. WILLMOT (Eds.): *Studying Management Critically*, London (Sage Publications) 2003, pp. 197-219.

PHILIPPS, R.: *Stakeholder Theory and Organizational Ethics*, San Francisco (Berret-Koehler Publishers) 2003.

POWER, M., LAUGHLIN, R.: "Habermas, Law and Accounting", *Accounting, Organizations and Society*, 21 (1996), pp. 441-465.

RASCHE, A., ESSER, D.: "Managing for Compliance and Integrity in Practice", in: C. CHATER ET AL. (Eds.): *Business Ethics as Practice*, Northhampton (Edward Elgar) 2007, pp. 107-127.

RASCHE, A., ESSER, D.: "From Stakeholder Management to Stakeholder Accountability – Applying Habermasian Discourse Ethics to Accountability Research", *Journal of Business Ethics*, 65 (2006), pp. 251-267.

REED, D.: "Stakeholder Management Theory: A Critical Theory Perspective", *Business Ethics Quarterly*, 9 (1999), pp. 453-483.

SCHNEBEL, E.: "Values in Decision-making Processes. Systematic Structures of J. Habermas and N. Luhmann for the Appreciation of Responsibility in Leadership", *Journal of Business Ethics*, 27(1), (2000), pp. 79-89.

SEN, A.: "Does Business Ethics Make Economic Sense?", *Business Ethics Quarterly*, 3 (1993), pp. 45-54.

SOCIAL ACCOUNTABILITY INTERNATIONAL (SAI): *About Social Accountability 8000*, http://www.sa-intl.org/AboutSAI/AboutSAI.htm, Accessed Sept. 6, 2005.

TREVIÑO, L. K., WEAVER, G., GIBSON, D. G., TOFFLER, B. L.: "Managing Ethics and Legal Compliance – What Works and What Hurts", *California Management Review*, 41 (1999), pp. 131-151.

TULDER, R. V., KOLK, A.: "Multinationality and Corporate Ethics: Codes of Conduct in the Sporting Goods Industry", *Journal of International Business Studies*, 32 (2001), pp. 267-283.

ULRICH, P.: *Integrative Economic Ethics – Towards a Conception of Socio-Economic Rationality*, Berichte des Instituts für Wirtschaftsethik der Universität St. Gallen No. 82, St. Gallen 1998.

UNERMAN, J., BENNETT, M.: "Increased Stakeholder Dialogue and the Internet: Towards Greater Corporate Social Accountability or Reinforcing Capitalist Hegemony?", *Accounting, Organizations and Society*, 29 (2004), pp. 685-708.

WATSON, S., WEAVER, G.: "How Internationalization Affects Corporate Ethics: Formal Structures and Informal Management Behavior", *Journal of International Management*, 9 (2003), pp. 75-93.

WHITE, S. K.: "Reason and Authority in Habermas: A Critique of Critics", *The American Political Science Review*, 74 (1980), pp. 1007-1017.

ZADEK, S., PRUZAN, P. M., EVANS, R.: *Building Corporate Accountability: The Emerging Practice of Social & Ethical Accounting, Auditing & Reporting*, London (Earthscan Publication) 1997.

Chapter 8

Sustainable Finance and the Stakeholder Equity Model

ALOY SOPPE

I. Introduction

Over the past decades the ideology of shareholder value has become entrenched as one of the basic principle of corporate governance among companies in the western market economies. Based on an historical analysis, Lazonick/O'Sullivan (2000) argue that not only the merger and acquisition market in the US until the 1970s encouraged this development[1], but also the reverse process of downsizing of corporate labour forces and distribution of corporate earnings to shareholders over the 1980s and 1990s. Numerous types of (leveraged) buy-outs or buy-ins changed the traditional character of a company. Companies became more and more a tradable itself. In the same period, capital and derivatives markets expanded exponentially and became matured.[2] The above factors enabled flexible company boundaries and fuelled the success of the shareholder model.

A more recent development in the global economy is the emergence of stakeholder participation. In business ethics, an impressive body of literature has emerged in which it is argued that the interest in stakeholder approaches to strategic management is growing around the world. Seminal articles on this topic are e.g. Freeman (1984), Donaldson/Preston (1995), Clarke (1998). More recently Friedman/Miles (2002) distinguish between four different types of stakeholders in order to explain theoretically the changing stakeholder relations. In today's network economy there are many agency relationships such as between employees and management or between creditors and management. While the shareholder/management relation is theoretically well studied and often solved by aligning the interests through performance dependent fees for management, the research on the relation between employees and management and between suppliers and management are in a premature stadium. Empirically hardly any research has been performed.

Apart from the emergence of stakeholder participation, there are more reasons which challenge the traditional shareholder paradigm. Zingales (2000), in search for new foundations of corporate finance, stressed that the nature of the firm is changing. The traditional corporation, which emerged at the beginning of the twentieth century, is an asset-intensive and highly vertically integrated firm with tight control over its employees. The modern firms have relinquished direct control of their suppliers and moved toward looser forms of collaboration. Human capital is emerging as the most crucial asset, which influences the power relations within a company. Margolis/Walsh (2003) present compelling social reasons to challenge the shareholder paradigm. Based on major inequalities of the social life in the world's most populous nations, they make a strong case to rethink social initiatives by compa-

1 As financed by the retention of corporate earnings and reinvested in corporate growth.

2 See various IMF annual reports.

nies and provide innovative solutions based on a normative theory of the firm. Engelen (2002) focuses on strong conceptual reasons that can be identified why the concern about shareholder value is increasing.[3] Another relevant aspect of changing power positions in companies is the growing interest in corporate social responsibility (CSR), which is strongly connected to stakeholder theory. In an article that reviews the existing research on CSR in the past 50 years, Kakabadse, Rozuel and Davies (2005) highlight many challenges and implications of the stakeholder approach. They conclude that as the network economy intensifies, new forms of cooperation are needed and that the shareholder is not necessarily the only ultimate owner of the residual claim of the company.

In the traditional shareholder model agency costs for other stakeholders than shareholders and management are hardly studied because these parties all have fixed contracts with the company. Due to increasing (global) competition and a strong market position of management and shareholders, many stakeholders with fixed contracts are successfully pressurized. The resulting unequal market positions of different stakeholders may increase governance costs and hence threaten sustainable development. Sustainable development and sustainable finance is considered the reference framework in which the stakeholder equity model is proposed. Sustainable finance will be discussed as the underlying framework in section 2.1. The primary goal of this paper is to argue that agency costs may be reduced by changing equity ownership of companies. In that sense it aims to contribute to the discussion on efficiency and ethics in the debate about shareholder primacy (see Lee 2006). First we need to explain that the wealth of the society may increase if contracting relations between different stakeholders change. Finance and financial theory will be used to describe payoff diagrams not just for the shareholder alone but also for the other stakeholders. Section 2 starts off by analysing the shareholder model from an economic, a sustainable and a legal perspective. Then, in section 3, agency costs and governance costs are introduced as the theoretical setting for gaining shareholder value. Section 4 presents and explains an example of potential payoff diagrams per stakeholder and their mutual differences. Also the main drivers of the market, against the background

3 Engelen distinguishes between prudential, functional and moral claims to justify the shareholder as the ultimate claimholder of the firm. By debunking all three claims extensively he concludes that corporate democracy should be a proper solution to the unequal power relations within the company.

of an option approach for allocating the company assets are addressed. In section 5 the corporate governance implications of the stakeholder equity model are discussed and section 6 concludes on the model.

II. Sustainable Corporate Finance and the Shareholder Paradigm

Shareholders as the ultimate claimants in the company are deeply rooted in economic and financial theory. Based on the free markets arguments as posed by economist like Smith, Friedman and Hayek, freedom of choice is the major driving force behind shareholders' ownership. Already Hayek (1948) and M. Friedman/R. Friedman (1980) argued that free markets utilize dispersed information most efficiently. By freedom (individual liberty) Hayek means the state in which a man is not subject to coercion by the arbitrary will of another. The liberal or free society to which Hayek aims is a society in which the subjugation of individuals to the will of others and the use of coercion is minimised. But also coercion does not involve the absence of choice. An individual that is faced with an agent that can dispose of overwhelming force and decides to obey still made a rational choice. The freedom of choice is very much represented by trading in financial markets, but also in organising the firm and its goals. To that background, sustainable finance and sustainability in general are very much the result of free choices of shareholders, managers and their co-operators. In search for an instrument to lower transaction costs in the long run, the next subsection first introduces the concepts of sustainable development and sustainable corporate finance.

1. Sustainable Corporate Finance

In recent years, lively discussions have taken place regarding the uniformity of the concept of sustainable development. Fergus/Rowney (2005a) reviewed the concept extensively and built a semantic framework of sustainable development in which the neoclassical economic model for business is an accepted, but not necessarily implemented, tool within the development of social relationships. The semantic roots, as identified by Lélé (1991)[4], were later extended by Fergus and Rowney within the context of an economical, ecological and social future direction of human progress. Implementing the neo-classical dominant paradigm, Fergus and Rowney finally identify 'sustaining growth' as an objective in itself. They argue that a definition, in general, is intended to clarify things in order to free us for action. But a definition can easily become a means of control – and that is what happened to the well-known Brundtland definition of sustainable development[5]. Fergus/Rowney (2005a) conclude that new insights and perspectives are necessary; reminding us that the neoclassical market approach is not necessarily the only context within which sustainable development can be attained.[6]

Today, many countries and companies have embraced and implemented the concept of sustainable development at different levels. There is a growing understanding that sustainability is not the exclusive responsibility of one society, country or sector. Sustainability, in practice, constitutes a set of actions; sustainable development is therefore incremental and builds on what already exists. Boadi (2002) discusses three arguments in favour of sustainable development. First, there is the '*healthy environment*' argument, which emphasises the need to stop the environmental degradation caused by traditional economic development.[7] A second approach maintains that sustainability is a *holistic* concept that is based on the idea that the whole is greater than

4 The literal meaning of 'sustain' is: *to maintain or to prolong*; 'develop' means: *to build on or change the use of.* LÉLÉ (1991), p. 608, described these words as 'contradictory and trivial'. Fergus and Rowney therefore conclude that the context itself is crucial in providing a meaning.

5 A widely used definition of *sustainable development* is the one established by the Brundtland Commission (G. H. BRUNDTLAND: *Our common future: The world commission on environment and development*, Oxford [Oxford University Press] 1987) and generally accepted by the WCED 1987. There, sustainable development is defined as, "development that meets the needs of the present without compromising the ability of future generations to meet their own needs" (p. 43).

6 The neoclassical model, as one extreme in social relationships, just emphasizes the economic responsibilities of man and neglects social responsibilities that also influence economic output.

7 Because the environment is not a priced stakeholder in the traditional finance concept, there is an economic impulse to externalise these costs, which deteriorates the quality of the environment.

the sum of the parts.[8] This is a powerful aspect of sustainability, but at the same time a major obstacle for progress, in practice. Sustainable development avoids the shortcomings of approaching social policy from the single perspective of the market-based economy. However, an integrated approach of economics, environment and social equity calls for a critical mass in favour of collective care; this is difficult (if not impossible) to obtain in a world that is evolving in the direction of individualism. Free riders, in particular, are endangering social cohesion. The third argument, used by Boadi to illustrate the necessity of sustainable development, is the inherent *promotion of equity*. Sustainability basically incorporates a two-dimensional commitment to equity: between present- and future generations, and between the rich and the poor of the world's population. Boadi argues that the art of sustainable development, from the perspective of the policymaker, is to ensure a fair distribution between the current costs and both current- and future benefits.

In this paper on the development of stakeholder equity, CSR literature is used as a footing for the sustainable corporate finance concept as developed in Soppe (2004). Although the financial policy of the firm is merely one aspect of its strategic decision-making, it is a crucial aspect. The major problem is that finance explicitly or implicitly interferes with all decisions in the firm. Orlitzky/Benjamin (2001) make a strong case that CSR is directly related to financial risk. Based on a meta-analysis of over 1200 US and international business- and trade journal articles from 1970 until 2000, they developed six hypotheses linking CSP (corporate social performance) to financial firm risk. A minority of the articles measured financial risk explicitly. However, those that were integrated quantitatively were separated according to the temporal order of measures taken: (a) prior CSP → subsequent risk, (b) prior risk → subsequent CSP, and (c) contemporaneous (cross-sectional) measures. They concluded that the empirical study supports the theoretical argument that the higher a firm's CSP, the lower its financial risk. More specifically, according to Orlitzky and Benjamin the relation between CSP and risk appears to be one of reciprocal causality, because prior CSP is negatively related to subsequent financial risk, and prior financial risk is negatively related to subse-

8 Human behaviour is not considered to be above and apart from nature and laws of nature, but embedded in nature and responsible for nature as described by e.g. the deep ecology concept of A. NEASS: "Ecosophy T", in: B. DEVALL, G. SESSIONS (Eds.): *Deep Ecology – Living as if Nature Mattered*, Layton/Utah (Gibbs M. Smith) 1985, pp. 225-228.

quent CSP. Additionally, CSP is more strongly correlated with measures of market risk than with measures of accounting risk. Of all CSP measures, *reputation regarding social responsibility* appeared to be the most important one in terms of risk implications.

Taking into account the general relationship between CSR and financial risk as described above, it is important to develop an 'exchange syntax' to transmit sustainability developments into the (traditional) financial literature. The term *sustainable corporate finance* could be used as an example of such exchange syntax. In Soppe (2004), the term is defined in the conclusion as: '*a multi-attribute approach to finance the company in such a way that all the company's financial, social and environmental elements are interrelated and integrated'*. The paper further deduces sustainable corporate finance from traditional finance theory by identifying four criteria by which sustainable corporate finance distinguishes itself from traditional finance and behavioural finance. Through a closer look at a) the consisting elements of the 'theory of the firm', b) the assumed behaviour of the economic agents, c) the discussion on the ownership of the firm and d) the ethical framework of the company, the paper proposes an alternative financial policy. It is concluded that a sustainably financed company is a multi-attribute optimiser of goals wherein the assumptions of, and approach to, human behaviour are based on cooperation and trust, instead of selfish behaviour. This change in human behaviour may lower agency conflicts in general and therefore reduce agency costs.

This paper elaborates on the third element of the classification of sustainable finance above: the optimal ownership of the firm. Seeking to increase corporate democracy and reduce agency costs, the sustainable company is one that is owned by a portfolio of stakeholders (Soppe 2004, p. 220). The analysis starts off by describing some of the legal footings of the shareholder paradigm.

2. The Legal Approach

Analysing the core features of modern company law, Davies (2002), outlines three main groups of people who dominate the activities of companies: 1) shareholders (or 'members' of the company; 2) its directors and, to a lesser extent, its senior managers, whether they are directors or not; and 3) its creditors, who may be secured or unsecured. The law seeks to regulate the relationship between this trinity of stakeholders. The legal function of the director is to manage the company – although what that entails can vary according to the size of the company and the distribution of its shareholding. Shareholders, who may or may not be the directors of the company, usually provide the company with a particular type of capital: risk capital. In return, they generally receive two types of rights. The first is to exercise ultimate control over the company, notably by selecting or removing the directors and setting the terms of the company's constitution. The second type of right is merely to receive a financial return on their investment in shares. Since the shareholders' rights are essentially a matter of contract with the company, each company may wish to issue shares on its own terms. The third major group of participants in the company are the creditors – and these also come in many varieties. The most obvious are the suppliers of goods yet to be paid for, and the banks that provide medium- or long-term loans to the company.

Of crucial importance in shareholder analysis in law is the fact that a company is a *separate legal entity* – separate from its shareholders, directors, creditors, employees and anyone else. This complicates legal abstraction because company law does not always establish definite legal relations between these groups directly, but instead only mediates between them through the company as a legal person. Bigger companies mostly concern Public limited companies (Plc) with limited liability. 'Limited liability' means that the rights of the company's creditors are confined to the assets of the company and cannot be asserted against the personal assets of the company's members (shareholders)[9]. Thus, directors will owe duties over the company rather than over shareholders, and shareholders may have rights to the company rather than against the directors. The commonly heard expression 'limited liability companies' can be explained by the above fact, but this is really a misnomer. The liability of the company is not limited at all. Creditors' rights can be asserted to the full against company assets. But: *it is the liability of the members (i.e. shareholder) that is limited* (Davies 2002, p. 11). There are some good rationales for limited liability: the encouragement of public investment and facilitation of public markets in shares. The question, however, is whether today's financial markets really need that encouragement. The increasing importance of private equity, project finance and the development of the markets of venture capital signal the availability of capital in the high-risk segment of the capital market.

9 In Dutch law, this principle is legally anchored in Art 2:64 lid 1BW.

Summing up, the core features of the modern company are as follows: separate corporate personality, limited liability, centralized management under a board structure, control executed by shareholders and free transferability of shares. There is a clear positive correlation between the size of the company and the likelihood of manifestation of all five of the core features[10]. The analysis in sections 3 and 4 will focus on shareholder control of this type of company, where all of these core features are present. Stakeholder powers are derived mainly from the company's constitution, rather than company legislation. In other words, a company may always choose to change the statutes in such a way that other governance rules are applied. This study does not aim at that objective, but the substantive question needs to be addressed of whether and how shareholder control still can be justified in the rapidly changing (financial) markets of the last decades. Davies' arguments in favour of shareholder control boil down to a perceived necessity of attracting risky capital, which cannot be successful without inherent control rights. The next section elaborates on that issue.

III. The Shareholder Paradigm and Agency Costs

In an extensive analysis on the ownership of the firm, Hansmann (1996) perceives the regular stock company as a special type of producer cooperative, or more specifically: a 'lenders cooperative' or 'capital cooperative'. This theoretical generalisation of contracting parties in a company is useful in analysing the company in an objective way. He compares the 'lenders cooperative' with a farmers' cheese cooperative in which the cheese factory is owned by the farmers who supply the factory with raw milk. In the latter case, the firm pays its owners (or 'members') a predetermined price for their milk. This price is set low enough so that the cooperative is almost certain to have positive net earnings. Then, at the end of the year, the firm's net earnings are divided pro rata among the members according to the volume of milk that the member sold to the factory. Upon liquidation of the firm, any net asset value is divided among its members, according to some measure of the relative value of their relative patronage.

10 See DAVIES (2002), p. 27.

1. Transaction Costs Derived from Agency Relations

The structure of the cooperative, as described above, is basically similar to the organisation of modern companies that are quoted on stock markets. In an investor-owned firm, the transactions between the firm and its patrons – who supply capital instead of milk – occur within the context of ownership, while all other transactions take the form of market contracting. The providers of capital are legally the 'members' or 'owners' of the residual result of the production process. The accompanying voting rights – dependent on the amount of capital provided – are exclusively held by the shareholders. It is important to note that this prerogative equips them with the right to 'set the prices'.[11] With the goal of obtaining the highest societal wealth, the essential question from a theoretical perspective is the following: what governance model of the company brings the lowest cost of assignment of ownership? Or, in terms of lowering transaction costs: what organization of the company (corporate governance) brings the lowest governance costs? According to Hansmann (1996), the answer depends on the character of the market. The theoretically optimal position is to assign ownership to that class of patrons for whom the problems of market contracting – that is, the costs of market imperfections – are most severe (p. 21). Severe market conditions cause a natural motivation for that group of patrons to organize the production process in the most cost-efficient way.

Hansmann goes on to distinguish between two types of transaction costs: 1) costs of market contracting for those classes of patrons that are not owners (costs of contracting); and 2) costs of ownership for the class of patrons that own the firm (governance costs). Examples of the latter are the costs of making collective decisions among the owners (resolving conflicts and bureaucratic threats), the costs of monitoring managers (monitoring and bonding), the costs of poor decisions and excessive managerial discretion that results if monitoring is imperfect. And, of course, there are also the costs of risk-bearing associated with the receipt of residual earnings. The costs of contracting depend on the market power of the contractor, the risk of long-term contracting, and the level of asymmetric information (e.g. on the quality of the products sold), for example. Other problems are the communication of the relevant patron's preferences and the alienation of workers. The scope of this

11 Implying ultimate control of the conditions of the production process of the company.

study does not allow for elaboration on all of these possible costs. It is sufficient for now to model the transaction cost function for company y (T_y), which has to be minimized in order for the company to be cost efficient:

$$T_y = C_j^O + \sum_{i \neq j} C_{ij}^K \qquad [1]$$

where C^O_j is the cost of ownership (governance costs) for the group of patrons in class *j,* and C^K_{ij} is the cost of market contracting for the group of patrons in class *i* when class *j* owns the firm. Consequently, in order to decide on the optimal ownership of the firm, we must consider both the transaction costs for those contractors who are not owners and the governance costs for the class of owners of the firm. A change in ownership may influence *both* variables in the cost function. In order to increase societal wealth, the (reduction of) agency costs are defined then as the total of the costs of market contracting and the governance costs.

2. Why Agency Costs Decline in the Sustainably Financed Company

There are two theoretical reasons why agency costs may decrease if the ownership is transferred from the provider of capital alone to a portfolio of stakeholders. First is the alignment of interests that occurs within a much broader set of stakeholders than between shareholder and management alone. As a result, the motivation of especially workers and creditors (suppliers and contractors) to serve the company well may increase. Second, the reallocation of the risk premium to different stakeholders may diversify the risk to more market participants and therefore lower the required return on capital. Let's briefly discuss these elements in turn.

In corporate governance practise, the policy of aligning interests through the provision of stocks or options on stocks of the own company is well established in the Anglo-Saxon market economy. If such a policy reduces agency costs in that stakeholder relation (shareholder – CEO), why shouldn't this model be extended to the other stakeholder relations? Theoretically, a similar effect may be expected from the employee-shareholder agency relation. If employees and suppliers provide capital to the company, then the incentive to shirk or to cheat diminishes, theoretically.[12] Workers and suppliers become financially involved, which encourages morally responsible behaviour. There is an extensive and interdisciplinary literature on ESOPs (Employee Stock Ownership Programs) to illustrate this phenomenon.[13] This is not the place to discuss extensively this line of argument, since the focus here is on capital market theory as a new element in the discussion.

The second argument, based on the sustainable finance concept, is an extension of capital market theory in combination with the earlier mentioned concept of the 'severity' of the market for different potential ultimate claimholders. A 'severe'[14] market is identified in this paper by the risk-return characteristic of a stakeholder in the market economy. A severe market, then, is characterised by high competition in a specific market, little opportunity to diversify risk (either through insurance or through diversification), and a relatively low liquid market with low market power of the specific stakeholder. In modern asset-pricing models (CAPM and APT), a high risk incurs a high expected return. An extension of the capital asset model to a stakeholder model, assuming the value additivity of all stakeholders' wealth, will include the risk position of all stakeholders and is therefore by definition broader than the risk position of shareholders alone. And, more importantly, the preferences of dual stakeholders[15] that provide capital are different from the preferences of the regular providers of capital. According to theory, the required return on capital will be maximised at any given level of risk (see e.g. the CAPM of Sharpe 1964 and Lintner 1965). In the sustainable company, the providers of capital are diversified among the direct stakeholders of the com-

---

12 For example, excessive remuneration easily incurs shirking behaviour by workers, but may be interpreted differently if the workers also realize the importance of the stock price (or the value) of the company.

13 See e.g. D. KRUSE: "Research evidence on the prevalence and effects of employee ownership", in: *Journal of Employee Ownership Law and Finance*, 14 (2002), pp. 65-90; J. BLASI, D. KRUSE, A. BERNSTEIN: *In the company of owners: the truth about stock options (and why every employee should have them)*, New York (Basic Books) 2003; D. E. HALLOCK, R. J. SALAZAR, S. VENNEMAN: "Demographic and attitudinal correlates of employee satisfaction with an ESOP", *British Journal of Management*, 15 (2004), pp. 321-333.

14 In terms of competitiveness.

15 Dual stakeholders are stockholders that also work for the company, provide services to the company (creditors) or otherwise have a stake in the company where they own stocks.

pany (a portfolio of the providers of factor services) and because dual stakeholders have more diversified preferences, they are theoretically expected to lower the required return for capital because of their dual interest in the company. This implies a lower riskpremium on capital and implicitly a lower cost of capital.

A modern example of a balanced position of shareholder interest is represented by the 'Universal Ownership' hypothesis,[16] and the 'fiduciary capitalism' concept of Hawley/Williams (2000). Universal ownership addresses the economics of well-diversified portfolios, drawing on the lessons from welfare economics in such studies as Stiglitz (2000), and is especially relevant for large pension funds. The universal ownership hypothesis states that worldwide investment returns are affected by both positive and negative externalities, as generated by the entities invested in. Because universal owners own cross-sections of the economy they inevitably find that some of their holdings are forced to bear the costs of other sectors or firms' externalities. If this hypothesis holds, it can be interpreted as a capital market incentive to develop sustainable growth. Bogle (2005) referred to this as *the battle for the soul of capitalism.* In this paper, equity held by a portfolio of stakeholders (stakeholder equity, SE) is applied to lower the risk premium of the provider of capital and therefore to lower agency costs and, *ceteris paribus,* to increase societal wealth.

There is one major conclusion to draw from the analysis as presented in this section: there is no theoretical reason that helps to understand why it is the provider of capital alone who should hold the ultimate rights to residual claims of most public companies in the world. Neither the costs of ownership, nor the costs of market contracting are theoretically lower because of capital providers holding the residual claim. According to the above line of argument, the question at hand now is whether the market circumstances for the shareholder are more 'severe' than those of the other stakeholders. The Hansmann cost function implies, *ceteris paribus*, that agency costs can be reduced by a change in ownership. To estimate the 'severity' of the market for different stakeholders, the next section will apply an expected risk and return analysis for each distinguished stakeholder.

16 *Corporate Governance. An International Review*, 15, nr 3 (May 2007), devoted a special issue to the concept of 'universal ownership'.

IV. The Stakeholder Risk Model

The new element of this model is applying the well-known expected risk and return analysis of the shareholder theory not just to shareholders but also to other stakeholders. It is well admitted that statistical data, as abundantly available for shareholder analysis, is scarce or nonexistent yet for the other stakeholders. Because of a lack of empirical evidence at this moment in time, the model is purely conceptual and needs quite some additional assumptions. On the other hand, following the clear logic of the Hansmann analysis of the former section, which deals with all stakeholders in an equal way, applying financial theory to other stakeholders is just a rational extension of financial theory. We start off with the general description of the model.

1. The Stakeholder Expected Return Diagrams

The first step to develop payoff diagrams for stakeholders is to suppose an aggregated theoretical economy with (in our example) 5 stakeholders. Let us assume that only companies produce economic output. The selected stakeholders in this example model are: 1) shareholders, 2) management (represented by CEO's), 3) suppliers, 4) employees and 5) the government, representing the general community's interest. Preferable would be a representative of the environment and a representative of local communities, but there is no way to estimate relevant cash flows of these stakeholders. For all different stakeholders there is a different claim at stake. First there are the strict financial claims of the shareholder. For this group an upfront financial payment (investment) is at stake. Then there are the CEO's and employees that hold (long lasting) regular contractual labour relations with the company. For the government it is the receipt of taxes or the payment of social security allowances that runs risk, and last but not least, there are the suppliers who invest (sell) goods & services in the companies (financial creditors like banks and bondholders are not included in this model).

A theoretical problem we encounter is that every stakeholder expects a different financial return, to be earned in a different (segmented) market. In order to compare these risks and returns it is needed to bring them under the same denominator, here called *expected return on stakes* ($E[r^{stake}]$). For the shareholder the $E(r^{stake})$ is the expected return on the stock containing cash dividends, stock bonuses plus stock price changes (total returns). The CEO aims for fixed salaries together with performance dependent bonuses in terms of own company stocks and options. The supplier expects money as a result of the goods & services delivered to the company. Employees are generally dependent on fixed salaries and the government earns taxes from healthy firms or pays subsidies and/or social security payments if companies are in trouble or go bankrupt. Of importance is the fact that all returns at stake are set in different market segments that are well developed, liquid and enabling informationally efficient market pricing. Only then we are able to compare the returns in similar financial terms.

The second step involves the definition of the drivers of the both upside and downside risk. First there is the **market liquidity** where a liquid market is typified by assets that can be sold rapidly with minimum loss of value at any moment in time. In liquid and complete markets it is easier to create a diversified portfolio of assets enabling different hedging strategies. As a result it is concluded that the more liquid the market, the stronger is the relative position of the stakeholder compared to a stakeholder operating in a less liquid market. The second aspect of the downside risk of expected return on stakes is the general **market power** of a stakeholder. Market power is defined as the ability of a specific stakeholder to set the prices of their own services in the total market economy. The more powerful a stakeholder, the better are the market results. For example, in the labour market the market power of CEO's is assumed to be stronger than the market power of employees. Both market liquidity and market power are considered equally important in the following subsections where the payoff diagram per stakeholder will be presented. It is important to realise that these two factors alone are considered to be dominant in positioning the distinguished stakeholders' risk and expected return.

2. Payoff Shareholder

Figure 1 presents the potential payoff diagram of the shareholders. The expected return on stakes (in this case shareholder returns) is measured on the vertical axis. The horizontal axis represents the aggregate normal profitability of the companies as a proxy for the success of the whole (stakeholder) economy. With normal profitability we mean a macro-economic definition of profit being equality between total revenues and total costs of a company. In this concept of normal profits the rate of return then matches the minimum rate required by equity investors to maintain their present level of investment. The aggregated profits of companies can be positive and negative. Zero profit is placed in the middle of the profitability range of firms. The general relationship between expected return of stakeholders and the profitability of the economy is assumed to be positive.

Figure 1

Expected payoff diagram of the shareholders

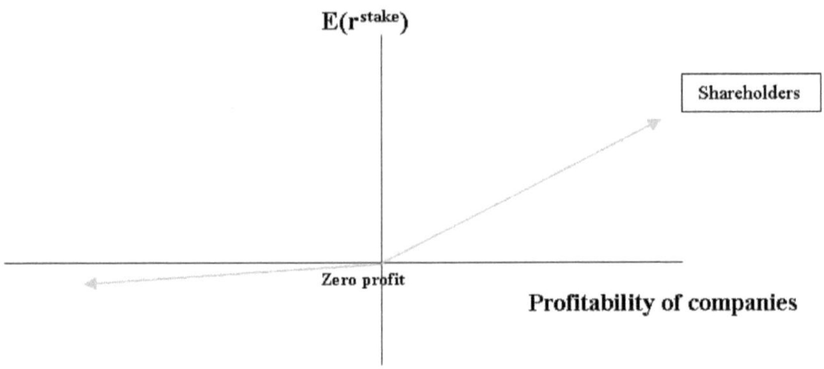

Black/Scholes (1973) were the first to provide the insight that the equity of the firm which has debt in his capital structure (a leveraged firm) is really a call option on the value of the firm. Proof of this can be read in many textbooks on finance (e.g. Weston/Copeland 1992, pp. 457-458).[17] For our analysis we take this as the starting point for analysis. The shareholders as a group are entitled to the complete upward potential of the residual returns. On the other hand, from the downside risk the idiosyncratic part can completely be diversified away. What remains at an aggregated level is the systematic risk (the market risk). Because stock markets are liquid in general and a diversification of a portfolio of stocks can easily be reached, the downside risk of an average investor is limited to the potential negative market

17 This insight beautifully represents that shareholders primarily have a right where all other stakeholders primarily have duties.

return.[18] A second and even more important explanation of the asymmetrical risk position of shareholders is based on the 'limited liability' of the shareholders. If a company defaults, shareholders lose their initial investments but are not sued for any further losses that may occur because of management failures. These costs are externalised to other stakeholders like customers and creditors for example. In figure 1 the shareholders' asymmetrical market risk is represented by the green solid line.

3. Payoff Management

Figure 2 inserts similar lines for the management of the company. Because CEO's earn fixed salaries plus bonuses like stocks and options of the own company, their upward potential is less than that of a shareholder but still with good potential. Dependent on the relative share of the performance dependent part of their total fee, CEO's upward market position is considered strong.

Figure 2

Expected payoff diagram of management

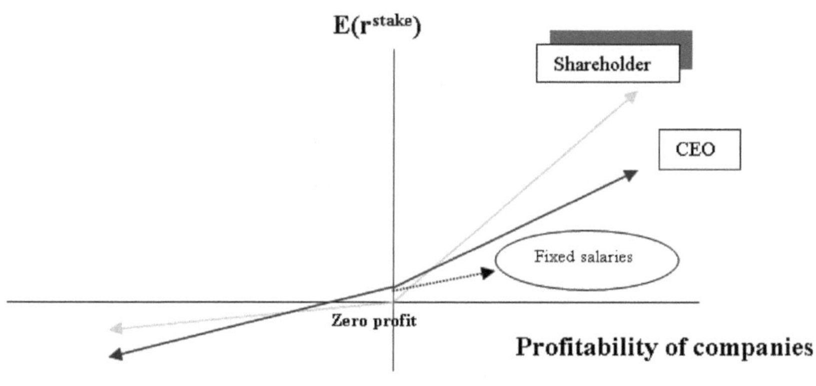

18 In addition there are a lot of hedging opportunities in the matured derivatives markets. Because of the high market liquidity shareholders have a stronger market position compared to other stakeholders.

The down side risk of CEO's is limited because of fixed salaries and the strong contracting position of (top) management in general. In the short run, sometimes even bad performing CEO's are able to leave the company with substantial financial bonuses. These bonuses are usually paid as a compensation for the (perceived) risk a manager takes when changing positions. Also the (international) market for corporate control is well developed implying good alternative job positions and therefore low downside risks. Nevertheless there is empirical evidence that CEO's of target firms who lose their jobs in company takeovers generally fail to find another senior executive position in any public corporation within three years after the bid (see Agrawal/Walkling 1994). Because of the fact that the labour market of CEO's is less flexible than the very liquid capital markets, the downside risk is perceived to be riskier CEO's compared to shareholders.

4. Payoff Suppliers

From a cash flow perspective especially the supplier (one specific form of creditors) is an important stakeholder in the company. A problem of modelling the contracting position of creditors is that the legal positions of different creditors vary widely. Where banks in general have strong positions in the sense that they are able to require collaterals, suppliers of good & services are in general more vulnerable. The risk position of the supplier is also dependent on the expansion policy of the management in a company and the expected growth rate of the economy in general. In low growth scenarios, suppliers do not have strong bargaining positions. As a result they are considered worse off than the shareholder, but on the other hand during high growth periods with scarce production capacity, the wealth easily goes to the creditors in general. Figure 3 presents an average modelled payoff for creditors.

Figure 3

Expected payoff diagram of suppliers

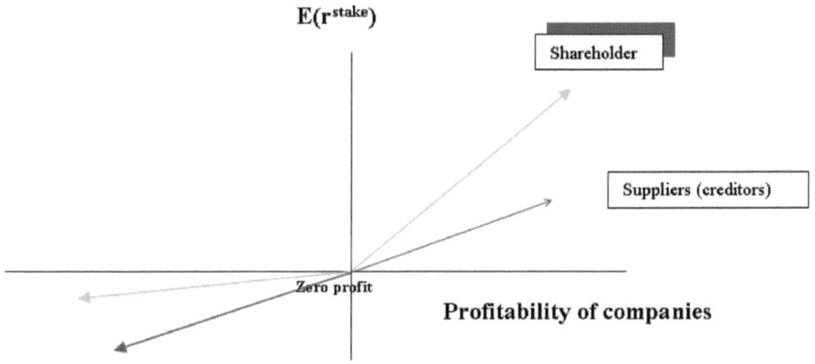

Similar to strong upward potential of creditors in an upward market is the downward risk in a declining market. As a protection, creditors can diversify their portfolio of clients, and thereby diversify that risk. However, because creditors operate in less liquid markets compared to the stock market, the downward risk is worse for creditors than for shareholders. Another problem for creditors is their relative weak bargaining positions in case of bankruptcies. Of course, specific contractual arrangement may result in different individual risk positions, but in most cases creditors are legally vulnerable.

5. Payoff Employees

Then there are the employees. Because they have in general long term fixed contracts, the upward potential is relatively limited. In a growing economy, labour unions do negotiate some gains, however, because of the strong competition with other stakeholders also fighting for the residual results, employees, as a massive homogenous group, are often the last stakeholder to share in profits. Figure 4 presents the modelled positions.

Figure 4

Expected payoff diagram of employees

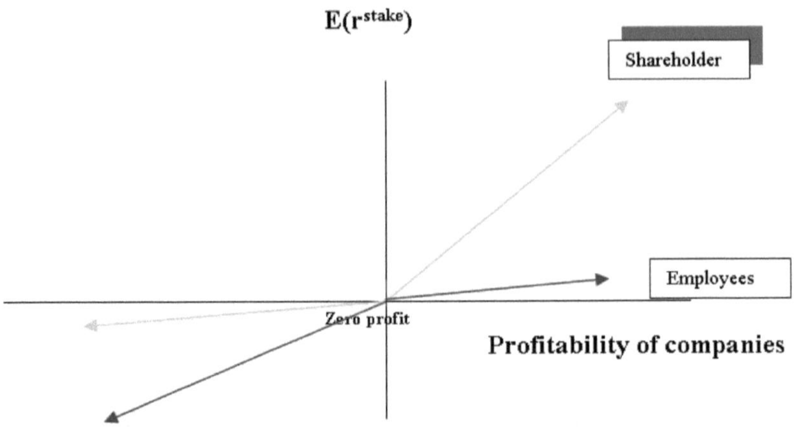

The downside risk of the employee is considered the most severe of all stakeholders. Because of long term education and long term fixed contracts, employees have a vulnerable bargaining position in the sticky labour market. Most important is the fact that employees cannot easily diversify their labour contracts. This makes the individual employee the most vulnerable party in this stakeholder's approach of the market economy. In the aggregated stakeholder model above, we see a declining downside expected return implying that more people are laid off when profits fall further. It is important to note that the economically vulnerable employee position is derived from weak economic power and low job flexibility of employees in the modern network economy. From a social and legal perspective employees are generally better protected.

6. Payoff Government

Finally, we take a closer look at the position of the government in the stakeholder economy. The government is supposed to reflect the interest of the community concerning social security, safety, legal infrastructure and the environment. The market liquidity of the government is non-existent because the state is by definition ultimately responsible for the performance of the market and therefore cannot leave the scene. On the other hand, because the government is in a strong position to incur political and legal changes (e.g. tax changes) they are considered better off than the employees. Figure 5 positions the upward potential of the government between the suppliers and the employees. The upward potential of a government is restricted in this case by an international competing tax rate of for example 30%.

Figure 5

Expected payoff diagram of the government

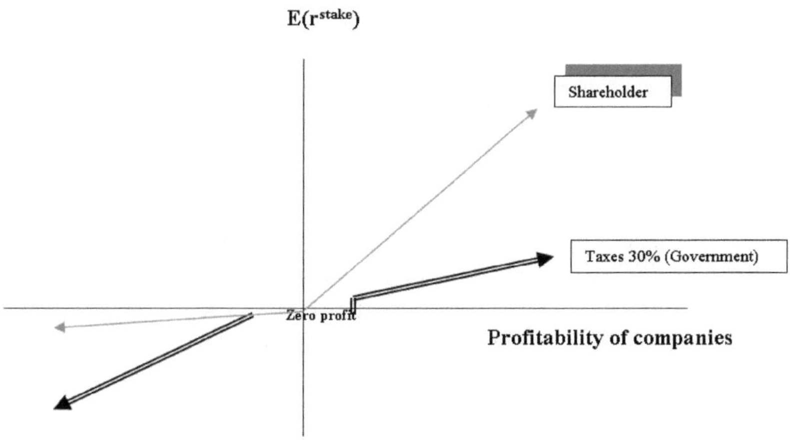

Especially the governments' downward risk is complicated to estimate. In period of recession or depression, the costs coming from additional unemployment payments, increasing subsidies, lower tax income etc. can be estimated. More troublesome are the costs coming from environmental threats, such as public health and natural disasters. Most important is that environmental costs are still externalised by the private sector and as such has become the responsibility of the government. This makes the position of the government weak in the downward risk segment. But then again, if the stakeholder economy is able to flourish, these risks are exactly the ones to be controlled by the private sector itself.

Finally it is of importance to put the above analysis in perspective. The graphs, as depicted above, are much more complicated than the result of just liquidity and market power arguments. There are other explaining factors and there are mutual influences of stakeholders and movements between shareholder risks etc. For example, what happens to the risk of pure shareholders if the influence of the employee stocks become stronger? These are all topics of further research. For now we contribute to the discussion of e.g. Stout (2002) on the shareholder primacy and make the case that in a sustainable economy, shareholder primacy can be attractive under the condition of the right distribution of shareholder ownership among relevant stakeholders.

7. Conclusions on the Payoff Diagrams

Let's first go back to the analysis of Hansmann (1996) in section 3, stating that "the theoretical optimal position to assign ownership is to that class of patrons for whom the problems of market contracting – that is the costs of market imperfections – are most severe" (p. 21). In that section we ended with the question whether the market circumstances for the shareholder are more severe than that of the other stakeholders. As based on the above approach with the general factors: **market power** and **market liquidity**, the general conclusion coming from figures 4.1 till 4.5 is that of all stakeholders, it is the shareholder and management[19] who hold the best risk / return pay-off positions in the market economy. Employees, government and suppliers all have lower expected returns and higher downside risks. For that reason it is concluded that because the market circumstances are not 'most severe' for shareholders in the modern economy, there is no valid theoretical economic argument to point towards shareholders alone to hold the ultimate risk and return of the modern stock market quoted company. Shareholders are primarily providers of risky capital, however that does not make them automatically the optimal stakeholder to control management. Depending on the character of the company, or the sector in which it performs, other stakeholders than shareholders may be optimally suited to own the residual rights. According to the Hansmann model, this could theoretically lower agency costs and therefore increase total wealth.

19 Financial creditors like bondholders and banks are not considers in this model.

The contribution of the above model is that it criticizes the hypothesis that shareholders are always the optimal owners of the residual claim as caused by their own 'severe' market position. The market position of other stakeholders is not *a priori* better. Despite the abstract character of the model, allowing for a lot of criticism on the exact relative positions of risk and return between different stakeholders, it is illustrative in the sense that from a strict economic efficiency perspective more stakeholders are candidates to own the residual claim of the firm. Monitoring management may improve when other stakeholders are involved financially. From an economic perspective it is crucial to find that governance model that minimises the corporation's transaction costs.

V. The 'Stakeholder Equity' Model

What are the consequences of a potential change from shareholder governance to stakeholder governance to the company's transaction costs? Theoretically it is argued above that the agency costs, as defined by the cost function in equation [1] in section 3, may decrease because of changing ownership of the residual risk (governance costs). Based on the assumptions of agency theory in general – that the economic agent primarily maximizes its own utility function – the diversification of interests in the sustainable economy reduces agency conflicts between stakeholders because their interests are more aligned. Equal distribution of the ownership rights in the company may lower agency conflicts and hence reduce transaction costs. On the other hand, it can also be argued that the very same portfolio of owners of a company increases governance costs because decision processes become more complex. This study does not answer that question. Additional research is needed to study the consequences of such a corporate governance change. In this paper the stakeholder equity model is primarily introduced to facilitate sustainable corporate finance. A stakeholder approach then is considered crucial for a sustainable economy.

1. The Stakeholder Model

Only few discussions in economics are as debated as the (perceived or real) controversy between shareholder and stakeholder value. For example, in a gentlemen's debate in the journal: Organization Science, Sundaram/Inkpen (2004) cynically accuse Freeman/Wicks/Parmar (2004) of confounding issues of 'value' (economic value) and 'values' (human values). Stakeholder theory begins with the assumption that values are necessarily and explicitly a part of doing business, and rejects the separation thesis. The separation thesis begins by assuming that ethics and economics can be neatly and sharply separated. Many proponents of the shareholder view of the firm distinguish between economic and ethical consequences and values. The sustainable market approach and sustainable finance tries to find the parallels between the stakeholder valuation of the firm and the shareholder valuation.

Also Szwajkowski (2000, pp. 382-384) makes a case that stakeholder management does not inherently conflict with sound conventional economics. They show that companies with good reputation ratings, as measured by the in the US widely used Fortune Reputation Survey (FRS), have low systematic risk (beta < 1) during recession periods and then higher betas (>1) in periods of growth. So there is a clear suggestion that high quality companies are less vulnerable to economic recessions than companies with a low reputation. Of crucial importance for the stakeholder view is to know that reputation ratings are arithmetic averages of eight attributes, five of which are non-financial (relating to employees, product quality, environmental quality etc.). In other words, the traditional shareholder view, in which stock prices reflect the value of the firm, does value reputations that depend on stakeholder relations.

Accepting stakeholder management, now the question is raised whether corporate governance changes can be used to attain more sustainable company policies. Jansson (2005) argues that it is not practical to give full property rights to more than one group of stakeholders. In some countries decision rights to employees[20] and creditors are already in place and the right of stakeholders are well protected legally, reducing the need to give them more formal decision rights. More specifically, Hillman/Keim/Luce (2001) empirically tested the hypothesis whether stakeholder representation on the board

20 Especially Germany has a reputation in accepting employees in the board of directors.

will be positively associated with stakeholder performance. Based on a data-set of 250 randomly chosen S & P 500 firms in 1995, their answer was a clear no. They presented a possible explanation by claiming that maybe the inclusion of community directors are useful in an attempt of the firm to gain legitimacy in the eyes of the public. The importance of the reputation of a company supports that hypothesis, but that question remained unanswered. In the next section, some changes are suggested in the corporate governance of the sustainable firm. The main goal of the proposal is to lower agency costs through lower ownership costs.

2. Stakeholder Equity

Let's first quote Fama/Jensen (1983):

> … whenever decision makers are not owners, decision management and decision control will be separated. Only when the decision maker is also the residual claimant – the person with legal rights to the profits of the enterprise once all the other claimants of the firm (for example, bondholders and employees) are paid – does it make sense to combine decision management and control.

To this background, it is proposed that a sustainable company emits a substantial amount of the equity of the company (at least 51%) to the major stakeholders of the company. The percentage of stocks held by internal stakeholders is called: stakeholders' equity (SE). This brings the legal claim of the companies' residual profits (including the potential losses), from the capital providers alone, to new shareholders who provide capital on the one hand but also have other stakes in the company (e.g. employees, environmental NGO's or suppliers). The purpose is to strengthen the interest in – and the responsibility of – different stakeholders beyond their conventional stakeholder interest. The old shareholders on the other hand still get the same reward for investments (although short term expected return – as caused by highly speculative projects- may diminish). The crucial difference is that capital providers lose ultimate control because ownership is now dispersed among the relevant stakeholders of the company. So, the stakeholder model does not reject the shareholder model. On the contrary, it builds completely on shareholders as ultimate claimants of the company results. The crucial difference though is with regard to the ownership of the shares.

In regular agency theory, the alignment of interests by providing the management with options and shares as part of their remuneration package is a well accepted tool to lower agency costs. Sustainable finance (see Soppe 2004) extends this traditional model to other stakeholders. In a sustainable financial system, agency relations cannot be restricted to shareholders and management alone. Other stakeholders, who also have big financial claims in terms of cash flows of the company, may be better motivated to manage the company efficiently. Suppose that the majority of a companies' cash flow is distributed to creditors, employees and shareholders (see figure 5 in Appendix 1 as an example). Then, shares could be sold to supplier organizations, labour unions, and the traditional shareholders. As a result all three stakeholders have a (financial) interest in the residual claim. This so-called stakeholder's equity (SE) should align the interests of the major stakeholders, and may therefore reduce the governance costs. Additionally, the government could propose a law to sell a minimum of shares (5%) to environmental NGO's to force these institutions to 'dirty their hands' (Wempe 1998) and make their financial result dependent on the performance of the local economy. All these measures align the financial interests of companies in an economy. In this way we create two types of shareholders: 1) 'pure' shareholders being the traditional (and strict financial) shareholder and 2) 'dual' shareholders implying other stakeholders that also own shares. Dual shareholdings encourage corporate democracy and aims at a more fair distribution of corporate results without lowering shareholder value.

VI. Conclusion

The basic conclusion of this paper is based on the analysis of Hansmann (1996), stating that "the theoretical optimal position to assign ownership is to that class of patrons for whom the problems of market contracting – that is the costs of market imperfections – are most severe" (p. 21). In the analysis, as presented in figures 4.1 until 4.5, the shareholder is not considered to be 'that class of optimal patrons of the investor owned company whose market position is most severe'. In fact, based on the factors market power and market liquidity as portrayed in figure 4.5, shareholders in general have a relative good risk/return position compared to other stakeholders of the company. For that reason it is concluded that there is no valid theoretical argument that it is the pure shareholder, in its role as capital provider, who should hold the ultimate risk and return of the modern stock market quoted company.

Therefore, using sustainable finance in its multi-attribute approach, it is proposed to reduce governance costs by introducing a corporate governance rule for the sustainable company. The rule proposes to sell a majority of the companies' equity to the major stakeholders of the company, as based on the distribution of the companies' cash flow. This part of the equity is called stakeholder equity (SE). The major goal of the stakeholder's equity is to prevent one specific stakeholder from being the only owner of the company's residual risk and return. The SE approach widens the interest and the responsibility of stakeholders from one specific interest group to a two dimensional interest and responsibility. Dual shareholders are stakeholders that also provide capital. For example, employees get a broader responsibility than just saving jobs if they have a financial stake as well, and suppliers get a more sophisticated financial interest and responsibility than maximising their own turnover. It is argued that the agency costs of the company may decrease because of: a) the alignment of interest between stakeholders and b) the creation of a more diversified portfolio of shareholders allowing for a lower risk premium. Sustainable corporate finance is considered to be the theoretical framework in which the company makes a free choice to select his own shareholders.

References

AGRAWAL, A., WALKLING, R. A.: "Executive careers and compensation surrounding takeover bids", *Journal of Finance*, 49 (1994), pp. 985-1014.

BLACK, F., SCHOLES, M. J.: "The pricing of options and corporate liabilities", *Journal of Political Economy*, 81 (3), (1973), pp. 637-654.

BLASI, J., KRUSE, D., BERNSTEIN, A.: In the company of owners: the truth about stock options (and why every employee should have them), New York (Basic Books) 2003.

BOADI, K.: "The concept of sustainable development: a critical analysis", Internet: *www.ises.abo.fi/kurser/nat/Ecolecon/Seminars/Kwasi_boadi_Sust_dev.pdf* (2002).

BOGLE, J. C.: *The battle for the sole of capitalism*, New Haven, CT (Yale University Press) 2005.

BRUNDTLAND, G. H.: *Our common future: The world commission on environment and development*, Oxford (Oxford University Press) 1987.

CLARKE, T.: "The stakeholder corporation: A business philosophy for the information age", *Long Range Planning*, 31 (1998), pp. 182-194.

DAVIES, P.: *Introduction to company law*, Oxford (Oxford University Press) 2002.

DONALDSON, T., PRESTON, L. E.: "The stakeholder theory of the corporation: Concepts, evidence and implications", *Academy of Management Review*, 20 (1995), pp. 65-91.

ENGELEN, E.: "A conceptual critique of shareholder ideology", *Economy and Society*, 31 (2002), pp. 391-413.

FAMA, E. F., JENSEN, M. C.: "Agency problems and residual claims", *Journal of Law and Economics*, 26, (1983), pp. 327-349.

FERGUS, A. H. T., ROWNEY, J. I. A.: "Sustainable Development: Lost meaning and Opportunity?", *Journal of Business Ethics*, 60 (2005), pp. 17-27.

FREEMAN, R. E.: *Strategic Management: A Stakeholders Approach*, Boston (Pitman) 1984.

FREEMAN, R. E., WICKS, A. C., PARMAR, B.: "Stakeholder theory and the 'Corporate objective revisited'", *Organization Science*, 15 (2004), pp. 364-369.

FRIEDMAN, A. L., MILES, S.: "Developing stakeholder theory", *Journal of Management Studies*, 39 (2002), pp. 1-21.

FRIEDMAN, M., FRIEDMAN, R.: *Free to choose*, San Diego (Harcourt inc.) 1980.

HALLOCK, D. E., SALAZAR, R. J., VENNEMAN, S.: "Demographic and attitudinal correlates of employee satisfaction with an ESOP", *British Journal of Management* 15, (2004), pp. 321-333.

HANSMANN, H.: *The ownership of enterprise*, Cambridge, MA (The Belknap Press of Harvard University Press) 1996.

HAWLEY, J. P., WILLIAMS, A. T.: *The rise of fiduciary capitalism; how institutional investors can make America more democratic*, Philadelphia, PA (University of Pennsylvania Press) 2000.

HAYEK, F. A.: *The meaning of competition*, in Hayek, Individualism and economic order, Chicago, IL (The University of Chicago Press) 1948.

HILLMAN, A. J., KEIM, G. D., LUCE, R. A.: "Board composition and stakeholder performance: Do stakeholder directors make the difference?", *Business & Society*, 40 (2001), pp. 295-314.

JANSSON, E.: "The stakeholder model: The influence of ownership and governance structures", *Journal of Business Ethics*, 56 (2005), pp. 1-13.

KAKABADSE, N. K., ROZUEL, C., DAVIES, L. L.: "Corporate social responsibility and stakeholder approach: a conceptual review", *International Journal of Business Governance and Ethics*, 1 (2005), pp. 277-302.

KRUSE, D.: "Research evidence on the prevalence and effects of employee ownership", *Journal of Employee Ownership Law and Finance*, 14 (2002), pp. 65-90.

LAZONICK, W., O'SULLIVAN, M.: "Maximizing Shareholders Value: A New Ideology for Corporate Governance", *Economy and Society*, 29 (2000), pp. 13-35.

LEE, I. B.: “Efficiency and ethics in the debate about shareholder primacy“, *Delaware Journal of Corporate Law*, 31 (2006), pp. 533-587.

LÉLÉ, S. M.: “Sustainable development: A Critical Review”, *World Development*, 19 (1991), pp. 607-621.

LINTNER, J.: “The valuation of risk assets and the selection of risky investments in stock portfolios and capital budgets”, *Review of Economics and Statistics*, 47 (1965), pp. 13-37.

MARGOLIS, J. D., WALSH, J. P.: “Misery loves companies: Rethinking social initiatives by business”, *Administrative Science Quarterly*, 48 (2003), pp. 268-305.

NEASS, A.: “Ecosophy T”, in: B. DEVALL, G. SESSIONS (Eds.): *Deep Ecology – Living as if Nature Mattered*, Layton/Utah (Gibbs M. Smith) 1985, pp. 225-228.

ORLITZKY, M., BENJAMIN, J. D.: “Corporate social performance and firm risk: a meta-analytic review”, *Business & Society*, 40 (2001), pp. 369-396.

SHARPE, W.: “Capital asset prices: a theory of market equilibrium under conditions of risk”, *Journal of Finance*, 19 (1964), pp. 425-42.

SOPPE, A. B. M.: “Sustainable corporate finance”, *Journal of Business Ethics*, 53 (2004), pp. 213-224.

STIGLITZ, J.: *Economics of the public sector*, New York (W. W. Norton & Company) 2000.

STOUT, L. A.: “Bad and Not-So-Bad Arguments For Shareholder Primacy”, *Southern California Law Review*, 75 (2002), pp. 1189-1209.

SUNDARAM, A. K., INKPEN, A. C.: “Stakeholder theory and 'the corporate objective revisited' : A reply”, *Organization Science*, 15 (2004), pp. 370-371.

SZWAJKOWSKI, E.: “Simplifying the principles of stakeholder management: The three most important principles”, *Business & Society*, 39 (2000), pp. 379-396.

WEMPE, J. F.: *Market and morality. Business ethics and the dirty and many hands dilemma*, dissertation Erasmus University Rotterdam1998.

WESTON, J. F., COPELAND, T. E.: *Managerial Finance*, Hinsdale, IL (Dryden Press) 1992.

ZINGALES, L.: “In search of new foundations”, *Journal of Finance*, 55 (2000), pp. 1623-1653.

Appendix 1

Example of stakeholder interest

This example is generated from the Philips Sustainability Report 2004. Figure 5 represents the stakeholder's distribution of the Philips cash flow in that year.

Figure 5: Distribution of economic benefits 2004

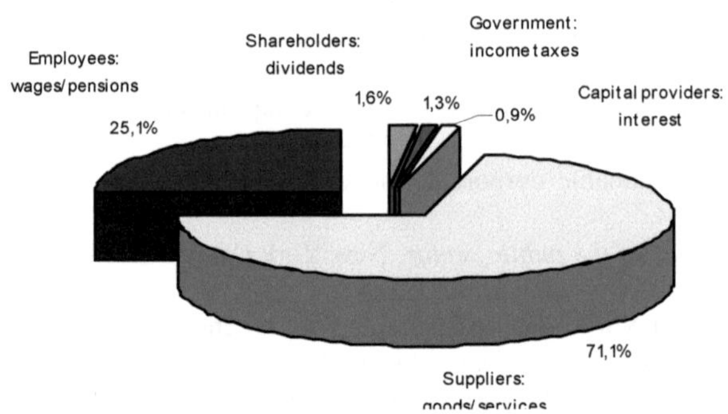

Source: Philips Sustainability Report (2004), p. 74.

The interesting signal from the cash flow distribution in Figure 5 is the substantial role of the suppliers: 71.1% of the total Philips cash flow in 2004 is redirected to this stakeholder. On the other extreme we find the stake of the capital providers (0.9%), the government (1.3%) and the dividends of the shareholders (1.6%). This example suggests that the success of Philips is relatively more important for the suppliers and the employees of the company than for the capital suppliers and the government. Concerning the shareholders it must be noted that only dividends are scheduled as the return on stocks. The majority of the expected return on stocks – a potential stock appreciation – is not reflected in this cash flow picture. Also should be noted that this example reflects the situation of one company in one sector in one single year. The long term distribution of stakes in a company is of course highly dependent on the sector and the timeframe in the economy.

Chapter 9

Theory, Practice, and Education: On the Role of Business Ethics for Management Education at Business Schools or Universities

MICHAELA HAASE

I. Introduction

Management scandals[1] have received much public attention throughout the last years. Opinion polls[2] demonstrate that managers' reputation has suffered

---

1 To refer to just one recent example in Germany, the *Financial Times Deutschland* headed "Bandenkriminaliät bei Siemens" (gang crime at Siemens) on Thursday, 11/23/2006.

from these events and that an increasing number of people are convinced that company leaders are not trustworthy. Despite this, corporate social responsibility has found its way into the executive suites of many businesses,[3] numerous indexes report on the ethical quality of firms' decisions,[4] and many managers participate in advanced training programs where they attempt to improve their understanding of the ethical aspects of management decisions and actions.

What can be concluded from the sketch above is that, at least in Germany, the level of trust in business leaders' decisions and activities is low. Nevertheless, activities like the participation of managers in vocational training programs, or measures like the adaptation of organizational structures in order to cope with ethical problems or requirements resulting from daily business, indicate that there is a "demand" for business ethics: Many managers are interested in improving their skills in this regard. As the ethical or moral dimensions of actions are usually not self-evident, this is not surprising. Even when managers intend to improve their decisions in an ethical respect, it is not easy to decide among the various options. Notwithstanding, management students frequently lack reflection on the ethical dimensions of their to-be decisions and actions throughout the course of their education. With respect to the "supply side," i. e., those places where many of today's managers are educated, the reaction to this "demand" has been rather weak so far, leading to a deficit or "education gap."

The paper does not provide a detailed analysis of this gap. One reason for it might be that many business schools or universities[5] (BS/U) do not have

---

2 A survey executed by TNS-Emnid by order of the World Economic Forum found that 70% of Germans believe that leaders of large groups are not to be trusted; 80% hold the opinion that the company leaders' influence or power is too great. Published in the Welt, 11/19/2006; http://www.welt.de:81/data/2004/11/19/362495.html?prx=1.

3 See, for example, the *Financial Times Deutschland*'s Sonderbeilagen (print supplements) on that issue.

4 See, for example, the journal's *Business Ethics* list of the 100 Best Corporate Citizens (http://www.thecro.com?q=be_100best) or the *Fortune Reputation Survey* (http://www.timeinc.net/fortune/datastore/index.html).

5 Concerning business schools, the paper mainly draws on discussions from the US and Australia. Particularly in the US, business schools began to teach "hard science" and analytical skills from the last century's sixties on. By that, business schools changed into "business universities" focused on the education of

enough resources at their disposal needed to enhance the number of fields of study within their walls. It could also be the case that they do not believe that a particular instruction in business ethics is really required, or they believe they should limit the impartment of knowledge to that stemming from their core disciplines, i. e., economics[6] and management studies. In primarily referring to the before-mentioned fields of study, the paper discusses assumed benefits of implementing business ethics at BS/U with respect to its contribution to the development and impartment of management knowledge, on the one hand, and the application of management knowledge by future managers, on the other.

Throughout the paper, "management practice" means the to-be practice of future managers, e. g., (universitary) further education of practising managers is not addressed. The paper assumes that management practice can be influenced by scientific[7] or scholarly knowledge; by that, it refers to a discussion among management scholars on issues of management education.[8] However, there are other kinds of knowledge also relevant for management practice. The particular knowledge which emerges as an outgrowth of management practice cannot be gained by means of management education. As Mintzberg/ Lampel (2001) have put it, "true managing" cannot be simulated in lecture halls. However, BS/U can provide their students with some of the cognitive prerequisites which will help them to meet the requirements later on.

The paper's arguments are developed from the following background: First, a theory of the firm is used that assumes co-production of a good or service by the supplier and the buyer of that good or service, as well as a competence-based perspective from which the term "core competence" is borrowed.[9] Second, the analysis of knowledge systems has resulted in the distinction between two modes of knowledge production (Mode 1 and Mode-2 knowledge). Third, from the history of economic and ethical thought, the view is taken that economics and ethics are intimately related by reference to

management. The paper does not deal with the fact that not all business schools in the world resemble these.

6 Economics holds a particular position among the disciplines relevant for management education (DONALDSON 2002, p. 97).

7 In the paper, "science" is understood as comprising both the natural and social sciences.

8 Cp. LEAVITT (1989); BAILEY/FORD (1996), PFEFFER/FONG (2002), MINTZBERG/ GOSLING (2002), GHOSHAL (2005).

9 Cp. GERSCH ET AL. (2005).

deliberative action. BS/U are interpreted as organizations which supply services[10] (education, degrees etc.[11]) for their clients (students[12]). By means of the competence-based perspective, the paper refers to the structure and nature of input required for the common production of the intended output. The paper argues that business ethics can contribute to the development of BS/U's core competences which, generally speaking, are seen in knowledge production (research) and knowledge impartment (education), as well as in the development of students' skills with respect to theory application, discernment, and moral reflection.

As the paper aims at precisely working out the consequences of distinctions, it often simplifies where things are complex and interwoven, or it refers to polarizing arguments where history meanwhile displays a rapprochement. The reason for this is purely methodical; it does not mean that the importance of, for example, historical developments that have led to "mixed cases" or scenarios is disputed.

II. Knowledge Sources of Management Practice

Knowledge sources are not independent of the ends which are to be achieved by them. Recently[13], educational goals have been the subject matter of dis-

10 It is not necessary to adopt this view on BS/U in order to follow the paper's line of argumentation. The approach, however, provides an adequate framework for the discussion because it assumes that both parties involved in the production of the good or service take a (more or less) active part throughout the process of production.

11 The output of management education at BS/U can be described from different perspectives. What is handed over, after the end of the transaction, is a sheet of paper documenting that the student has achieved a certain degree. From an ethical point of view, to-be managers graduating from a BS/U should be able to understand the ethical dimensions of decisions and actions.

12 Since the paper restricts its discussion to future managers who graduate from a BS/U, it can avoid a discussion of cases in which, for example, businesses pay for the further education of employees, i. e., cases where it is at least open to discussion who the client is, the student or the company.

13 From the point of view of ancient ethics, the relationship is, of course, not completely new.

cussions which are related to business ethics as, for example, "science education for citizenship and/or for social justice" (Zembylas 2005) or "education for sustainable development" (Reid et al. 2002). Although education has to adapt to evolution within society,[14] it is not required to follow each demand. The paper discusses demands on business ethics education that are independent of particular ends, like the two mentioned above. Its analysis deals with the understanding and accomplishment of management education in general. Among management scholars, there is a long discussion on the relations of theory and practice, in particular on the actual influence of BS/U's education on management practice.[15] Management scholars have pointed out that BS/U's education has either executed little (or no) influence on the minds of students (Pfeffer/Fong 2002), or a bad influence which, from an ethical point of view, leads to a change of social reality in the wrong direction (Donaldson 2002, Ghoshal 2005). The paper summarizes this debate among management scholars as follows: Theory-based knowledge can actually take effect on the mind-sets of to-be managers, but the consequences which they draw from theories, as well as the decisions and actions which rest on them, can take the wrong course.

The importance of theoretical knowledge notwithstanding, the education of future management requires that the degree holders will later on be able to solve problems which at first glance arise in businesses but not in theories. In this regard, the paper addresses the following questions: Do the theories taught at BS/U have an impact on students' minds? Is the knowledge embodied in theories and taught at BS/U relevant for future actions of to-be managers? Or are most of the educational efforts tantamount to "window dressing" (Pfeffer/Fong 2002) and the students mainly enroll "to get drunk" (ibid., p. 82)?

In order to find an answer to these questions, the paper first addresses the distinction between Mode 1 and Mode-2 knowledge, and then the manner in which theory application and management practice are related.

---

14 "A teaching programme is an 'artefact' that should be subject to permanent scrutiny, this being the only way in which it can adapt to evolutions in society" (SZYMKOWIAK 2003, p. 184).

15 For references see note 8.

1. Mode 1 and Mode-2 Knowledge

According to Gibbons et al. (1994), there are different kinds, institutions, and realms of knowledge production. Academic disciplines produce what they call Mode-1 knowledge.[16] It is a result of a high degree of academic division of labor and develops from a common point of view, approach, or theory. If academic researchers at BS/U undertake research in their fields of origin, i. e. economics, sociology, or psychology, they produce Mode-1 knowledge. Research is based on theory-guided identification of problems[17] and subsequent attempts by researchers to solve them. Mode-1 knowledge is related to particular "theoretical worlds" that express scholarly knowledge in a rather pure form. In this regard, researchers solve the problems identified by their theories; by that, they attempt to enlarge and refine the theories. Gibbons et al. (1994, p. 3) characterize Mode-1 knowledge production as being, at least for many, "identical with what is meant by science. Its cognitive and social norms determine what shall count as scientific problems, who shall be allowed to practise science and what constitutes good science."

Mode-1 knowledge production has been described and analyzed by historians of science like Thomas Kuhn. Mode-2 knowledge, in comparison, seems to be a relatively new phenomenon in the history of knowledge production.[18] It results from the emergence of such places of knowledge production as R&D departments, research institutes, think tanks, etc. where researchers from different scientific communities come together in order to work on particular problems which are located beyond disciplinary borders. Compared to disciplinary research which leads to Mode-1 knowledge, trans-

---

16 NOWOTNY ET AL. (2005) argue that in the meantime universities are also producing Mode-2 knowledge to an increasing degree. Because the paper wants to emphasize the differences and not the rapprochement, it mainly draws on the earlier work by GIBBONS ET AL. (1994).

17 This does not exclude scholars addressing problems which are put on the agenda by practitioners.

18 As GIBBONS ET AL. (1994, p. 6) state, "Mode 2 knowledge is thus created in a great variety of organizations and institutions, including multinational firms, network firms, small hi-tech firms based on a particular technology, government institutions, research universities, laboratories and institutes as well as national and international research programmes."

disciplinary research gives rise to Mode-2 knowledge.[19] Table 1 juxtaposes commonalities and differences between disciplinary and transdisciplinary research:

Disciplinary research	**Transdisciplinary research**
Knowledge is first produced and then applied. Problems are set and solved in a context governed by the interests of a specific community.	Knowledge is produced in the context of its application.
Research teams are interested in general unifying principles.[20] Knowledge tends to preserve its form.	Research teams are interested in particularities or idiographic attributes rather than in general unifying principles. Knowledge is transient.
Standards of quality control apply.	The development of particular criteria for assessing the results is required.
The produced knowledge is rather homogeneous.	The produced knowledge is rather heterogeneous.
Research teams look for additional problems or more specific solutions after a problem is defined or solved.	Research teams dissolve after a problem is defined or solved.
Kuhn's analysis of what he calls normal science applies.	The development of new theoretical structures, research methods, and models of practice might be required. The relationship between research team and approach is rather loose.

Table 1

Mode-1 knowledge is a source not only for scholars of new insights or views; it can change practitioners' views on social reality, too. As regards management education at BS/U, one can expect that students are busy with the learning of disciplinary conceptual frameworks, problems, and problem solutions. They are thus mainly involved in Mode-1 thinking. Because of this, it is rather disciplinary than interdisciplinary knowledge which gains influence on

19 Interdisciplinary research is located between disciplinary and transdisciplinary research. Cp. NOWOTNY ET AL. (2005, p. 117).

20 This depends, of course, on the subject matter and the degree to which a researcher or community is disposed to assume that unifying principles can describe her or its field of study. An interest in particularities or idiographic attributes is in no way excluded by that.

their mind sets. By means of their theoretical education, they are provided with particular "glasses" which help them to reduce the complexity of social reality. Besides knowledge, there are other entities located within the social domain (which can be distinguished from the individual level of analysis) like ideology, value judgments, or morality. These entities are also able to reduce the complexity of social reality, but their influence on decisions and actions is rather seldomly systematically dealt with at BS/U. In this section, the paper mainly refers to the knowledge dimension; in section III it adds the value and ideology dimensions.

The worth of academic education of to-be managers would be questionable if they were later unable to connect the theoretical worlds and their *conceptions of social reality*,[21] or, as Hambrick (1994, p. 15) has put it, "worlds of scholarship and practice." The academically educated manager should prove to be able to match theory-based descriptions of a problem and conceptualizations which arise from practice.

The connection between both types of "worlds" is made up by knowledge. Social reality is not a contrast to theory inasmuch as it is unaffected by theory. In fact, social reality is indirectly shaped by multiple theories which people have in mind since they were introduced to them at school, college, or university.[22] The difference between conceptualizations of social reality which have their origin in everyday knowledge and "theoretical worlds" introduced by scholarly theories is based on the exclusivity of knowledge embodied by present-day theories. The main reason for this exclusivity is that scholarly communities dispose of the theories which embody knowledge: The closer this knowledge is to the frontiers of research, the less likely that it has passed through steps of justification assumed as required by a community, and the smaller the chance that it will already inform a broader public at BS/U and beyond.

Mode-1 knowledge is not the only kind of knowledge of importance for future managers. Activities within social reality, as well as learning processes

21 It is not possible to directly match theory and reality. Thus, independent of how social reality is constructed according to the one or the other social-theoretical approach, one can only match conceptualizations of social reality of first order, on the one hand, and of second order, on the other (SCHUTZ 1982).

22 As MACHAN/CHESHER (2002, p. XXI) point out, "apart from the highly technical and developed levels of understanding, there is also common sense. We are all commonsense physicists, chemists, sociologists, economists, moral philosophers, and political theorists – at least amateurs in these areas of concern."

based thereon, are a source of "practice-based knowledge" (Clegg/Ross-Smith 2003, p. 87[23]). Gibbons et al. (1994, p. 6) do not subsume activities related to management under the term "Mode-2 knowledge". There are, however, intersections of the characterizations of Mode-2 knowledge, as given by Gibbons et al. (1994), and "practice-based knowledge," as given by management scholars like Clegg/Ross-Smith (2003) or Mintzberg/Lampel (2001). Accordingly, Hargreaves (1999) and McIntyre (2005) have already discussed a gap between educational research and educational practice in terms of the distinction between Mode 1 and Mode-2 knowledge. As regards Mode-2 knowledge, the following (incomplete) list of attributes draws on Gibbons et al. (1994). In comparison to Mode 1, Mode-2 knowledge is characterized by

- operation within a context of application;
- discovery that occurs in the fields where knowledge is developed for, and put to, use;
- problems that are not set within a disciplinary framework;
- a constant flow back and forth between the fundamental and the applied;
- knowledge production that does not take place within university structures;
- knowledge production that is more socially accountable;
- a wide range of criteria in judging quality control; and
- knowledge production that takes place according to the producer's own set of cognitive and social norms.

Compared to that, practice-based knowledge

- is based on the interaction and communication among people influenced by different backgrounds in education, knowledge, and experience;
- results from the activity of managing, not from studying it; and
- develops from the identification of problems which have their reason, not in theory, but in the course of business or management activities and managers' subsequent attempts to solve these problems as well as the learning processes resulting from this.

---

23 CLEGG/ROSS-SMITH (2003, p. 87) do not refer to the distinction between Mode 1 and Mode-2 knowledge. They criticize that management knowledge has separated "itself sufficiently from mundane practice and assume some of the characteristics of an abstracted science."

In the following, the paper subsumes practice-based knowledge under the more general heading "Mode-2 knowledge." Practice-based knowledge, in the sense of knowledge that has its origin in the practice of management, is *non-scholarly* Mode-2 knowledge.

As Gibbons et al. (1994 et al., p. 14) have pointed out, Mode 1 and Mode-2 knowledge are different but nevertheless related: (Scholarly) Mode-2 knowledge is "an outgrowth" of Mode-1 knowledge; "Mode 2 is not supplanting but rather supplementing Mode 1" (ibid.). Mode-1 knowledge and non-scholarly Mode-2 knowledge are not contrary to each other either: Managers need Mode-1 knowledge in order to identify or "find" a problem from the perspective of a theory, and they need practice-based knowledge to correctly identify the problems of the business. However, that a manager's mind set has a stake in both of the worlds mentioned above does not yet sufficiently enable him to solve a business' problems. For that purpose, a particular kind of knowledge is required – knowledge related to previous theory applications and the experiences resulting from them. In ethics, in particular in Aristotelian ethics, this is paralleled by the knowledge and "application" of both (general) principles and practical wisdom: "we can apply principles but must be wise about it" (Hartman 2006, p. 76).

2. Theory Application and Management Practice

According to Stenhouse (1981, p. 105), there are two kinds of theory applications: First, predictions which provide individuals with information about the context of action; and second, predictions which, by application of general laws, provide information about the outcomes of specific acts. The first kind of prediction is directed at the framework of actions; it tells us, for example, that the sun will rise tomorrow as it has risen today or that in an economy there are rules which prevent or induce particular actions. The second kind of prediction is based in end-means relations described by causal laws (or what is held for that). If translated into the language of economists, the first kind of prediction aims at conditions of action and the second at concrete options of action. Donaldson (2002, p. 103) emphasizes the second type in the conclusions of his discussion of the main management theories' usefulness for management education: "The curriculum of management education should draw upon knowledge that offers theoretical models of a kind that managers can use, causal models in which the causes are variables that managers can influence (...) and the effects are variables that managers care about (...)." [24]

Both Stenhouse and Donaldson's characterizations do not distinguish between a theory application undertaken by a scholar and one undertaken by a practitioner. In either case, specialized knowledge is required that connects knowledge embodied in theories and knowledge necessary to fit the concrete circumstances of application. For this reason, fields of study within scholarly communities have developed called "applied sciences" or "policies." As Wagner/Wiegard (2002) have pointed out, theory application and, by that, the accomplishment of predictions or policies which are directed at a change of social reality require individuals endowed with particular skills not widespread even within scholarly communities. In economics, under the heading of "economic policy," the combination of rather general knowledge, related to a particular theory, and more concrete knowledge, related to the description of a current situation or problem, has led to the development of a class of specialized knowledge workers.

Wagner/Wiegard (2002) further argue that the successful execution of a theory application requires an "Actus der Urteilkraft" (act of discernment) which – in a kind of double-loop learning – is also informed by training and experience (Bailey/Ford 1996, p. 10). According to Kant, "Urteilskraft" (discernment) is required in order to evaluate the moral rightness or reasonableness of decisions. "Discernment" is as well an expression of the special, often idiosyncratic knowledge required for the mediation of general, abstract theories, on the one hand, and concrete, situation-specific descriptions by which the subject matters of applications are characterized, on the other.

Principally, if discernment is required for economic policy, then it is also required for practitioners who intend to decide and act on the basis of theoretical knowledge. The ability to weave together and to make use of different kinds of knowledge characterizes theory applications by academia as well as by non-academia. This ability can be learned, at least in part, by the participation of students in BS/U's research activities (where they can achieve an understanding of a theory and the problems for which it is thought to be the solution), and in practical studies (where they can learn how the problems identified by a theory are interpreted in organizations or businesses). Both scholars and managers have to deal with the fact that the application of theo-

24 As BACON (1902, p. 11) has put it: "Knowledge and power are synonymous, since the ignorance of the cause frustrates the effect ..."

ries requires an understanding of specific contexts and situations to which the respective theory is applied. For this reason, the ability to apply scientific knowledge is not simply an epiphenomenon of the impartment of theoretical knowledge and analytical techniques. Thus, BS/U which are only engaged in the impartment of theoretical knowledge, but do not address the ability of to-be managers to apply that knowledge, deliver only half the good.

The above distinction between Mode 1 and Mode-2 knowledge (or practice-based knowledge) gives BS/U reason to reflect again on the importance of "practice" in their educational programs. As management scholars have argued, it is not possible, at least not to a degree which comes sufficiently close to "true management," to simulate the production and application of practice-based knowledge within the walls of BS/U. According to Mintzberg, "Management is, above all, a practice, where art, science, and craft meet" (Mintzberg quoted by Reingold 2000, p. 290). No wonder then that this complex socio-cognitive endeavor cannot, as Mintzberg/Lampel (2001) have put it, be replicated in the classroom: If Gibbons' et al. (1994) characterization of Mode-2 knowledge (cp. the list in section II.1) applies to practice-based management knowledge, then BS/U cannot instruct future managers in that regard.

Case studies are helpful in improving the students' ability to recognize problems[25] and find solutions to them (at BS/U, mainly from the theoretical perspective to which the students are introduced), but they cannot substitute for management experiences that, for example, result from endeavors to enforce such solutions. Hartman (2006, p. 77), who advocates the use of case studies particularly in business ethics education, emphasizes that case studies sharpen the moral imagination like experiences do, that they are a basis of analysis, and thus they can bring forward the process of moral maturation. The paper agrees on the importance of the case method for business ethics education. However, by means of the case method, a BS/U cannot contribute to the development of what is called in Aristotelian terms *practical wisdom*.

What BS/U can do, of course, is extend the time students have to spend with practical studies in order to provide students with an enhanced opportunity to make "true management experiences." From an economic point of view, then, "cannot" is synonymous with "too expensive." To sum up: With

25 See PORTER/MCKIBBIN (1988), who criticize that there is insufficient emphasis on problem finding in contrast to problem solving. Problem finding by students can only occur if they are familiar with pertinent Mode-1 knowledge.

one eye on its core competences and the other on the costs, any BS/U has to decide how much importance it will ascribe to practice-related knowledge compared to theoretical knowledge, and how much – in terms of time and other resources – this will be allowed to cost. Most BS/U will probably have to limit their activities to the provision of access to practical studies for students and the subsequent reflection on the experiences resulting from them. Because BS/U cannot simulate "true managing" or can only substitute for it to a limited degree by "second-hand" experience, they should prefer to concentrate on their core competences, which can be seen in the development of their students' ability to understand and apply (social-) scientific knowledge. Table 2 adds particular competences based on the implementation of business ethics to the characterization above.

An educational program based on Mode-1 knowledge as main pillar does not speak for a supersession of scholarly Mode 1 by *scholarly* Mode-2 knowledge[26], because scholarly Mode 2 is not tantamount to Mode-2 knowledge resulting from "true managing." The concept of scholarly Mode-2 knowledge can help to better understand the nature of management studies (or science), as well as of business ethics, which is the subject of the subsequent section.

III. Business Ethics and the Study of Businesses: A Formal View

In the following, the distinction between Mode 1 and Mode-2 knowledge is applied to a delineation of the main characteristics of business ethics, as they are seen from the perspective of this paper. The paper does not aim at providing a complete and detailed description of today's business ethics; it is rather a description distorted by the use of certain "lenses" which are known in advance to be crooked in a specific manner. As a consequence, the picture that emerges from the use of these lenses does not provide a "true" image of the depicted entity. Since any description presupposes the use of "lenses" or pre-adjustments, there is, of course, no true image that could be drawn.

26 Scholarly Mode-2 knowledge, i. e., inter- to transdisciplinary knowledge is of remarkable importance for both management studies and business ethics.

As sketched in the paragraph below, the emergence of business ethics is an outgrowth of an increasing academic division of labor that has led to separated Mode-1 knowledge productions in fields of study which earlier were connected. Business ethics is interpreted as an attempt to reintegrate the divided strands of economics and ethics. With respect to the examples below (economics ethics), this has already led to business ethics approaches which produce Mode-1 knowledge.

1. Gains and Losses from Academic Division of Labor

With the development of different disciplines from philosophy, economics has become separated from ethics. Then, because of the development of other disciplines beyond economics, a further increase of the number of theories and research areas has taken place. These theories rest on a diversity of principles, ideas, and methods of which they make use in order to analyze social reality.

The ongoing division of labor among the separated disciplines has given rise to remarkable net gains in terms of knowledge. This development, however, has not only led to gains, but also to losses: Gains of specialization expressed by increasingly sophisticated theories are associated with losses following the increase of the number of disciplines (and herewith the number of theories and problems identified by them). As a start, knowledge increases by specialization. Losses can arise if the identification of or solutions to problems presuppose interdisciplinary research or applications of theories from different disciplines which are not undertaken (or at least not in a sufficient or adequate manner).[27] One palpable example for an issue or a realm of problems which requires an integration of analyses having their origin in disciplines which are currently separated is research on the course of the globalization process: it has to consider, for example, comparative cost advantages and specialization, on the one hand, and justice, or misuse of power, on the other (see Ehret et al. 2007). A second example is the modelling of the economic actor as "a faceless economic calculator, losing almost all personality" (Danner 2002, p. 150). In the analysis of concrete actions (Danner 2002, p.

27 BAILEY/FORD (1996, p. 8) describe how "knowledge that is generated (at modern business schools, M. H.) has become increasingly technical and sequestered; so much that a professor in one department can need years of training to understand the research of an colleague in another department."

154), this has been interpreted in terms of a disconnection of moral and economic values, or a disconnection of the moral or social dimensions of human behavior, which has taken place in economics after Adam Smith (De-Juan/ Monsalve 2006, Wagner 2001).[28]

Regarding the examples above, knowledge losses arise from a division of labor concerning the analysis of activities which are of the same type, namely, scholarly knowledge production. The potential remedy for this kind of knowledge loss is interdisciplinary research. In the beginning of or throughout the process of interdisciplinary work, the prevalent separation of disciplines conjoined with the subsequent development of different theories, methods, conventions etc. has to be partially reversed. This endeavor will not be undertaken without sufficient reason because of the costs which, of course, also arise from interdisciplinary research. In order to outweigh these costs, there must be a kind of promise related to interdisciplinary research: the promise of solving an important problem or of achieving scientific progress by means of the pursuit of interdisciplinary research. Despite the promises of interdisciplinary research, it does not aim at rolling back the degree of specialization. Nevertheless, interdisciplinary research can be institutionalized over time and, by that, begin to assume features of transdisciplinary research (Nowotny et al. 2005, p. 117).

Besides interdisciplinary research, the losses which arise from division of labor can be coped with by a systematic re-integration of fields of study as has taken place, for example, in economic ethics (Koslowski 1998, Homann/ Suchanek 1987) or in some strands of socio-economics (Wagner 2001, Samuels 1989). Systematic re-integration aims at the implementation of an enduring field of study that gives rise to the development of new ethical-economic theories which surmount the separation of economics and ethics. For example, Machan/Chesher's (2002) combination of a neo-Aristotelian approach and Austrian economics refers to two main pillars of business ethics: individual ethics and order ethics. As with other approaches within economic ethics, this one embodies both lines of argument developed throughout this paper: free will of economic actors, actors' ability to critically reflect on issues of interest, and (re-) integration of economics and ethics.

From this paper's perspective, business ethics is a composed discipline (or field of study) which has its main sources in both economics and ethics.

28 SMITH'S "Wealth of Nations" and "Theory of Moral Sentiments" are an expression of this decomposition.

Business ethics is thus a field of study dealing with ethical-economic problems, problems which have their origin in economics *and* ethics. In other words: business ethics is more than a cooperation between economics and ethics which recognizes both disciplines as being independent and equally important (Enderle 1996, p. 47); for this paper's sake, this view is not wrong but only a starting point. In order to institutionalize itself as an academic discipline, business ethics has to become more than just a cooperation between two disciplines; it has to transcend them. Business ethics (as an academic field of study) is thus seen as an intended, long-term coproduction of knowledge within a field of study to which economics and ethics have primarily contributed but which allows – if not demands – its own theory development and subsequent application. At the first glance, the business-ethics concept is thus interpreted very narrowly, excluding organizational, behavioral, cultural and political aspects. At the second glance, however, one can see organizational and behavioral aspects within economics.[29] Whereas political and cultural aspects are not on the main agenda of most economic approaches,[30] they can gain influence in the case of application. In addition, as management studies (with economics as its core discipline) is involved in scholarly Mode-2 knowledge production, the problems dealt with can have their origin not necessarily in economics, but also in sociology or psychology (cp. section III.2).

Business ethics is not homogeneous as a field of study; it can refer to different approaches in ethics and economics as well. Because the paper does not aim at delving into the similarities and varieties of those approaches, it takes what it calls a formal stance. By use of the term "composition," nothing is said about the particular shape or form of the composition: According to this paper, "composition" means either that economics and ethics are arranged at the same level, or that one party is subordinated to the other one. Even economic ethicists disagree on this issue.[31]

29 See, for example, Oliver Williamson's work in the organizational economics. For the matter of behavioral economics, cp. BRUNI/SUGDEN (2007) or JOLLS (2007).

30 For works on the intersection of law and economics, see JOLLS (2007) or VERMONT (1999).

31 HOMANN/SUCHANEK (1987) distinguish the conviction that ethical norms are justifiable by economics from the view that it is the task of ethics alone to justify ethical norms (model of application of ethics to economics); they argue against the application model. Compared to that, MACHAN/CHESHER (2002) advocate the view, that business ethics is a subfield of philosophy.

Ethics is a part of philosophy which can itself be more or less "empirically informed" (Musschenga 2004). Normative ethics can generate an interest in getting empirically informed and, for this reason, look for opportunities to collaborate with empirical disciplines. Empirically informed ethics are normative ethics that, with respect to their application, consider contextual, historic, or pragmatic aspects. Contextually and historically informed ethics can take into account, for example, the Western coining of many of their ideas and convictions.[32] The amount and kind of empirical information assumed as required by ethicists can change from problem to problem. In any case, the process of empirical information gathering and processing is limited (it stops if the aspired "level of satisfaction" is achieved), and the main theories of ethics will probably not change after they have been run through such a process of "information-loading." Such "empirically informed ethics" seem to be an instance of what is called *application model* (cp. Note 31). Rather than the application model, an "equal-status" model of business ethics can lead to conjoint theory developments, that is, theories which go beyond both current ethics and economics.

There is another source of losses which arise if knowledge of different origins ought to be combined but is not; but they are not the consequence of a scholarly division of labor. Typically, this is the case if there are problems the solutions to which require the combination of knowledge based on both academic research and knowledge resulting from social practice.[33] Examples are provided by scholarly analyses of management problems and their subsequent translation into management practice, or by the relationship of educational research and educational practice.[34]

32 One striking example is the common reference to a reason-based religion (Vernunftreligion) in Europe.

33 Academic knowledge production can also be interpreted as a kind of social practice, but at this point, the distinction between diverse realms of social practice is in the foreground.

34 WHELDALL (2005, p. 573), in his introduction into a special issue of *Educational Psychology*, bemoans „that much educational contemporary research has little relevance to, or has little potential to inform, educational practice."

2. Interrelations Between Management Studies and Business Ethics

Management studies and business ethics – their subject matter as well as their conceptualizations – "overlap" in a threefold manner: First, as emphasized by both ethics and economics, because of the free will of those who are prepared for decision-making within and for organizations (businesses). A common source of economics and ethics is the idea of intentional or deliberate action (cp. Ghoshal 2005, p. 77,[35] Wyller 2002, Koslowski 1998). This idea assumes actors who base their decisions on knowledge, values, beliefs, religion, or ideologies[36] which serve as the foundation for the formation of their intentions.[37] The impact of these factors will vary depending on the actors' socialization, education, and experiences. At the cost of other bases of beliefs and convictions like religion or ideology, the paper mainly refers to knowledge. This does not mean that religion or ideology are not important; it follows rather from the fact that religion or ideology are usually not taught at BS/U, at least not with the aim of making students believe in or advocate it.

Second, there is an overlap by reason of the ethical nature of the *activities* executed within and for both organizations and markets.[38] Examples for such ascriptions of an inherent ethical nature to economics can be detected in the evaluation of economic activities as fundamentally "right" or "wrong." Advocates of the first position are Milton Friedman, according to whom it is the whole social responsibility of a firm or manager to make a profit, or Machan/Chesher (2002) who maintain that there is something morally right about

35 GHOSHAL (2005, p. 77) is right in stating that "ethics is inseparable from human intentionality" but erroneously seems to believe that this does not apply to economics.

36 This is, of course, not a complete list of all factors which can be of importance for decision-making. The list mainly refers to factors related to cognition and neglects the influence of emotional factors as well as the interaction of cognitive and emotional factors.

37 The assumption of a free will as a presupposition of the freedom to deliberate on decisions and act accordingly is not worked out in all economic theories. The conceptualization of individual action on the basis of individuals who are able to reflect on their preferences and decisions (KOSLOWSKI 1998, pp. 69 f.) is opposed to that expressed in the highly abstract Walrasian equilibrium model.

38 The paper does insofar agree with business ethics conceptions that are "oriented fundamentally towards *doing – decision making and taking action in business* (…)" (ENDERLE 1996, p. 46; italics in the original).

business.[39] According to them, individuals arrive at conclusions on the grounds of personal prudence[40] and act on the basis of their right to possess private property (as a concrete expression of individual liberty which is guaranteed as part of the institutional order).

Third, the overlap exists because of the ethical dimensions of *economic* concepts and theories which are applied to the analysis of businesses. Market theories as well as organization theories are based on assumptions which express evaluations or can be evaluated from an ethical point of view. A reflection on the value dimensions of the knowledge imparted to future managers throughout their academic education is of an ethical nature, too.

The close relationship of business ethics and economics notwithstanding, economics is by far not the only social science duly qualified or responsible for the study of businesses. In this regard, business ethics (with economics as the main source) is similar to management studies whose scholars stem from different disciplines (economics, sociology, psychology, cp. Ghoshal 2005, p. 82, Clegg/Ross-Smith 2003, p. 85) and analyze management problems from the perspectives of their theories or approaches (Bailey/Ford 1996, p. 8).[41] Because management education is not only based on economics, business ethics education at BS/U will be confronted with non-economic theories, including specified problems or points of view. In order to deal adequately with, for example, issues of ethical leadership or value communication within a business, business ethics can become involved in common research with psychology or organization theory. It is thus involved in what is called by Gibbons et al. (1994) Mode-2 knowledge production.

Today, as an academic field of study, business ethics is mainly anchored in departments of economics and business administration at BS/U. As in

---

39 MACHAN/CHESHER (2002, p. 16) bemoan "that many believe that businesses gain moral credit solely from such pro bono work, a perspective not widely embraced concerning the moral work of other professions such as medicine, education, or science."

40 The availability of prudence, however, is nothing taken for granted by MACHAN/CHESHER (2002, p. xx): "People are far from automatically prudent and are, indeed, very often reckless, inattentive, and lacking in industriousness and ambition."

41 OTTEWILL/MACFARLANE (2002, p. 11) argue that "the study of business is already an example of mode 2 knowledge produced within a broader social and economic 'context of application' compared to traditional, disciplinary, mode 1 knowledge." Compare however BAILEY/FORD'S (1996, p. 8) appraisal as quoted in note 27.

other parts of the Western world, the reputation, and subsequently, the financial as well as personal resources of BS/U are related to their success in (social-) scientific research. In the US, business schools achieved academic respectability and legitimacy by becoming social-scientific departments in the nineteen sixties (Pfeffer/Fong 2002, Bailey/Ford 1996). Though BS/U's educational programs have been criticized for a long time, this has not changed the anchoring of their research programs within the social sciences. Strength in research is also of importance for a discipline's ability to provide doctoral programs and thereby to attract and educate its offspring. Consequently, it cannot be assumed that business ethics' influence at BS/U can increase without participation in research there.[42]

It does not seem to be an exaggeration to state that business ethics research is demanding since, first, the business ethicist needs to possess a profound knowledge of ethics.[43] Second, the business ethicist needs an in-depth knowledge of economics, theories as well as applications (including its applications to management studies). Third, since business ethics research might not be adequately executed by the exclusive use of business ethics theories, the business ethicist needs to be able to engage in interdisciplinary research, too.

3. Core Competences of Business Schools and Their Amendment by Business Ethics

At a BS/U, business ethics has to bring about the ethical dimensions of the problems management studies and economics deal with (including the above-mentioned Mode-2 dimensions). For this purpose, business ethics has to become informed about the ethical dimensions of the problems singled out by

42 A presupposition of business ethics' research activity is that it is an independent field of study which can give rise to its own problems as, for example, the relation of profitability and social responsibility, or wealth production and distribution.

43 Bowie (2000, p. 17), who reports from the US that philosophers rarely take courses in business ethics, believes that business ethics' future offspring will be rather educated at business schools than in philosophy departments. If this tendency consolidates and endures not only in the US, then particular efforts are required in order to maintain the philosophical education of business ethics' offspring.

economics and management studies. Table 2 delineates outcomes of the deployment or activation of BS/U's core competences as assumed by the paper. It also states what, from its point of view, can be achieved by the implementation of business ethics as a field of study at BS/U. As addressed in more detail below, BS/U's core competences are potentiated and extended by the implementation of business ethics, which is seen as the source of what is called below *BE competences*. With respect to BE competences, the paper distinguishes between competences which are related to theoretical knowledge, and competences which are related to the moral development of personality or character.

The answer to the question if and to what degree BS/U can promote or build character is, presupposing an adequate definition of "character," partially an empirical one. If the concept of character could be derived from an empirical theory and related to empirical information in adequate manner, then, in their endeavor to develop their students' characters, BS/U could make use of it. At this time, it seems that "character" is a concept of ethics, in particular of virtue ethics, that has no or no sufficiently accepted counterpart in empirical theories.[44] From this situation, however, the paper does not draw the conclusion that it does not make sense at all to speak about character or personality development in business ethics education. It rather means that, from the perspective of empirical theories like social psychology (not necessarily from that of ethics), the meaning of concepts like "character" or "personality" is not (fully) understood or that these concepts cannot be derived from them. Not enough knowledge seems to be currently available to take a well-informed stance on this issue.[45]

Acting from an ethical perspective, as well as the search process directed at finding possible solutions to ethical problems are both guided by the individual, particularly by the individual's knowledge, experience, belief, and emotions. A BS/U that only addresses the students' cognitive abilities and

---

44 According to HARMAN (2003, p. 92), "the ordinary conception of a character or personality trait is of a relatively broad-based disposition to respond in the relevant way with acts of the corresponding sort. (…) Now, the evidence indicates that people may differ in certain relatively narrow traits but do not have broad and stable dispositions corresponding to the sorts of character and personality traits we normally suppose that people have."

45 HARTMAN'S (2006) Aristotelian answer to this question is rather conceptual in nature. Cp. also KLIMOWSKI (2006) on this issue.

neglects their personal, emotional, and social development, as well as the related ethical aspects, will probably not tap its full potential.

Core competences of BS/U
are the source of the impartment of theoretical knowledge as well as the development of analytical and practical skills directed at students' ability to • understand "worlds of theory," their advantages as well as their limitations • understand the specific contributions of different theories • find problems based on theories • apply theoretical knowledge in order to cope with problems • match theoretical worlds and conceptualizations of social reality
BE competences (related to theoretical knowledge)
• Identification of value dimensions and ideologies related to theories • Improvement or development of the ability to make ethically informed decisions • Reflection not only on the means but also on the ends of end-means relations • Knowledge about ethical principles, procedures and values • Ability to provide ethical salient descriptions of particular situations • Ability to match ethical principles with particular situations
BE competences (related to character)
• Ability or disposition to undertake ethical choices • Ability to understand and arrange own values • Ability to develop a coherent moral system

Table 2

Table 2 presents the subject matter in a mainly formal manner. As regards *content*, the formal perspective needs a supplement like the walls and girders of an otherwise uncompleted building need further equipment and furnishing in order to become a place to work or live in. The formal dimension itemized above has thus to be completed by the concrete fields of study or by the approaches which business ethics scholars or communities use. This paper is mainly interested in the "walls" and "girders;" it thus neglects the "equipment."

a) Business Ethics Competences Related to Theoretical Knowledge

Business ethics can play multiple roles in the process of intermediation between theoretical worlds and social reality: First, business ethics pays attention to theories on the basis of which a problem is identifiable and analyzable. Second, business ethics is helpful in the process of problem identification and solution insofar as it, from an ethical point of view, directs attention to the desirability of a solution or the means to achieve it: Whereas the applied theory states that an *x* is a solution to a *y*, business ethics encourages the decider to bear in mind the values related (or relatable) to the ends strived for or the ethical consequences to be expected from an action. By this, business ethics is not seen as an immediate source for the rightness or wrongness of a decision or action; furthermore, it is a framework helpful for the reflection on and evaluation of ethical relevant matters. Third, business ethics can itself provide such problem-solving theories. Fourth, even though principles (such as, for example, the categorical imperative) are not an exclusive source of ethical decisions and actions, without taking them into consideration one will run into the danger of overvaluing aspects related to particular situations. The same holds true for values in the sense of second-order desires (Frankfurt 1981) or the *ethical good*: In order to develop the faculty to provide ethically relevant or salient descriptions of particular situations (Hartman 2006, p. 74), students at BS/U have particularly to match the economic and the ethical good. Fifth, principles can be applied to particular situations, but in order to be successful, the individual has to make sure that principle and (the description of a) situation match each other. As Enderle (1996, p. 49) has pointed out, knowledge of principles is not sufficient for ethical decision making and acting: "ethics does not give security once and for all but it makes reflection inevitable by weighing concrete and general considerations against each other and by looking for possible solutions of acting from an ethical perspective."

b) Business Ethics Competences Related to Character

In virtue ethics, "character" is defined along the lines issued by Aristotle (Solomon 2003, p. 50). Hartman (2006, p. 69) defines "character as one's standard pattern of thought and action with respect to one's own and others' well-being and other concerns and commitments." By means of the term "character," the paper thus refers to mind sets of individuals, their way of thinking and their dispositions of acting. Particularly virtue ethicists (for references see Hartman 2006, p. 68) have emphasized that the "mere knowledge of principles" (ibid.) will not suffice to become an ethical person, whereas knowledge and disposition will. But there is no reason to assume that character alone will suffice in order to predict the behavior of the ethical person in all circumstances.[46]

As mentioned above, it is the competence of business ethics to attract attention to the ethical dimensions of both economic activities and theories. Management education should enable students to be more conscious of ideologies or values that have an impact on scientific theories (Hoover 2003). This is not only the subject matter of knowledge based on both theoretical and meta-theoretical reflection. A BS/U should, at least to some degree, take responsibility for the manner in which its students go through these processes of reflection and how they are assumed to act on its basis. With respect to the advantages of pluralism in economics, Barone (1991) refers to Perry's different-level model of intellectual growth defined in terms of knowledge, values, and personal identity. According to Perry's model, the belief in absolute knowledge determined by authorities belongs to the lowest level of development. This is followed by knowledge tied to different perspectives and values.[47] Business ethics strengthens the position of critical reflection on activities insofar as it provides concrete reasons for it and adds content to it. This reflection can refer to different subjects, such as, for example, the ends intended to accomplish by theory applications, or practical activities, the moral rightness of particular decisions and their respective consequences, the conception of the self which a person has to develop, etc.[48]

As with any other discipline, ethics is not a source of secure and definitely right choices. The reasons which can guide ethical choices have thus to be made as explicit as those which guide any other choice. Especially in the Western world, morally unequivocal instances that might function as secure bases of recognition and decision have diminished or no longer exist (this

46 As SOLOMON (2003, p. 45) has pointed out, "character is never fully formed and settled. It is always vulnerable to circumstances and trauma. (…) People (…) respond in interesting and sometimes intermediate ways to their environment, their peers and pressures from above. Put in an unusual, pressured, or troubled environment, many people will act 'out of character,' sometimes in heroic but more often in disappointing and sometimes shocking ways."

47 The achievement of the second level thus presupposes the availability of different perspectives and, by that, pluralism.

48 See DAVIES (2004) for his analysis of the potential of collaborative work between science educators and citizenship educators.

applies even to people who are members of a church or believe in a religion, cp. Horster 2004). Knowledge, experiences, and evaluations can change over time; thus, moral obligations based on them can come into conflict with moral obligations which have their origin in unchanged convictions and beliefs. Rawls' concept of reflective equilibrium can be used as a guideline to develop a coherent system of moral convictions.

As academic education is more than vocational training, the fortification of decision-making abilities of actors which enable them for reasonable action and the impartment of knowledge required for this is of particular importance. From an ethical point of view, actions are related to values, obligations, or principles, all of which (in particular on the basis of experiences and/or learning processes) are in need of continuous evaluation. An individual who is unconscious about his or her own values is probably not able to understand the values of others and other cultures: In case of, for example, cultural differences and the possible ways to come to grips with them, students should first "develop a deep understanding of their own values and then have opportunities to experience the values of another culture" (Eastwood et al. 2004, p. 3).

4. Sizing Down the Education Gap

Recently, management scholars have extended the list of skills which students are required to develop throughout their education at a BS/U: Pfeffer/Fong (2002, p. 84) mention communication abilities, leadership and wisdom; Leavitt (1989) lists interpersonal skills, teamwork skills, negotiating skills, and political skills, and then asks: "Why hasn't MBA education focused more on factors like leadership, determination, sense of duty?" Many other authors and many other selections of wished-for skills could be quoted: What they all have in common is the claim that there is a missing element in current management education, something beyond "mental rigor and hard analysis of environment" (Leavitt 1989, p. 40), namely, in terms of Leavitt (ibid.), "effective implementing," or, "getting things done through and with other people," or, "effective pathfinding" which requires "soul, imagination, personal commitment, and deep belief."

Chapter III.1 has referred to systematic interrelations between management studies and business ethics: free will, activities which take place in social reality, and the conceptions or theories which are applied to their analysis. A BS/U can size down the education gap (with respect to those aspects for which it has responsibility) by implementing business ethics. Ethical discernment requires the students to be able to identify ethical dimensions of choices or situations. As there is no single and unique basis for ethical decisions, there are different theoretical approaches which compete in their endeavor to systematize and explain social reality. Based on Perry's model of intellectual growth, there is an ethical argument for pluralism.

a) Pluralism as One Presupposition of Choice

Higher education provides knowledge-based input as well as the critical reflection on it. It is one main goal of BS/U to provide students with the Mode-1 knowledge necessary to find and solve problems based on those theories made familiar to them. In addition, students need training in order to understand the merits as well as the limitations of theories, and to be prepared for the comparison of different theories. If, for example, one theory can identify a problem but cannot solve it, at least not in a sufficient manner, then the students ought to be able to consider the application of other theories that might contribute to a pertinent problem solution.

Competition among different theoretical perspectives takes place rather seldomly within lecture halls. Reflection on the advantages as well as shortcomings of different theories presupposes that contending theoretical perspectives are available. A debate among economists[49] about the merits of pluralism in economics illustrates how this can work. In economics, despite today's dominance of neoclassical economics, several approaches have emerged which compete against each other. Economists have brought forth concrete proposals aiming at curricular reforms which allow for the integration of contending perspectives in economics education. Pluralism can have an effect on economic research, or on the teaching of economics, or on either of these. As Barone (1991, p. 18) points out, even if the neoclassical paradigm is not to be called into question by the introduction of contending perspectives, it helps to "introduce a healthy intellectual debate" or to "diversify the value premises of economics and raise the level of dialogue and understanding of the range of human values underlying human economic action and choice" (ibid.).

Compared to economics, management studies seems to be not in urgent need of implementing additional perspectives: if one abstains from econom-

49 See for example SENT (2003), DOW (2004), and GARNETT (2005).

ics, management studies' anchorage in sociology or psychology has given rise to a great number of perspectives which compete in the identification (finding) of problems as well as proposals to their solution. BS/U's students benefit from the opportunity to reflect on different assumptions, approaches, or ideas.[50] In many cases, a problem cannot be solved by means of only one approach, but requires an application of two or more approaches from different perspectives. Psychological, economic, and sociological theories shed light on specific problems from different perspectives.

Pluralism does not mean that every available position has to be presented or valued as being equally important as each of the others. Pluralism assures that there are enough approaches from which to choose with respect to both disciplinary research (or discussion) and interdisciplinary research (or discussion). The availability of different approaches is advantageous, since they are the "input" in a critical discussion of distinct assumptions, models, and action opportunities based on them.

b) Functional Equivalents for Business Ethics Education

It is obvious that BS/U can meet the challenge of developing students' ethical discernment without having implemented business ethics beforehand. It is possible that a BS/U can offer the suggested add-ons on the basis of the capacities already available to it. In particular, with respect to theory comparison and theory application, training of students in the philosophy of science will also work. The philosophy of science and business ethics are different but related building blocks for academic education: First, the concept of the philosophy of science can be interpreted in a wider sense, including such approaches as the sociological, historical, and aspects of scientific recognition and their embodiment in scientific theories. Second, some of the business ethics competences like the identification of value dimensions and ideologies related to theories are close to what can be called *philosophy of science competences*. Third, the development of both business ethics and philosophy of science competences requires stepping back from imparting knowledge about "what is;" and is a means to take over a meta-perspective and to reflect on this basis on the issues at hand. Nevertheless, as Table 2 shows, business ethics is the main source for those parts of academic education which are responsible for the development of skills related to ethical

50 See SCHWARTZ (1997) for intriguing examples of the impact of ideas on social reality.

reflection, deliberation and choice. The implementation of business ethics at a BS/U is a signal that a systematic reflection on the subject matter of business ethics takes place or is appreciated there.

c) Responsibility of Students

So far, the paper has dealt merely with BS/U's option to implement business ethics as a field of study and its assumed consequences on students' skills. However, there is also a responsibility of students for their learning[51] which, at least in part, is expressed in the degree of their active participation in the learning processes.[52] Students are not passive consumers of contents selected and justified by their teachers (and others), but are active co-producers of the outcomes of their education. For this reason, the results of BS/U's education may vary to a great extent, even though the curricula are quite similar across schools (Pfeffer/Fong 2002, p. 84[53], Leavitt 1989[54]).

The statement that both BS/U and students are involved in the process of co-production (i. e., the learning process) of the good or service of the BS/U has two dimensions: It matches with the presupposition that economics and ethics share basic convictions concerning the conceptualization of individual action. Second, if, economics as well as ethics assumes individuals act by reason and deliberate on their decisions, then this idea should also guide the manner these fields are taught.[55] BS/U are mainly responsible for offering opportunities to students and supporting students in their endeavor to make use of them; students are responsible for making use of these opportunities.

51 PFEFFER/FONG (2002, p. 83) complain that students are relieved of any sense of responsibility for their learning.

52 MCINERNEY (2005, p. 595) calls for an "active, transforming role of the learner."

53 Another reason for the situation that there are no economic gains from an MBA degree unless one graduates from a top-ranked school may be, as PFEFFER/FONG (2002) argue, that pedigree counts more than learning.

54 LEAVITT (1989, p. 39) points out „that almost all MBA programs now look very much alike, having gradually converged around a few key ideas born in the fifties".

55 "There (in the family, M. H.), we went right on encouraging our children to act independently, autonomously, and self-reliantly – for a while. Then we reversed direction. We sent them off into the university, the army, and General Motors – there they learn to conform and obey" (LEAVITT 1989, p. 41).

IV. Conclusions

If BS/U decided to implement business ethics, they could enhance the potential of their core competences with respect to research and education. As regards research, this improvement can be stated by means of the terms suggested by Gibbons et al. (1994): Business ethics is a source of Mode-1 knowledge production, and, as regards inter- or transdisciplinary work with management studies, it is also involved in scholarly Mode 2. In regard to education, the paper's arguments partially parallel those of management scholars who advocate a change of management education: It is not enough to impart Mode-1 as well as *scholarly* Mode-2 knowledge to future managers. In addition, because BS/U cannot provide situations or conditions under which "true" management experiences are achievable, they should rely on their core competences (i. e., the impartment of scholarly knowledge, the development of to-be managers' ability to apply theoretical knowledge to problems which arise within social reality, the ability to critically or morally reflect on that knowledge as well as on the practice which can be based on it). From the paper's point of view, Bailey/Ford (1996, p. 8) are right in demanding a "separate education model" for business schools; they are wrong in stating that management should not be taught as a science but as "practice or craft."[56]

Advancements, however, do not simply occur by the addition of a new subject matter to the list of those already available: A clear conception of the role that business ethics is thought to fulfil is required. To put it in terms used by (Ghoshal 2005, p. 87), "tokenism," that is, just adding courses on ethics to an otherwise unchanged program (cp. ibid.) will not unfold the full potential of an implementation of business ethics at BS/U. That notwithstanding, presumably there is no single, or unique, or best way to close the education gap. BS/U can, for example, ethically "empower" the curricula of the established subjects or implement business ethics as a field of study of its own. Separate courses on business ethics, however, do not make superfluous a critical reflection on contents of other academic fields of study. A critical reflection and (re-)evaluation of all fields of study do not imply that all curricula have

56 BAILEY/FORD (1996, p. 9) do not reject the idea that the scientific approach is appropriate to the study of management. They rather doubt its value as an approach to teaching management studies.

to be rewritten. Reflection and (re)evaluation rather mean that the ethical dimensions of the subject matter are noticed. If pluralism and a culture of reflection are already anchored at a BS/U, the better is business ethics' starting position.

References

BACON, LORD: *Novum Organum*, New York (P. F. Collier & Son) 1902 (Edited by Joseph Dewey, first edition in 1620).

BAILEY, JAMES; FORD, CAMERON: "Management as Science *versus* Management as Practice in Postgraduate Business Education", *Business Strategic Review*, 7 (4) (1996), pp. 7-12.

BARONE, CHARLES: "Contending Perspectives: Curricular Reform in Economics", *Journal of Economic Education*, Winter (1991), pp. 15-26.

BOWIE, NORMAN E.: "Business Ethics, Philosophy, and the Next 2005 Years", *Business Ethics Quarterly*, 10 (1) (2000), pp. 7-20.

BRUNI, LUIGINO; SUGDEN, ROBERT: "The Road Not Taken: How Psychology Was Removed from Economics, and How it Might be Brought Back", *The Economic Journal*, 117, January (2007), pp. 146-173.

CLEGG, STEWART; ROSS-SMITH, ANNE: "Revising the Boundaries: Management Education and Learning in a Postpositivist World", *Academy of Management Learning and Education*, 2 (1) (2003), pp. 85-98.

DANNER, PETER L.: *The Economic Person: Acting and Analyzing*, Lanham et al. (Rowman & Littlefield) 2002.

DAVIES, IAN: "Science and Citizenship Education", *International Journal of Science Education*, 26 (14) (2004), pp. 1751-1763.

DE-JUAN, OSCAR; MONSALVE, FABIO: "Morally Ruled Behaviour: The Neglected Contribution of Scholasticism", *The European Journal of the History of Economic Thought*, 13 (1) (2006), pp. 99-112.

DONALDSON, LEX: "Damned by our own theories: Contradictions between Theories and Management Education", *Academy of Management Learning and Education*, 1 (1) (2002), p. 96-106.

DOW, SHEILA C.: "Structured Pluralism", *Journal of Economic Methodology*, 11 (3) (2004), pp. 275-290.

EASTWOOD, KAREN; LÄMSÄ, ANNA-MAIJKA; SÄKKINEN, AILA: "About Ethics and Values in Business Education – A Cross-Cultural Perspective", *Electronic Jour-*

nal of Business Ethics and Organization Studies, 9 (2) (2004), pp. 1-9 (http://ejbo.jyu.fi/index.cgi?page=articles/0301_2; access on 2/28/2005).

EHRET, MICHAEL; HAASE, MICHAELA; KALUZA, MARTIN: "Concepts of Globalisation: The Institutional Prerequisites of World Market", in: KARL HOMANN, PETER KOSLOWSKI, CHRISTOPH LUETGE (Eds.): *Globalisation and Business Ethics*, Aldershot/London (Ashgate) 2007, pp. 11-26.

ENDERLE, GEORGES: "Towards Business Ethics as an Academic Discipline". *Business Ethics Quarterly*, 6 (1) (1996), pp. 43-65.

FRANKFURT, HARRY G.: "Freedom of the Will and the Concept of a Person", in: GARY WATSON (Ed.): *Free Will*, New York (Oxford University Press) 1982, pp. 81-95.

GARNETT JR., ROBERT F.: "Whither Heterodoxy?" *post-autistic economics review*, 34 (October 2005), article 1, pp. 2-21. http://www.paecon.net/PAEReview/issue34/Garnett34.htm.

GERSCH, MARTIN; FREILING, JÖRG; GOEKE, CHRISTIAN: *Grundlagen einer "Competence-based Theory of the Firm": Die Chance zur Schließung einer „Realisierungslücke" innerhalb der Marktprozesstheorie.* Arbeitsbericht Nr. 100 des Instituts für Unternehmensführung (ifu). Bochum: Ruhr-Universität Bochum 2005.

GHOSHAL, SUMANTRA: "Bad Management Theories Are Destroying Good Management Practices", *Academy of Management Learning & Education*, 4 (1) (2005), pp. 75-91.

GIBBONS, MICHAEL; LIMOGES, CAMILLE; NOWOTNY, HELGA; SCHWARTZMANN, SIMON; SCOTT, PETER; TROW, MARTIN: *The New Production of Knowledge: The Dynamics of Science and Research in Contemporary Societies,* London et al. (Sage) 1994.

HAMBRICK, DONALD C.: "What if the Academy Actually Mattered?" *Academy of Management Review*, 19 (1) (1994), pp. 11-16.

HARGREAVES, DAVID H.: The Knowledge-Creating School, *British Journal of Educational Studies*, 47 (2) (1999), pp. 122-144.

HARMAN, GILBERT: "No Character or Personality", *Business Ethics Quarterly*, 13 (1) (2003), pp. 87-94.

HARTMAN, EDWIN M.: "Can we Teach Character? An Aristotelian Answer", *Academy of Management Learning & Education*, 5 (1) (2006), pp. 68-81.

HOMANN, KARL; SUCHANEK, ANDREAS: "Wirtschaftsethik – Angewandte Ethik oder Beitrag zur Grundlagendiskussion?", in: BERND BIERVERT, MARTIN HELD (Eds.): *Ökonomische Theorie und Ethik*, Frankfurt am Main (Suhrkamp) 1987, pp. 101-119.

HOOVER, KENNETH E.: *Economics as Ideology: Keynes, Laski, Hayek, and the Creation of Contemporary Politics*, Lanham u. a. (Rowman & Littlefield) 2003.

HORSTER, DETLEF: "Gibt es einzig richtige moralische Entscheidungen?", *Archiv für Rechts- und Sozialphilosophie*, 90 (2) (2004), pp. 226-236.

JOLLS, CHRISTINE: *Behavioral Law and Economics*, Yale Law School Research Paper, No. 130 (2007), http://papers.ssrn.com/abstract=959177.

KLIMOWSKI, RICHARD: "Introduction: Aristotle as a Business Ethics Professor", *Academy of Learning & Education*, 5 (1) (2006), pp. 66-67.

KOSLOWSKI, PETER: *Ethik des Kapitalismus* (mit einem Kommentar von JAMES M. BUCHANAN), Tübingen (Mohr Siebeck) 1998.

LEAVITT, HAROLD J.: "Educating our MBAs: On Teaching what we Haven't Taught", *California Management Review*, Spring (1989), pp. 38-50.

MACHAN, TIBOR R.; CHESHER, JAMES E.: *A Primer on Business Ethics*, Lanham (MD) (Rowman & Littlefield) 2002.

MCINERNEY, DENNIS M.: "Educational Psychology – Theory, Research, and Teaching: A 25-year retrospective", *Educational Psychology*, 25 (6) (2005), pp. 585-599.

MCINTYRE, DONALD: "Bridging the Gap between Research and Practice", *Cambridge Journal of Education*, 35 (3), (2005), pp. 357-382.

MINTZBERG, HENRY; GOSLING, JONATHAN: "Educating Managers Beyond Borders", *Academy of Management Learning & Education*, 1 (1) (2002), pp. 64-76.

MINTZBERG, HENRY; LAMPEL, JOSEPH: "Do MBAs Make better CEOs? Sorry, Dubya, it Ain't Necessarily so", *Fortune*, 143 (4) (2001), pp. 244-244.

NOWOTNY, HELGA; SCOTT, PETER; GIBBONS, MICHAEL: *Wissenschaft neu denken: Wissen und Öffentlichkeit in einem Zeitalter der Ungewißheit*, Weilerswist (Velbrück) 2005.

OTTEWILL, ROGER; MACFARLANE, BRUCE: "Assessing the Pedagogic Challenges Faced by Business and Management Education in UK Higher Education" (2002), http://www.business.heacademy.ac.uk/resources/reflect/conf/2002/ottewill/index.html (access on 3/2/2006).

PFEFFER, JEFFREY; FONG, CHRISTINA: "The End of Business Schools? Less Success than Meets the Eye", *Academy of Management Learning & Education*, 1 (1) (2002), pp. 78-95.

PORTER, L. W.; MCKIBBIN, L. E.: *Management education and development: Drift or thrust into the 21st century*, New York (McGraw-Hill Book Company) 1998.

REID, A., SCOTT, W., GOUGH, S: "Education and sustainable development in the UK: an exploration of progress since Rio", *Geography*, 87(3), (2002), pp. 247-255.

REINGOLD, JENNIFER: "Henry Mintzberg", *Fast Company*, November 2000 (40), pp. 286-294.

ROSS, DAVID: *The Right and the Good* (ed. by Philip Stratton Lake), Oxford (Clarendon) 2002.

SAMUELS, WARREN J.: "Four Strands of Socio-Economics – A Comparative Interpretation", in: MARK A. LUTZ (Ed.): *Social Economics: Retrospect and Prospect*, Boston, Dordrecht, London (Kluwer) 1989, pp. 269-309.

SCHUTZ, ALFRED: *Collected Papers I. The Problem of Social Reality* (Edited and Introduced by MAURICE NATANSON), The Hague, Boston, London (Nijhoff) 1982.

SCHWARTZ, BARRY: "Psychology, 'Idea Technology,' and Ideology", *Psychological Science*, 8 (1) (1997), pp. 21-27.

SENT, ESTHER-MIRJAM: "Pleas for Pluralism", *post-autistic economics review*, 18 (February 2003), article 1.

SOLOMON, ROBERT C.: "Victims of Circumstances? A Defense of Virtue Ethics in Business", *Business Ethics Quarterly*, 13 (1) (2003), pp. 43-62.

STENHOUSE, LAWRENCE: "What Counts as Research?", *British Journal of Educational Studies*, XXIX (2) (1981), pp. 103-114.

SZYMKOWIAK, SOPHIE: "Why Build a Network about Introduction of Sustainable Development into Scientific Education?" *European Journal of Engineering Education*, 28 (2) (2003), pp. 179-186.

VERMONT, SAMSON: "Why 'Law and Economics' is not the Frankenstein Monster", *Economics and Philosophy*, 15 (1999), pp. 249-267.

WAGNER, GERT G.; WIEGARD, WOLFGANG: *Economic Research and Policy Advise – Also a Note to Immanuel Kant's „Actus der Urteilskraft"*, DIW Research Note 10, Berlin 2002.

WAGNER, WALTER C.: "Market Management of the Essential Economy: An Essay", *Journal of Socio-Economics*, 30 (2001), pp. 533-537.

WHELDALL, KEVIN: "Introduction to Special Issue: When Will we ever Learn?", *Educational Psychology*, 25 (6) (2005), pp. 573-584.

WYLLER, TRULS: *Geschichte der Ethik: eine systematische Einführung*, Paderborn (Mentis) 2002.

ZEMBYLAS, MICHALINOS: "Essay Review: Science Education: For Citizenship and/or for Social Justice?", *Journal of Curriculum Studies*, 37 (6) (2005), pp. 709-722.

List of Authors

ALEXANDER BRINK is Professor for Applied Ethics, University of Bayreuth, Bayreuth, Germany.

CHRISTOPHER J. COWTON is Dean of the Business School, University of Huddersfield, Huddersfield, United Kingdom.

DIRK ULRICH GILBERT is Professor of Management, University of Erlangen-Nürnberg, Germany.

MICHAELA HAASE is Assistant Professor at the Marketing Department, Freie Universität Berlin, Germany.

BERNARD HODGSON is Professor of Philosophy, Trent University, Peterborough, Ontario, Canada.

PETER KOSLOWSKI is Professor of Philosophy, Vrije Universiteit Amsterdam, Amsterdam, Netherlands.

HANSRUDI LENZ is Professor for Business Administration, Accounting and Consulting, University of Würzburg, Germany.

ANDREAS RASCHE is Assistant Professor, Helmut-Schmidt-University, University of the Federal Armed Forces in Hamburg, Germany

YUICHI SHIONOYA is Professor emeritus of Economics, Hitotsubashi University, Tokyo, Japan.

ALOY SOPPE is Assistant Professor of Financial Ethics, Erasmus University Rotterdam, Rotterdam, Netherlands.

Index of Names

Page numbers in italics refer to quotations in footnotes or references

INDEX OF NAMES

INDEX OF NAMES

INDEX OF NAMES

INDEX OF NAMES

MIX
Papier aus verantwortungsvollen Quellen
Paper from responsible sources
FSC® C105338

If you have any concerns about our products,
you can contact us on
ProductSafety@springernature.com

In case Publisher is established outside the EU,
the EU authorized representative is:
Springer Nature Customer Service Center GmbH
Europaplatz 3, 69115 Heidelberg, Germany

Printed by Libri Plureos GmbH
in Hamburg, Germany